Born

in the

Country

Revisiting Rural America
Pete Daniel and Deborah K. Fitzgerald, Series Editors

Mary Neth. *Preserving the Family Farm: Women, Community, and the Foundation of Agribusiness in the Midwest, 1900–1940*

Sally McMurry. *Transforming Rural Life: Dairying Families and Agricultural Change, 1820–1885*

David B. Danbom. *Born in the Country: A History of Rural America*

BORN

in the

COUNTRY

A History of Rural America

DAVID B. DANBOM

The Johns Hopkins University Press

Baltimore and London

© 1995 The Johns Hopkins University Press
All rights reserved. Published 1995
Printed in the United States of America on acid-free paper
04 03 02 01 00 99 98 97 96 95   5 4 3 2 1

The Johns Hopkins University Press
2715 North Charles Street
Baltimore, Maryland 21218-4319
The Johns Hopkins Press Ltd., London

Design: Christine Taylor
Composition: Wilsted & Taylor Publishing Services

ISBN 0-8018-5039-8
ISBN 0-8018-5040-1 (pbk.)

Library of Congress Cataloging-in-Publication data
will be found at the end of this book.

A catalog record for this book is available from the British Library.

For Karen,

this time,

all of the time

Contents

Preface
and Acknowledgments

In *The Age of Reform*, historian Richard Hofstadter wrote that "the United States was born in the country and has moved to the city."[1] Like many of the things Hofstadter wrote, this was deceptively simple. On the surface, Hofstadter was stating the obvious: the United States, once an overwhelmingly rural and agricultural country, had become urban and industrial. At the time of the American Revolution, over 90 percent of Americans lived in a rural setting, and the vast majority of them drew at least part of their livelihood from farming. In 1990, less than 25 percent of Americans were rural, and fewer than one in ten rural residents farmed.

In another sense, Hofstadter could be seen as trivializing the rural past by denying its relevance to the present. The farm was something left behind by a maturing nation, like a skirt that was no longer in style or shoes that did not fit anymore. Hofstadter was part of the generation of American historians that discovered urban history and considered it the disciplinary wave of the future. A native of Buffalo who spent his career in New York City, Hofstadter portrayed farmers as hypocritical and self-serving manipulators, as country slickers who hoodwinked urbanites (unlike such scholars as Frederick Jackson Turner and John D. Hicks, who sympathized with them).[2]

But while he felt no attachment to the countryside himself, Hofstadter recognized that most Americans did. After all, the United States *was* born in the country and remained emotionally attached to it long after it had moved away. Hofstadter knew that many Americans considered rural living preferable to urban living and farmers superior to nonfarmers. He considered the agrarian myth to be mainly myth, but he was too good a historian to discount its power. He knew that rural America had exercised an influence on the American mind and public policy far out of proportion to the numbers of farmers in the population. Even as he tried to dismiss it, then, Hofstadter recognized the powerful influence that the countryside had on our national life. Unfortunately, not all of his contemporaries were wise enough to share that observation.

Hofstadter's remark about the countryside introduced a chapter on the Populist movement during the 1890s. Hofstadter's interest in Populism reflected the reality that agrarian politics was a major preoccupation of historians in his day and had been at least since the publication of John D. Hicks's *Populist Revolt* in 1931. The agricultural frontier also provided grist for historians' mills, ever since Frederick Jackson Turner suggested its significance in 1893. The history of agricultural economics and technology continued to command a fair amount of scholarly attention, as did land policy, the preserve of the redoubtable Paul Gates and his many students.[3] But the history of rural society was ignored in Hofstadter's day. In 1936 Joseph Schafer wrote *The Social History of American Agriculture*, but the "social" in the title was an exercise in literary license—Schafer's book was mainly about farm politics and economics.[4]

Hofstadter and Schafer and the contemporaries of both can be excused for slighting rural society, because little of what we would call social history was being done for anyone, urban or rural. There was little scholarly interest in the day-to-day lives and relationships of ordinary people, especially when such ordinary people failed to leave written documents in conventional depositories. History was still mainly the story of great men and their significant public acts.

All of this began to change in the 1960s, as young historians—as well as some older ones, such as Hofstadter himself—began exploring the lives of ordinary people and the roles they played in the history of the United States. For many young scholars, this avenue of inquiry represented a political commitment to blacks, ethnic minorities, women, workers, and others who were downtrodden when they lived and ignored after they died. For all social historians, models provided by European scholars and new and imaginative ways of defining and analyzing evidence played a significant role in shaping their products.

The emphasis on social history was important to the study of rural America, because most rural Americans have been, and remain, quite ordinary people. Beginning in the midsixties there was such an outpouring of work on such topics as rural ethnicity, slavery, kinship, and early American communities that it was possible by 1981 for Robert Swierenga to write of the "new rural history."[5] Since then this outpouring has become a flood, with such topics as women's lives and roles, market consciousness and behavior, and the cultural interpenetration of city and country commanding particular interest. This rural social history—much, but unfortunately not all, of which is cited at the back of this book—made *Born in the Country* possible.

There are a couple of things that need to be said about this book. First, what I have attempted to do here is write a synthetic history of rural America that integrates the new social history with the old—and new—political and economic history. Agriculture, rural culture and society, and agrarian politics are so intertwined, to my way of thinking, that separation of them is misleading and excessively artificial. The second thing that needs to be said is that, while the title promises a study of rural America, what the book delivers is mainly a study of farm people in America. I chose to focus on farm people for two reasons, one theoretical and one practical. On the theoretical side, I believe that farm living is enough different from small town living that the two are not easily or valuably integrated into a synthetic treatment. On the practical side, I am limited by the very reality that has made this book possible—the vast bulk of the rural social, economic, and political history produced in the past generation has focused on farm people.

So far I have written about what this book is and what made it possible, but I would like to conclude with a few words about what made it necessary. For about fifteen years I have taught a course entitled History of Rural America. It has been frustrating to me and to the students in the class that there is no synthetic treatment of this subject. Students from rural backgrounds, of whom I have had many, feel dispossessed by this lack of scholarly attention, and students from urban backgrounds wonder why such an important part of American history has received so little attention. It was to begin to fill this gap in our history that I wrote this book. I do not expect this to be the last comprehensive attempt to address the history of rural America; indeed, I hope it is the first of many. But I hope that, at the very least, it will give all students who read it, whatever their background might be, an appreciation for what it means and has meant to be "born in the country."

Several people were kind enough to share their time and their thoughts with me regarding this manuscript. Gerald Anderson read the entire manuscript, making a number of valuable comments and throwing in an occasional joke to keep me loose. Barbara Handy-Marchello provided a very useful and sensitive commentary that made this a better book. Tom Isern and Doug Hurt, both of whom know much more about agriculture than I do, saved me from some embarrassing gaffs. Peter Argersinger read the manuscript for the Johns Hopkins University Press and provided a careful, thoughtful, and judicious commentary. Hiram Drache, Gary Goreham, Mark Harvey, Michael Lyons, and Jim Ross also favored me by reading selected chapters on which they had special expertise.

I would like to thank Bob Brugger of the Johns Hopkins University Press for his interest in and commitment to something that has never been done before and for which there was no model. It's not easy being first. I also wish to thank Katherine K. Buxton for her careful and skillful copyediting. The chair of my department, Larry Peterson, provided a supportive atmosphere for my work and helped me get a developmental leave in 1992–93 to write the first draft of this book. I also thank North Dakota State University and the taxpayers of North Dakota for making that leave possible. H. Roald Lund, former director of the North Dakota Agricultural Experiment Station, has provided steadfast support for this project as well as for my other scholarly endeavors, and I thank him. Karen, Elizabeth, and Mark put up with my highs when things were going well and my lows when things were not, and I appreciate that. Finally, I especially appreciate the work of our departmental secretary, Amy Ochoa. Amy turned chapters out promptly and accurately, bore numerous revisions with good humor (at least in public), and deciphered writing about which even I was uncertain. You should all be so lucky.

ONE

Rural Europe
and Pre-Columbian America

If you form a mental picture of the American countryside today, what you probably see is a large expanse of open country, sprinkled with farmsteads surrounded by fenced lands. You probably envision a family living in the farmhouse, enjoying the same conveniences and using the same products as families in towns and cities. You can see a car in the drive, electrical wires and phone lines coming into the house, and a television antenna on the roof or a satellite dish nearby. When you think about it further, you might imagine that the family has a fairly broad range of experiences, that it travels to market towns and nearby cities and vacations periodically; that at least some of its members have been in the armed service, attended college, and are members of national social and economic organizations. You probably recognize that, outwardly at least, rural Americans are little different from their urban counterparts.

When you reflect on the farm you might well think of it as a substantial business. You recognize the farmer as a sophisticated businessperson, a technical expert, and a skilled manager of a heavily capitalized and mechanized operation. You assume that, like other businesspeople, the farmer makes decisions on the basis of individual self-interest, restrained only by

2 economic, environmental, and public policy realities over which he or she has little control.

This picture would be generally accurate, for most farmers in the Western world. But it is also misleading, because it reflects developments that are very recent. Through most of world history rural people have been dramatically different from urban people, and rural life has diverged strikingly from urban life; that reality continues now in much of the developing world. Until very recently rural people in Europe and North America had unique experiences. They looked, talked, and acted differently from urban people. And they pursued an occupation that was at least as much a way of life as it was a way of making a living.

In order for us to understand where we are and how we got here, it is necessary for us to go back to the beginning. We must go back to rural Europe and rural America in the late fifteenth century, on the eve of the sustained contact that would transform both.

THE EUROPEAN VILLAGE

Today, most American farm families live on individual farmsteads, sometimes miles away from their closest neighbors. Some Europeans five hundred years ago lived the same way, especially in relatively wild and unsettled regions; but most European farmers lived in nucleated villages surrounded by the fields they worked.

The European village was not really comparable to the small town of today. It was not mainly a political unit or a physical place, and it cannot be understood as an aggregation of independent individuals. The European village at the time of Columbus was an organic community—almost a living essence, apart from and superior to the individuals who lived there. The village was much more than an address or a place to live. It was an educational institution, a welfare institution, and to a large degree, a self-contained and self-directive economic entity as well. In short, the village was central to the lives of most Europeans in 1492 in a way mere places are to very few of us today.

The village was at the center of a society in which people usually defined themselves by relationships rather than by profession, ethnicity, or religion. It bound families together, sometimes over many generations, providing them with a sense of place and identity and comfort. The families of the village bound parents and children and other kin together, providing not only defining and nurturing relationships but welfare services as well. The village church, to which all normally belonged, defined their relationship with God. And the village social structure, rather than separating people, bound the high and low together in an intricate web of loyalty and obligation.

In this world of intimacy few needed more of an identification than that provided by a Christian name. People distinguished themselves from one another on the basis of relationship or occupation. One John was Robert's son and another was William's son; a third was John the smith and a fourth John the brewer. My great-great-great-grandfather Gustav, being Edmund's son, took the name Edmundson to distinguish himself from the other Gustavs in his Swedish village. When he was recruited into the army he fashioned a name out of that of his village, Dansbo. When European governments required peasants to take surnames, in the eighteenth century in most of Western Europe, such names of convenience became permanent.

The web of relationships and the life of intimacy conveyed a sense of stability and permanence to the village that was misleading. The European village was the product of historical circumstances and was changed by historical circumstances. The oldest villages developed in the tenth century A.D., as powerful nobles formed estates, called manors. Peasants living on manors provided labor service to the lord on his lands in return for his protection of their lives and property. The manorial system broke down in the fourteenth century, largely as a result of the Black Death, a plague that killed half of the population of Western Europe. Many villages were abandoned entirely, and the peasant population was so reduced that they were in the unaccustomed position of being able to shape the terms of their labor. In some places, manorial obligations were dropped entirely; in most they were transformed into yearly payments of money or produce.

The end of the manorial system did not signal the beginning of village democracy or egalitarianism. Most villages did not have a noble in residence, but they did have a hierarchy that was rigid, not least because they believed it to be divinely ordained. Women were always subordinate to men, and children were subordinate to both. Substantial landowners dominated village society and comprised a stable village core. Under them were smaller landowners, renters, and landless laborers. The closer to the bottom one was, the less likely one was to enjoy common village rights and the more likely one was to move to a town or city or to another village.

Softening the rigid hierarchy of the village was a tradition of reciprocity

4 embodied in mutual claims and responsibilities. All were responsible for the maintenance of the village and for providing labor on common fields and facilities like roads and bridges. None were unemployed. There was labor for all, from milling grain to tending fields to watching livestock. The landless usually enjoyed the use of the forest for wood, the pond for fish, and the common lands (property owned by the village rather than by individuals) for grazing their livestock. After the crops were in, the village livestock grazed on farmers' fields. It was a society in which some were better off than others but in which people were expected to look after one another.

The village tended toward self-sufficiency and self-containment. Most of what was consumed by the village was produced there. Few men pursued just one occupation. John was a farmer and also a miller. William brewed beer and rented a little land. Robert had a few acres and also made shoes and harnesses. Even the priest often had crops to tend. The village fed itself from its fields and orchards and flocks; housed and warmed itself from its forest; clothed itself from the flax and wool it grew and sheared.

The traditional village did not need much contact with the outside world—nor did it want it. Now and then a peddler came through to barter a nutmeg or a few yards of silk for livestock or flour or honey. On occasion, people from a neighboring village came for a festival or to beg for help. Sometimes soldiers of a king or a local noble would come through to recruit or to collect taxes or tribute. Beggars passed through only to be driven on to the next village. But most of the time most people lived in relative ignorance of, and isolation from, the world beyond the village. As a consequence villages were insular, suspicious, and distrustful of strangers. Those who wanted to move in had to seek village approval, while those who offended the village faced banishment. Villagers lived in their own world, within their own small circle, so isolated that even their language could sometimes not be understood by compatriots a hundred miles distant.

Individuals' lives were controlled by the community in a variety of ways. Property was private in the sense that it was owned by individuals, but the village—sometimes operating through periodic meetings and sometimes through the substantial peasants who held public office—determined how it would be used. The village dictated which crops should be planted and where and when, how a gristmill should be used and what the miller should charge, how much barley should be brewed into beer and how much ground into flour. Those who lacked work were assigned work that served village needs, as woodcutters or shepherds or swineherds. The village functioned as a welfare institution, placing the indigent with families and orphans into servitude or apprenticeship. And the village controlled behavior, imposing a conformity that most modern people would find absolutely suffocating.

Village society was not for individuals. Indeed, the word *individual* was not applied to human beings before the seventeenth century. We can guess that those who did not fit in, whose behavior or personalities set them apart from the mass, did not fare very well. They were the people who were accused of witchcraft when times were bad, or were turned over to the army when it was recruiting, or were driven out of the village to join the "people without places," the wandering poor—the lepers, the insane, the petty criminals, and the other unfortunates who lived a hand-to-mouth existence in early modern Europe.

We would find village life stultifying and confining. Developing the personality is our major preoccupation; their society worked best when personal idiosyncrasies were suppressed. Life in the village, from our perspective, was not attractive, but being a person without a place was infinitely less so.

Even for those who did not offend the mass and did not lose their places, the enforced intimacy, conformity, and community controls of village life could produce anxieties and frictions. The ideal of mutual obligations and responsibilities tended to break down in times of hardship. Families and individuals feuded and bickered, and litigation or even violence was sometimes the result. Community divisions arose and sometimes became so serious that villagers would not attend church services with one another. As in all areas of human life, village reality often fell short of the village ideal.

VILLAGE AGRICULTURE

The 60 to 80 percent of Europeans who lived in villages five hundred years ago devoted most of their time and effort to feeding and clothing themselves. As individuals and as a group villagers strove to maintain self-sufficiency and to avoid or at least minimize risk. Villagers practiced a very conservative, safety-first agriculture not because they were ignorant or backward but because, as people who produced only slightly more than their subsistence, their very lives depended on prudence and care. So, while change did occur in agricultural methods and technology, its pace was glacial. Further, most information was passed by word of mouth. The vast majority of European

6

villagers in 1492 were illiterate. Even the priests, in many villages, had only the barest rudiments of learning.

Still, change was possible and did occur. Fifteenth-century Europe was technologically advanced for the age. While other cultures planted with digging sticks or hoes, Europeans used plows to break and turn the soil and harrows to pulverize clods and smooth and level the seedbed. Seeding, harvesting, and threshing, however, were done by hand.

In most villages, arable land was unfenced but was divided into long, narrow fields often less than an acre in size. Peasants seldom had consolidated fields, instead owning or renting strips of land in several different places. While this scattering of fields was inconvenient, and became more so with advances in mechanization, it was apparently a conscious tactic in the ever-present peasant strategy of minimizing risk.

By 1492 most of European agriculture operated under the three-field system, a major agricultural reform that had replaced the two-field system of the late Middle Ages. This system involved leaving one-third of the arable land fallow (unplanted) while the other two-thirds was cropped. Of the land that was planted, half was usually seeded to small grains, with the rest devoted to hay, turnips, or other fodder (feed for animals). Sometimes Europeans intercropped, planting rye with clover, for example, or oats with peas. The fact that one-third of the land was fallow imposed obvious limitations on agricultural productivity. The adoption of soil-restoring crops from America like beans and potatoes, beginning in the seventeenth century, allowed villages to go to a six- or seven-field system, improving productivity and helping stimulate a major population boom.

Of the grains produced, rye was most important in much of northern and central Europe. Rye is a hardy cereal that does well in cold climates. Its dependability made it the primary grain used for bread and thus the staple of the peasant diet. Oats, spelt (a hard and flinty grain), and barley were also commonly produced, the last of these being an important ingredient in the brewing of beer. Wheat, a more temperamental crop, was less often grown, but it was preferred by urban consumers and, as the peasants became more oriented to the market, more was produced.

Striving for self-sufficiency, the villages produced an impressive variety of other crops. Flax was grown in many places, and villages commonly maintained orchards and vineyards. Bees were kept for honey. Peasant families maintained impressive gardens. Village houses were built facing roads, with long, narrow lots, sometimes nearly an acre in size, behind the houses. In these house lots villagers grew onions, leeks, carrots, parsnips, peas, and cabbages, which could be preserved, as well as leafy green vegetables for immediate consumption.

Virtually all peasants kept cattle, hogs, sheep, and poultry, usually in pens at the front of their houses, but sometimes—especially in central and eastern Europe—inside their homes. Such solicitude for animals may seem touching but dramatically reduces whatever romance we might attach to peasant life. Aside from hogs, these animals also served other purposes: cattle were milked and drew farm machinery, sheep were sheared for wool, and poultry provided eggs.

Village agriculture was more impressive for its variety than for its abundance. Cereal yields averaged less than five to one (fewer than five bushels harvested for every bushel sown) in most places. By contrast, cereal yields in the U.S. wheat belt today average forty to one. We can surmise that the yields of other crops were similarly low and that animals did not reach maturity as quickly as they do today.

One factor that kept yields down was the absence of varieties of crops specially developed for local conditions. Another reality was that crops were vulnerable to vermin and insects and to fungal outbreaks. Grains produced in cool, humid areas—which is to say, much of continental Europe—are especially susceptible to rust, ergot, and other funguses. Peasants in a near-subsistence economy did not usually have the option of not consuming infected grain. One result was widespread ergotism, a condition manifested in convulsions, hallucinations, and temporary paralysis.

The main cause of low yields was probably low fertility. The three-field system allowed a third of the land to rest in any given year, presumably enhancing its fertility. Hay and turnips fixed nitrogen and thus helped restore fertility, though turnips spread only slowly over the continent and were not common everywhere until the eighteenth century. Peasants recognized the effects of animal manure on fertility, but they usually did not have enough of it or manage it carefully enough to make a significant difference.

In agriculture as in all areas of life, peasant understandings of cause and effect were premodern. Agriculture necessarily moved to the rhythms of the day and the seasons. Agricultural work was task—not time—oriented; only the rare village contained a clock. Within those broad parameters and enduring realities the timing of agricultural operations was set by traditions as

8 old as farming itself. The moon was an especially important governor of agricultural operations. Turnips were to be planted during one phase of the moon, rye under another. A new moon dictated that onions be harvested or that hogs be slaughtered.

In peasant agriculture every natural phenomenon had a supernatural cause. An abundant harvest meant that prayers had been answered, not that agricultural and meteorological conditions had been favorable. Droughts, hail, and epidemics were punishments. The peasant whose cow passed blood in her milk or whose sow gave birth to hairless piglets was the victim of a curse. The peasant did not go to an experiment station or county agent for help but fell back on traditional folk wisdom, passed orally, like most other information, from generation to generation.

DAILY LIFE IN THE VILLAGE

Daily life in the European village of five hundred years ago was extremely primitive. Most people lived in rude huts, sometimes stone but more often wood or mud and wattle, a composite of clay and sticks. Roofs were usually thatched, and floors were usually earthen. In a world of intimacy, the family lived in especially close contact. The typical peasant dwelling consisted of one large room in which the family ate, cooked, slept, and conducted all of the other affairs of family life, sometimes in the presence of their animals. It was an environment in which children rapidly learned the realities of emotional and physical relationships.

For most of the year, homes were dark and cold. Families that could afford more illumination than that provided by the ever-burning fire had to make do with a couple of smokey candles. Not until the eighteenth century were flues designed to put more heat into a room than went up the chimney. Consequently, people more than a few feet from the fire shivered. It is not hard to imagine peasants in northern Europe, where winters were cold and long and periods of daylight were brief, spending days at a time huddled together in bed or under blankets around a fire.

What are today considered minimal comforts were unattainable luxuries to most villagers five hundred years ago. Glass or even oiled paper for windows was beyond the reach of the average peasant. Most families had no chairs, using rude benches, instead, for seating. People slept on crude pallets, with mattresses of straw or heather. Cooking utensils usually consisted of a large iron pot and a knife. Plates and bowls were not possessed by all.

Ole Gjervø family and kin in front of a frame and sod house, Cavalier County, North Dakota, circa 1898.

Courtesy of the Fred Hultstrand History in Pictures Collection, North Dakota Institute for Regional Studies and North Dakota University Libraries, Fargo.

10 Many peasants still used trenchers, large wooden platters from which the whole family ate. Each family member had a wooden spoon, which he or she carried along when eating out of the home. Forks did not appear in Europe until the sixteenth century and then were used mainly by the rich. Most people had only one or two suits of clothes, usually made of rough wool or linsey-woolsey, a linen and wool blend. Underclothes were a luxury most peasants did not enjoy.

The peasant diet was generally bland, unbalanced, and unvaried. Bread, usually baked in the wall of the hearth or in communal ovens, was present at every meal, often with cheese. Meat or fish was usually served in a soup or stew, made with whatever vegetables were available. The reality that foods could be preserved only by drying, salting, or smoking imposed harsh limitations on dietary variety. People enjoyed fresh green vegetables for only a brief period in the late spring and early summer. Vegetables consumed during the rest of the year had to be of the type that could be dried or that did not spoil rapidly in storage. Vegetables were sometimes consumed in different forms. Cabbage, for example, could be eaten in the form of sauerkraut throughout the year. What was true of vegetables was true of fruits as well. Apples kept fairly well, but other fruits, if not quickly consumed, were turned into wine. Whatever the peasants ate and whenever they ate it, they had little but salt or honey to alter the taste. The spices of the Indies—pepper, nutmeg, cumin, cloves, and dozens of others—were so expensive that only the wealthy had access to them.

In a society living close to the margin, such as this one was, food was the major shaper of life and well-being. Low nutritional standards retarded population growth. Poor nutrition kept men and women from reaching sexual maturity until their late teens or early twenties. Breast-feeding women usually stopped ovulating, effectively preventing conception until toddlers were weaned, usually at one and a half to two years. The availability of food affected the timing of conception in other ways, as well. Rates of conception fell off dramatically in late winter and early spring, when stocks of food ran low, rising sharply in early summer when food again became abundant. This was a society in which there was but a thin margin of safety most of the time.

Sometimes food controlled population more brutally. Famine was not unknown in Europe in 1492. The poor were especially vulnerable. In extreme cases of famine they ate grass, leaves, human feces, and corpses—and still they starved to death. Famine did not usually result in starvation, but the weak—the very young and the very old—sometimes did not eat enough to maintain health. They were especially vulnerable to epidemic diseases, to pneumonia, even to influenzas that could kill people weakened by hunger. Even those able to sustain life could not long maintain their youthful vigor. Nutritional deficiencies contributed to rickets, skin diseases, and loss of hair and teeth.

The unsanitary conditions in which people lived also threatened health. People washed their clothes and bodies only rarely, considering bathing to be a cause of leprosy and plague. Rats, cockroaches, and lice were their constant companions. Living in filth and lacking any suspicion that dirt and disease were related, people were easy prey to infections. Even a relatively minor cut could turn into gangrene, and childbirth often resulted in puerperal fever. Social violence could also threaten life at various times and places. In time of war undisciplined armies lived off the countryside. Armed bandit gangs looted, raped, and killed villagers. Overtaxed and hungry peasants sometimes rose in violent rebellion, only to be suppressed with equal or greater violence.

Taken together, poor nutrition, hunger, filth, disease, and violence kept life expectancy down to about thirty-five years in most places. While the high infant-mortality rate makes this figure a bit misleading, it is nonetheless true that people who lived to be fifty were considered old.

In this fragile life assurance was hard to come by. People sought consolation and control through religion and superstition, which they yoked together in an uneasy but enduring team. All natural effects were assumed to have supernatural causes. God, Christ, the Virgin Mary, and the saints were thought to involve themselves freely and regularly in everyday life, but so too were elves, trolls, witches, and other spirits. Dealing effectively with these forces sometimes required prayer, sometimes amulets and spells, and sometimes a little of each.

Even at best, one could minimize life's uncertainties only marginally and temporarily. Men and women were ever-subject to the whims of capricious fate. The family was delicate and vulnerable. It is unlikely that in many families all—or even most—children reached adulthood without losing at least one parent. The delicacy and vulnerability of the individual and the family reinforced the importance of the village. It would always be there, enduring even when individuals and families did not, providing nurture and succor and care at best, providing a chance for survival at the very least.

This crude, uncertain, and brutal life was, paradoxically, a life of substantial leisure. Underemployment was the rule in most villages. Most people did not—and in light of their physical conditions, perhaps could not—work more than five or six hours a day. Moreover, peasants celebrated a stunning variety of religious holidays and saint days—over 150 a year in some places. Festivals and carnivals, sometimes combining pagan and Christian elements, were regularly held, especially at crucial points in the agricultural year. Weddings, baptisms, and funerals provided more occasions for village celebration—for feasting and drinking and pageantry. And always, the entire village was involved. As in most phases of life, the village was at the center, overshadowing all else.

CHANGE IN EUROPE

The measured pace of life, the ancient ways of doing things, and the weight of custom and tradition in European villages of five hundred years ago convey a misleading sense of stability and inertia. Beneath the placid surface of European life were currents of change. Some villagers were already being moved by those currents, and within the next century and a half few would be unaffected. Most of the forces for change in European economic, political, and intellectual life were located in cities, where new classes built economic power and political leaders established bases of support. But they were felt beyond city walls, throughout the countryside, across international borders, and even beyond the oceans.

The most powerful currents of change in the Europe of 1492 were economic, and of these none was more powerful or portentious than the interest in trade. In the two centuries after Marco Polo's trailblazing overland journey to China, Europeans became increasingly attracted to Oriental imports. To people living lives of material privation and tedium, such Eastern products as silks and spices offered an excitement that it is difficult for people in the Western world today to grasp. The desire to tap the lucrative Oriental market, dominated by the city-state of Venice, which controlled the eastern Mediterranean, was the main factor launching the voyages of discovery, of which Columbus's was the most famous.

Europeans needed to have something to trade for the marvelous and expensive products of the Orient. They traded foodstuffs, and they developed a manufacturing sector. Woolen textiles, metal goods, jewelry, and dozens of other products flowed out of European workshops and into the channels of trade. Commerce and manufacturing were concentrated in urban places. Old towns and cities grew, and new ones developed at natural harbors and the intersections of rivers, where trading activity was particularly intense. Those towns and cities came to be dominated by merchants, manufacturers, and financiers, people who had been peripheral in a feudal, insular, and self-sufficient Europe but who were crucial actors in a Europe that was developing a taste for trade.

Successful commerce was difficult in the absence of strong central political authority. Merchants in countries infested by robbers and bandit gangs demanded protection only a strong government could provide. Financiers and others engaged in economic activities longed for stable, standard currencies. Merchants bemoaned the existence of dozens of political subdivisions, each with its own laws, customs duties, and commercial regulations. A poorly developed, uncoordinated infrastructure of roads and bridges further inhibited commerce.

Merchants, manufacturers, and bankers looked to royal houses to provide strength and stability. Throughout the history of Europe after the fall of Rome, monarchs had often been kings in name rather than in fact. While theoretically subordinate to them, powerful local nobles like the Duke of Burgundy in France were actually often more powerful than those who sat on the thrones. This was changing, at least in some places. Merchants and bankers, such as the Fugger family of Augsburg and the Medicis of Florence, provided money to national monarchs. The monarchs turned money into power, raising armies sufficient in size to cow the independent local nobles. Power soon translated into more uniform legal practices and commercial regulations, greater security for persons and property, and infrastructure development.

These major economic and political developments did not begin in the villages, where a large majority of Europeans lived, but they had an impact there. The rise of national monarchs changed life in the villages. On the positive side, greater personal and property security benefited the peasants just as it benefited other orderly and law-abiding people, and improved roads and bridges facilitated marketing of crops and broadened social horizons. Less positive, perhaps, was the loss of local autonomy that accompanied the rise of the nation-state. Local people, for example, no longer dispensed justice. A centralized court bureaucracy with a standardized legal code now undertook that task.

14 The new monarchical nation-states also placed burdens on the peasantry. Central governments with expanded functions demanded taxes and soldiers that the villages were compelled to provide. Wedded to the rising urban classes and fearful of the urban masses, national monarchs saw to it that cities—especially capital cities—were relatively well fed and lightly taxed. The villages frequently suffered as a consequence.

The growth in population and wealth of towns and cities also had an impact on villages, especially those nearby, generally in the direction of making villagers more commercial and market oriented. Peasants had always been involved in the market to a degree, regardless of the self-sufficient and subsistence orientation of their production. Even subsistence farmers usually produced some sort of surplus, since no farmer, not even today, can control his or her yield. Subsistence producers who were prudent planted enough to try to assure family self-sufficiency and also to provide a cushion against adversity. Sometimes they fell short, and crises of subsistence resulted, but usually they produced a surplus, which they marketed locally.

As towns grew in population and affluence, as physical security and transportation were improved, and as tempting trade goods and manufactured products filtered into the countryside, villagers became more attentive to market factors. They began producing more wheat, the urban bread grain of choice. They were likely to keep more sheep for wool and more cattle for butter and cheese.

Expanding market opportunities, along with population growth in most rural areas, turned entrepreneurial farmers' minds toward thoughts of greater productivity. Some began to agitate for an end to the open-field system, division of the common lands, and consolidation of holdings and their enclosure behind fences or hedges. Detractors of traditional village agriculture complained that it diminished productivity. Not only was farming scattered fields inefficient, but sound management and restoration of fields was difficult when all villagers enjoyed certain rights on them.

Standing in favor of maintaining open fields and common lands were forces of self-interest and custom. In a conservative, risk-averse society, the very longevity of the open fields and the commons provided a powerful argument for their retention. But self-interest played a key role as well. Peasants with small holdings and laborers worried that, without access to their neighbors' fields and the commons, they would be unable to raise the livestock that sustained their standard of living.

The threat that market thinking presented to the traditional values of the village meant that struggles over consolidation, enclosure, and extirpation of common lands and common rights were intense and protracted. In individual villages the struggle went on for years and even decades, and it was often necessary to appeal to outside authority for resolution, as in England, where village enclosures often required acts of Parliament. In the course of these struggles village harmony was often shattered, as peasants divided along class lines.

The development of a more market-oriented economy in the villages was not an easy, smooth, or rapid process. As late as 1700 only half the villages of England had undergone enclosure, mostly in the east and south near London and continental markets. But every year more open-field villages were converted, and once enclosed they never returned to the old system. The rural future belonged to the entrepreneurs and innovators, not to the keepers of custom, partly because experience proved them right. A more productive agriculture provided more and better food to rural and urban people alike, and market-oriented farmers enjoyed a rising material standard of living. On the other hand, insecurity and impoverishment were often the result of the market revolution for the rural poor, and materialism, jealousy, and individual selfishness poisoned human relationships in villages where organic communalism had once been the ideal.

Changes in politics, economics, and habits of mind in Europe five hundred years ago thus affected villagers in complex and far-reaching ways, and the change was just beginning. In August of 1492 a tiny fleet set forth from Palos, Spain, under the command of Christopher Columbus. Appropriately enough, he was engaged in finding a new route to the Orient, a project that interested his patrons, national monarchs Ferdinand and Isabella of a newly united Spain. Instead, he found America, initiating a process that revolutionized both the world he found and the world he knew.

LIFE IN THE WOODLAND CULTURE

Rather than being one of the outlying islands of Japan, as Columbus surmised, the place he named San Salvador when he landed there in October of 1492 was on the periphery of two large and diverse continents. Over the next several centuries Europeans would find in the Americas geographic, climatological, biotic, and social variety far beyond what Europe had to offer.

In 1492 there were perhaps as many as 100 million people in the Americas.

16 Some lived in the frozen Arctic, while others dwelt in the treetops in equatorial rainforests. Some lived in highly bureaucratized and commercialized civilizations, such as those of the Aztecs of Mexico and the Incas of Peru, while others, such as the Bannocks and Paiutes of the Great Basin, were wanderers who lived on the roots and insect larvae they dug from the ground.

There was much about the peoples of the Americas that Europeans could not or would not understand. But many of those Columbus called Indians lived lives that were not all that different from those of European peasants. Consider, for example, the peoples of the Woodland Culture, which included most of the groups in what became British North America and the United States, that portion of the continent south of the Great Lakes and the St. Lawrence River, east of the Mississippi, and north of the Gulf of Mexico. Most of the people of the Woodland Culture lived in a village society dependent on an agricultural economy.

There were differences between Woodland Culture peoples and Europeans. For one thing, villages in the Woodland Culture tended to be a little smaller than those in western Europe, usually ranging from two hundred to five hundred people, at a time when five hundred was probably the average population in European villages. They usually laid claim to a larger territory than did their European counterparts. Moreover, most villages in the Woodland Culture were mobile. In summer they would be near arable land. Fall and winter would find them in the forest, where firewood and game were plentiful and shelter from the wind could be found. In spring they would be on the riverbanks, taking advantage of runs of spawning fish. Mobility had its advantages. It helped people escape vermin, albeit briefly, and made it more difficult for them to foul their water supplies. To us a movable village might not seem like a village, because we think of a village as a place. But to the people of the Woodland Culture the village was a social entity—it was people. It was the same thing to the peasants of contemporary Europe.

The typical village of the Woodland Culture was commonly part of—and encompassed—a complex social structure. Tribes, which our European forebearers tended to visualize as unitary political and social entities, were often rather loose aggregations of subgroups that identified with one another on some basis, often linguistic similarity. Most of the larger tribes consisted of a number of bands. Bands usually distinguished themselves from one another on the basis of culture, dialect, or geographic location. Many Euro-

Town of Secotan, in present-day North Carolina, in the 1580s.
Engraving by Theodore DeBry after a watercolor by John White. Courtesy of the Library of Congress.

pean parallels could be used for purposes of illustration. Sicilians, for example, are Italian, but their dialect, culture, and region provide them with a common identity that distinguishes them from the larger society of which they are part. In the Woodland Culture, bands often composed several villages, usually proximate to one another. Their cultural identity was underscored by the fact that they usually enjoyed a degree of political independence from the tribal groups with which they were identified.

At the subvillage level the most important social units in the Woodland Culture were kinship groups, extended families usually called clans. Clans were composed of people who traced their ancestry to a single source, commonly an animal such as a bear or a wolf. The inner cohesion of clans, reflected in the fact that all members sometimes lived together in large dwellings, occasionally threatened the unity of the village, especially when clans behaved as political organizations favoring particular agendas or courses of action.

One major difference between the Woodland Culture and rural Europe was that in the former, social status and political leadership were usually attained rather than ascribed, though in some groups at least some positions were inherited. People usually came to be respected, and assumed leadership positions, on the basis of accomplishments and demonstrated competence. People became sachems or shamans because they possessed political or spiritual skills. When a sachem could no longer demonstrate the ability to provide political leadership, or when a shaman could no longer mediate effectively with the spiritual world, he lost public confidence and was replaced. As in Europe, leaders were males, but women often exerted a good deal of power within clans, and the frequent absences of men gone hunting and fighting gave women effective control of the villages.

Most villagers of the Woodland Culture lived mainly by subsistence agriculture. Men would open fields by burning out grass, underbrush, and small trees. Trees too large to burn would be girdled (a strip of bark around the base would be removed, killing the tree by preventing the flow of water and nutrients to its leaves), allowing the sun to penetrate to the forest floor. By this method of clearing, called slash-and-burn or swidden in developing countries today, Indians opened fields that the English estimated at between one hundred and two hundred acres.

As in many developing regions today, women did the actual farming. Using mattocks (heavy implements combining features of hoes and axes), women would form hills in which corn, beans, and squash would frequently be planted together. These crops were mutually supportive. Corn formed a trellis for the beans, which in turn drew nitrogen from the air to fertilize the corn. Squash spread over the ground, impeding weed growth and the evaporation of essential moisture. When fields began to lose their fertility, the Indians simply abandoned them and opened new ones.

Squash would remain edible for a long time if kept cool, and corn and beans could be dried. Corn and beans are both high in vegetable protein, and when consumed together each releases an otherwise inaccessible protein in the other. These three crops, along with some minor ones such as artichokes, cucumbers, and pumpkins, supplied about 80 percent of the calories consumed by Woodland Culture villagers, the rest coming from game, fish, wild berries and fruits, nuts, roots, and dogs, the only domesticated animal possessed by North American Indians.

To English observers, life in the Woodland Culture was idyllic. Women produced a subsistence with relatively little labor, and men devoted themselves mainly to hunting. Moreover, villagers seemed to have ample time for ceremonies and celebrations, recreations that often revolved around milestones in life, seasonal changes, and natural phenomena. But appearances were deceptive. The people in America, like those in Europe, lived in cold and smokey dwellings. Vermin were their more-or-less constant companions. The Woodland Culture diet was sound but incomplete. It lacked variety, and the absence of fruits and vegetables for most of the year caused problems, as did the deficiency of calcium. People in the Woodland Culture lived on the margin. They got by in normal times, but a sudden increase in population or an unexpected shortfall in resources caused hunger and sometimes starvation.

Childbirth, infection, and pneumonia were all major killers, even before the Europeans introduced deadly viruses to which American Indians were not immune. The hunt presented dangers, as did warfare, which was more-or-less endemic in some areas. Arthritis, respiratory disorders, syphilis, and intestinal parasites were numbered among their chronic disorders. It was a precarious existence, in which life expectancy was probably about what it was for the European peasant.

Like all peoples in a prerational and prescientific state of existence, people in the Woodland Culture attempted to limit the precariousness of life and control the uncontrollable through religion and superstition. Shamans influ-

20 enced the natural world by appealing to some spirits and warding off others in attempts to make harvests abundant and hunts successful or to help individuals survive war or illness. Sometimes they were effective and sometimes they were not, but failure led people to question the shaman, not the existence of a controlling spirit world.

The people saw themselves as part of nature and part of society as well. The village, the band, and the clan defined individuals, providing their identity and imparting meaning to life. The individual lived for the group, and the group sustained the individual, providing for every one of his or her material and spiritual needs. It was a relationship that is hard for us to grasp, but one that the illiterate and unsophisticated European peasant would have understood implicitly.

THE COLUMBIAN EXCHANGE

The peoples of the Woodland Culture could not know it and would not begin to realize it for generations, but Columbus's voyage doomed their way of life. Over the next four centuries, the Spanish, the Portuguese, the English, the French, and the Dutch turned the Western Hemisphere into a creolized Europe, where people spoke European languages, practiced European religions, and lived under European political, economic, and legal systems. The Western Hemisphere served as a laboratory for an expansive Europe, and the experiment's success lay in the eye of the beholder.

From the perspective of agriculture and rural life, America was not exactly turned into a pale imitation of Europe, but it was altered dramatically nonetheless. The Europeans replaced what was usually a village-centered, subsistence system with a commercial agricultural regime in which the most important units of production were plantations. Among American Indians agricultural producers were usually free and female. Among the Europeans those working on farms were predominantly male and were often slaves.

European technology also made its appearance in the New World. The Europeans introduced wind- and water-powered mills to grind grain and saw wood, and they brought plows to break the soil. They introduced new crops, such as small grains, rice, and sugar, and a range of domesticated animals, such as horses, cattle, swine, and sheep.

Nearly as important as the intentional introductions were the unintentional ones. New weeds and grasses crossed the Atlantic as bedding or animal fodder. Clover, bluegrass, and the ubiquitous dandelion were among the flora introduced in this hemisphere in that manner. Likewise sparrows and rats, common stowaways aboard ships, were among the fauna accidentally transferred from the Old World to the New.

These alterations and introductions were disruptive and far from benign. European agricultural practices were far more intrusive than were American Indian ones. Fully cleared and plowed fields of the European type were especially vulnerable to water and wind erosion and to weeds; soon streams were choked with silt, indicating lost fertility. The European practice of devoting entire fields to single crops increased vulnerability to insect pests and fungal outbreaks, and sharp-hooved cattle and rooting swine laid waste to tender native plants. The face of rural America was altered so dramatically and completely that it is hard for us to say with any certainty what parts of it even looked like before 1492.

Interhemispheric contact was less revolutionary for Europe than it was for America, but its impact was significant nonetheless. In terms of major economic and political trends, contact with America had the effect of pushing Europe further and faster along the road toward capitalism and the dominance of the nation-state.

In the short run, the Americas enriched the earliest arrival, Spain, disproportionately and dramatically. The gold and silver that poured out of the mines of Peru, Mexico, and Bolivia made Spain the richest country in Europe and, at a time when the size of one's army depended entirely on one's ability to hire soldiers, the continent's most powerful nation as well. Eventually other well-unified and strongly led nation-states such as England and France followed Spain to the New World and competed with her there. They, too, were enriched and empowered by that process and moved ahead of the less well-organized and integrated Germans and Italians.

But the entire continent felt the economic impact of the exploitation of the Western Hemisphere. Spanish gold and silver flowed through Europe, raising price levels disruptively, hastening the replacement of a barter with a money economy, quickening trade, manufacturing, and urbanization, and simultaneously speeding the transformation to a more commercial, market-oriented agriculture.

The pace of commercial enterprise was further quickened by the introduction of seductive new products from America, such as cocoa, and the dramatically increased supply of such luxury goods as coffee, rice, cotton, and sugar. These products helped transform Europeans' lives. By the eighteenth century coffee had become the main import item of the Swedes, who had discovered in it the secret to staying awake, and most peasants had replaced the honey pot on their tables with a sugar loaf. Europeans were being pulled increasingly into a modern world of markets and exchange, a world in which Brazilian coffee, Barbadian sugar, and Virginia tobacco played a role as important in people's lives as that once played by local cheese, rye, and wool.

On a less exciting but equally enduring level, contact with America allowed the introduction of a number of new crops that revolutionized European farming and enriched European diets. Squash, pumpkins, and most varieties of beans were American introductions in Europe. Also important was the tomato, called the love apple by Europeans because of its supposed effectiveness as an aphrodisiac. Another significant introduction was American corn, or maize. Maize converts sunlight into more calories per acre than any other grain and can be used for human consumption as well as for wet or dry fodder for animals. Maize became an important European crop, especially in the Balkans and the Mediterranean region.

The most important American crop introduction in Europe was the potato. Potatoes are high in vegetable protein and other nutrients, grow well in cool, damp conditions and on marginal, sandy soils, and yield impressively. In the eighteenth century it was estimated that a peasant family could live for a year on the potatoes produced on an acre and a half.

It took a long time for the peasants to accept potatoes as human food, largely because they believed them a cause of leprosy and a source of flatulence. But by 1800 the potato had become the primary item in the peasant diet throughout northern and central Europe. Its adoption dramatically increased the capacity of the land to support people, thereby stimulating an increase in the rural population, freeing farmers to go to cities, and allowing the devotion of more acres to commercial crops.

In their own way, then, both gold and potatoes transformed Europe, and in the same general manner. They and the other products of the Americas moved the Old World further and more rapidly down the road to commercialism, unitary political authority, and agricultural capitalism.

TWO

The Rural Development
of English North America

England felt the impact of the Spanish exploitation of the Western Hemisphere as much as or more than any other western European country. Spanish gold and silver filtered into England, enriching merchants and artisans and encouraging those who considered growing wool for commercial markets. The wealth and luxuries of America excited English senses and stimulated English avarice. And Spain's strength made England cautious and induced her leaders to remain on peaceful terms with Europe's greatest power.

But England did not attempt to undertake its own colonizing ventures until a century after Columbus's voyage. Part of the reason for this delay was the preoccupation of the crown of England with conquering Ireland, a bloody and brutal struggle that took much of the sixteenth century. Internal political and religious disorder also held England's attention. Restive independent nobles periodically challenged crown authority, and the Scots were hostile. Henry VIII's creation of the Protestant Church of England in the 1530s stimulated religious dissent and, at a time when state and church upheld one another, political opposition as well from Catholics who wanted no Protestant Reformation and Protestants who wanted a more complete one than Henry provided.

Eventually, these factors that had delayed colonization stimulated it. Military officers who had learned their trade in Ireland sought new fields to conquer for crown and country. And religious dissenters, Catholics and Calvinists especially, thought about creating an English society without the Church of England in the New World.

Economic factors also played a role in stimulating colonization. Enclosure put increasing numbers of villagers out of their places, and even those who held land wondered how they could provide for their children. By diminishing available arable lands and shortening the growing season, the Little Ice Age curtailed agricultural opportunities for tens of thousands. Shrinking opportunities for some conspired with a growing population to create large numbers of paupers, orphans, sturdy beggars, and criminals, who represented a drag on society. Countless others avoided becoming public charges but saw little opportunity to improve their stations in life. Eventually, these social and economic forces created a stream of English colonists to the New World beside which the out-migrations from Spain, France, or the Netherlands paled into insignificance.

The portion of the New World where most of these colonists settled was known well enough by the English to make them confident but not well enough to make them cautious. In 1497 and 1498 John and Sebastian Cabot had explored the coasts of Newfoundland and Nova Scotia under commission from Henry VII, and English fishermen visited the region throughout the sixteenth century. The North American coast further south became increasingly familiar to English ships carrying on illegal trade with Spanish colonies or engaging in piracy. What the English knew about the North American coast—that it was heavily timbered, drained by impressive rivers, and inhabited by natives eager to barter furs for European goods—fed extravagant hopes that resulted in early colonizing ventures at Roanoke and Jamestown.

Eventually, and after much pain, America disabused the English of their fantasies. It was not a land where people could live without work, where gold and precious gems could be picked off the ground, or where the passage to the Indies could be found. But it was a land where agricultural societies could be developed that might provide comfortable lives, societies that were shaped by both the English experience and the American environment.

The first successful English colony in North America was founded in the Chesapeake Bay region in 1607 as a profit-making venture by a private company. There, in a portion of vast grant they called Virginia, after Elizabeth I, the Virgin Queen, the founders planted a settlement they called Jamestown, after James I, Elizabeth's nephew and successor. The Virginia Company of London hoped and expected to profit in a number of ways from their colony, but for many years its very survival was in doubt.

From the very beginning Jamestown suffered from a host of problems. The town was sited in a swampy area on the James River, which was unhealthy even before the colonists began fouling the water. Lacking knowledge of the region and short on agricultural experience, the early colonists could not feed themselves. The powerful Powhatan Indians who dominated the area were skilled at the production of such American crops as corn and beans, and colonists were awed by their fields that were sometimes larger than one hundred acres. But the Powhatans did not have a substantial surplus to trade, and when colonists tried to seize what they needed angry Indians drove them back into their pathetic stockade. As a result the company had to feed the colonists by sending relief ships from England. In the winter of 1609–10, known as the "starving time," the relief vessels failed to appear, and the colonists lived by eating cats, rats, dogs, and, eventually, the corpses of their fellow Virginians. While 1609–10 was the worst period in Jamestown, hunger, disease, and the Powhatans conspired to kill as many as three of every four colonists sent there between 1607 and 1622, usually within a year after their arrival.

All of this was a rude awakening for the company. It was expensive to send people to Jamestown just to have them die. Instead of turning a profit, the colony was a continual drain on the company's treasury, and the few commodities, such as potash and barrel staves, that Virginians produced did not begin to cover expenses. Exacerbating the company's financial crisis was the fact that the colony, six weeks distant by ship, was hard to supervise and control, and some managers were not above misappropriating company property and funds and using company servants on their own estates. Virginia enriched some people but not the investors from the London Company.

The company made a valiant effort to retrieve the situation in Virginia. It raised more money and redoubled its attempts to recruit settlers, tempting them with headrights, beginning in 1616. A headright was a grant of fifty acres for each person whose way was paid to Virginia by someone other than the company. Under this system, an immigrant to Virginia who brought a wife, three children, and a servant would receive three hundred acres and another fifty acres every time he brought in another servant. Later southern colonies also used headrights to encourage immigration in the early stages of settlement.

The English government, which saw Jamestown as a semipublic enterprise and a matter of national pride, did what it could to help. James gave the company the monopoly on tobacco production in the empire after Virginians started shipping it in 1617, and Parliament created a lottery, the proceeds of which were earmarked for the colony. The government exported undesirables—paupers and orphans, for example—to Virginia by the boatload, and judges gave criminals a choice of death or Virginia. The reputation of the colony is illustrated by the fact that a number of the condemned chose death.

These efforts had resulted in some progress when a surprise attack by Powhatans in 1622 killed one-fourth of the colonists. A colonial counterattack dramatically reduced the Indian threat but did not save the company from bankruptcy, and Virginia was still a place with an uncertain economic and demographic future when the crown assumed control in 1624. But it did survive and even attained a modest prosperity. Within a few years it was clear that, while it had met few of the high expectations of its founders, Virginia would be a successful colonial enterprise.

Part of the reason colonization succeeded in the Chesapeake region— where Maryland, founded by the Calvert family as a refuge for English Catholics, joined Virginia in 1632—was that the colonists learned to feed themselves. They subsisted on corn, pork, and beef. Corn converted sunlight into calories as efficiently for the English as it did for the Indians. And imported hogs and cattle multiplied rapidly in the Maryland and Virginia woods where they were allowed to roam, providing sustenance for colonists energetic enough to shoot them or round them up.

Another secret to the success of the Chesapeake colonies was tobacco. Tobacco was grown in both the New and Old Worlds, including in the British Isles, but when James I gave the company a monopoly in 1617 the government suppressed production of the crop in England. Tobacco growing became a virtual mania in Virginia, where people's lives largely revolved around it. It was a profitable product, and even though its price plummeted from three hundred to twenty shillings per hundredweight between 1617 and 1660, it returned a better income than anything else people in the Chesapeake could have produced.

Tobacco shaped both the human and the spatial organization of the Chesapeake. Tobacco's labor-intensive nature created high labor demands. Tobacco seeds were planted in flats in the late winter and early spring, where they were protected from direct sunlight by gauze awnings or brush. The seedlings were then transplanted in hills prepared with hoes. As the plants matured, they were weeded, topped and primed (topping prevented the plant from flowering and priming involved removal of coarse leaves at the base of the plant), and suckered (runners that might take plant energy that would otherwise go to leaves were pinched off) by hand, and insects were removed in the same way. When plants matured they were cut, hung on poles, and cured—a delicate and time-consuming process—and the finished product was carefully packed in large barrels for export.

One worker could handle about three acres of tobacco and could produce fifteen hundred to two thousand pounds per year. Because a farmer's income was highly dependent on the number of hands he could put in the tobacco fields, family labor was important, and there was a strong demand for indentured servants (people who sold their labor for a period of years in return for passage to America) and, later, for slaves.

Tobacco is also a crop that quickly drains nutrients from the soil. A tobacco field in the Chesapeake lost much of its natural fertility within three or four years. It was usually possible to follow tobacco with corn for a couple of years, but thereafter land had to lie fallow for about twenty years to recover its fertility. This meant that a farmer needed fifty or sixty acres of land for each hand; thus farms tended to be large. In 1668, for example, Thomas Tuggle maintained a family of six and a servant on a Middlesex County, Virginia, farm of one hundred acres.[1] While this was a substantial farm by English standards, it was sufficient to maintain only a small-scale tobacco farmer. The need for substantial acreage was the major factor encouraging the dispersion of settlement in the Chesapeake. In striking contrast to rural England, the Chesapeake was a land where most people lived on individual farmsteads and few lived in towns.

Life in the seventeenth-century Chesapeake was primitive. Most planters, as the farmers were called, lived in rudimentary conditions. Wooden huts, usually of only one room, were the norm, and physical possessions were few and expensive in a place where virtually all manufactured products had to be imported. A bedstead and straw mattress, a rude table and bench, a gun, a pot or two, a few wooden plates and cups, and a few crude utensils constituted the personal property of the common planter. Poor planters were worse off, usually lacking bedsteads and tables. The planter's days were spent in tedious service to the demands of tobacco and corn, and his nights were often spent alone. Because most immigrants to the Chesapeake were male indentured servants, many men never had the opportunity to marry. The diet consisted mainly of corn and pork, and recreation was crude and re-volved largely around liquor.

The deathrate fell slowly as more natives—relatively immune to the dis-eases of the region—were born and as planters fanned out from the pestilen-tial Jamestown site. But death was still an omnipresent reality in the Ches-apeake. A male of twenty-one who managed to live through the seasoning process in the early Chesapeake could expect to survive only until his early forties, and even natives had a life expectancy of less than fifty years.

The high deathrate and the uneven sex ratio were only two of the reasons why the population grew slowly. Because servants were prevented from mar-rying, most immigrants did not have that opportunity until their late twen-ties or early thirties. Those who did marry had an average of only two chil-dren, and fully one-third of unions were broken by death in less than ten years. Widows, in high demand in this male society, usually remarried quickly, creating blended families. Mary Tuggle, who brought a son from her previous marriage into her union with Thomas, was quite typical. Wid-ows were also sometimes able to acquire substantial property in those early decades, amassing substantial estates through several marriages.

The fragility of life translated into social instability. Individuals and fam-ilies came and went in a region where death was part of life, and the immi-grant population exceeded the native-born population until nearly 1700. Planters did not live long enough to develop substantial estates or become acknowledged and experienced community leaders. Those who became prominent could not perpetuate family status through sons who were not there. Paternal discontinuity prevented the emergence of the sort of strong patriarchalism that later characterized the region, and enduring kinship net-works could not easily develop in a situation of individual immigration, high deathrates, and low birthrates. The strong rural neighborhoods that later came to characterize the Chesapeake did make an early appearance, however. Colonists depended on neighbors for help in time of need, to look after widows, and to care for orphans. In an age before modern welfare systems and even before dependable kinship groups, neighbors provided a form of social security.

One might wonder why people came to a place where they were likely to die, and where, if they lived, they would work harder than in England in far more primitive surroundings. But the Chesapeake offered opportunity that was absent in England. In America people could become landowners and achieve a level of independence and self-respect that was, for them, virtually unattainable in England.

In the seventeenth century, land signified not only wealth but security. A man's ability to support himself and his family and to establish a position of respect in his community and participate in its affairs depended on his ability to control land. But in England landownership was moving further and further beyond the grasp of average people. For them, the future seemed to promise a hand-to-mouth existence, a life of hardship and dependency.

Immigration promised land. One who lived through the seasoning, survived indentured servitude, and worked hard could expect to acquire land. Thomas Tuggle came to the Chesapeake as an indentured servant, but when he died in 1689 he owned one farm of one hundred acres and another of 110 that he rented to a tenant. True, for every Thomas Tuggle there were two or three others who died in servitude or who lived only to struggle along in a brutal, marginal existence. But the fact that it was possible to acquire property and achieve status and self-respect there made the Chesapeake a magnet for thousands of ordinary English people.

NEW ENGLAND

In 1638, while Chesapeake settlers were still struggling with death and dispersion in their attempt to create a satisfactory rural society, a few hundred miles to the northeast in a region called New England, Peter Noyes and his fellow founders of the town of Sudbury were confidently electing officers, dividing land, and assigning work.[2] Their experience would differ dramatically from that of their fellow English men and women in Virginia. Unlike their contemporaries in the Chesapeake, they were able to recreate the English agricultural village in the New World. While Virginians found death and starvation in their early years, New Englanders enjoyed health and abundance. Relative to the Chesapeake, New England was a world of cer-

Worm fencing and cleared fields—typical of early-American practice.
Courtesy of the Library of Congress.

tainty and security, inhabited by a confident, expanding, and self-reliant population.

Virginia was founded by a company seeking profit and settled by people in search of opportunity. While these motives were not totally absent in New England, the settlers there were motivated mainly by religion. The early New England colonies were founded by Calvinists, Protestants who believed that the Reformation should have gone much further than the Church of England was willing to take it. The crown of England under James I and his son Charles I was decreasingly tolerant of Calvinists, convincing some of them that the New World offered the opportunity to create a model community based on Christian love.

The first Calvinist community in New England was the Plymouth Colony, planted by Pilgrims at the base of Cape Cod in 1620. The Pilgrims were separatists who had left the Church of England and, in many cases, England itself, fleeing to the Netherlands for sanctuary. The New World offered them the opportunity to recreate an English culture and society without suffering persecution by English authorities. The early years at Plymouth were difficult, but with Indian help the colonists mastered New World crops and methods, and the colony enjoyed a modest success until 1691, when it was merged with its larger neighbor, the Massachusetts Bay Colony.

The Rural Development of English North America

The Massachusetts Bay Colony was founded in 1629 by Puritans. These people were Calvinists who had tried to reform the Church of England from within but in the face of rising persecution had embraced colonization. Puritan successes were much more dramatic than those of their Pilgrim neighbors, and they quickly built the dominant New England society and the one that unintentionally gave birth to New Hampshire, Rhode Island, and Connecticut as well.

When contrasted with their counterparts in the Chesapeake, the New England colonies were stunning successes. The communities quickly achieved economic self-sufficiency, the people were relatively healthy, birthrates were high and deathrates low, and life expectancies were impressive—indeed, only slightly lower than they are in America today, for those who survived early childhood. Unlike Virginians, moreover, New Englanders successfully transferred the English agricultural village to the American environment.

There were lots of reasons to live in villages, as even the Virginians illustrated by clinging to the hellhole that was Jamestown far beyond the time dictated by common sense. Villages facilitated common work and afforded protection, not only from the Indians but also from the wilderness, which superstitious Europeans saw as the domain of Satan and the dwelling place of elves, trolls, and other creatures that could ruin a sturdy peasant's day. Most of all, villages were a familiar part of life, and recreating them in the American environment and giving them Old Country names like Worcester and Roxbury and Bristol made the New World less frightening to people who wanted to leave England but had no desire to cease to be English.

Villages were successful in early New England for several reasons. For one thing, New Englanders grew crops that did not encourage dispersion of farms in the way tobacco did. Moreover, the religious purpose of most early New Englanders imparted in them a devotion to communal living that people in the Chesapeake were less likely to have. Finally, while English villages had evolved prior to historical memory, their New England counterparts were carefully planned by colonial officials who knew what successful communities required.

In the Massachusetts Bay Colony the General Court (an elected body combining judicial and legislative functions) organized immigrants into towns, commonly consisting of between thirty and fifty families. On occasion the people in a town would be from one place in England, but usually they were drawn from several locations. In putting together a town, the General Court was attentive to the demands of self-government and social and economic self-sufficiency. It tried to assure that some of the townspeople brought governing experience from England. It also attempted to include in each town people with essential skills, such as milling and blacksmithing. Sometimes a minister was part of the original town, and sometimes he was called later. When the General Court was satisfied with the composition of the community it made a town grant, usually of twenty-five to one hundred square miles but sometimes larger. The size of the grant was determined by the population of the town and the perceived quality of the land, but towns in the colony were larger than their English counterparts; it seemed as if plenty of land was available in the New World, and the General Court hoped to provide for the children and grandchildren to come as well as the original residents.

The towns fulfilled the expectation of the General Court that they would be self-governing. One of the first decisions a town, as a corporate body, was called on to make was what sort of agricultural system to put in place. New Englanders most frequently instituted an open-field system with common lands and common rights on all lands, though this was not universal. Part of the reason for this preference was undoubtedly familiarity. Peter Noyes and the other leading inhabitants of Sudbury came from open-field villages, so it is not surprising that they would choose to replicate this system, but it is also likely that New Englanders were drawn to the open-field system for the same reason their distant ancestors had been—because it placed a premium on communal labor and minimized risk. Both of these were important considerations in the early stage of settlement.

Enclosure eventually came to these towns, sometimes quite quickly. While Sudbury sons continued to follow the system of their fathers a generation after settlement, nearby Andover was enclosing fields within fifteen years.[3] Some characteristics of the open-field system were retained, however. The continuing existence in so many New England towns, including Boston, of commons that have been transformed into parks is a living tribute to an ancient agricultural system.

The open-field system put a premium on communal labor and communal decision making. In March a town meeting was held to determine which farmers would plant what and when and on which of their fields it would be planted. Usually the town simply ratified decisions made by selectmen, elected officials analogous to city councilmembers today. Common rights and responsibilities, and such issues as when animals should be turned into the fields, called for further community discussion. The myriad responsibilities of communal labor also involved the filling of many offices, including such curious ones as hogreeve (literally, a sheriff for swine) and fence viewer, who had the job of seeing to it that temporary fences were erected in a timely manner and correctly maintained.

The most intense subject of community concern at the beginning of settlement involved the division of lands. All householders received grants of land, including house lots, in the village proper, and meadow and upland beyond. The amount of land granted varied, however, depending on the social status of the grantee, the importance of his occupation to the community, and the number of people depending on him. Peter Noyes, who had been a substantial tenant in England and had ten dependents, received 121 acres in Sudbury, a bit more than the minister, Edmund Brown, while the aptly named miller, Thomas Cakebread, got 174 acres. On the other end of the scale, Thomas Buckmaster, a single man of undistinguished origins, received ten acres.

The first division usually did not involve much land—in Sudbury a little more than 10 percent of the town was distributed, or about forty acres per family—but later divisions followed in response to settlers' demands for enlarged holdings to provide for growing families and to build farms for their children, and in response to requests from the second generation. These distributions were guided by the same considerations that had determined the first, with the result that the town elite often became substantial property owners. After four divisions in Andover, Massachusetts, for example, prominent settler John Osgood held 610 acres. It is essential to remember, however, that every householder in the original town, as well as such others as the town chose to admit, got land. In Andover Daniel Poor, who had come to America as a servant, left an estate of more than two hundred acres. While far inferior to Osgood's, it was an expanse of land he could not have dreamed of owning in England, a country in which both his condition and his fate were captured by his name.

Determining the agricultural system, selecting officers, and distributing land put the towns in the habit of governing themselves, directly and through selectmen. Towns made and enforced their own rules, provided protection and justice, created and maintained churches and schools, dispensed welfare services, warned off undesirables and approved the admis-

34

sion of new residents, and governed the colonies through their representatives in assemblies and general courts.

The towns also achieved a high level of economic self-sufficiency. Most villages included a miller, a smith, a brewer, a harness-maker, a cooper (who made barrels), and others whose skills supported agricultural production. Everybody—even ministers and skilled artisans—farmed. In the early years corn, beans, pumpkins, and squash were the most heavily emphasized food crops. Wheat and rye were also popular but demanded advanced technology. While one could grow the traditional Indian crops with a hoe, successful small grain production was difficult without plows and harrows. As late as 1633 there was only one plow in the entire Plymouth Colony, and elsewhere it was not uncommon for the farmers of a town to share one plow, sometimes designating one of their number a plowman. Further complicating wheat production was the presence of stem rust, a fungal infection common in New England and referred to by the colonists as the blast, that made its appearance in the 1660s and continued to be a problem thereafter. The colonists also maintained vegetable gardens, planted orchards, kept bees (a European introduction to America referred to by the Indians as English flies), and grew flax and hemp for cloth. They kept cattle, hogs, and poultry. Few sheep were raised in the early years, due to the close supervision they required and their vulnerability to the wolves that infested seventeenth-century New England.

Within the limits set by their technology and environment, New England settlers lived well. A difficult climate and thin soils limited yields to about fifteen bushels of corn and fewer than ten bushels of small grains per acre in most places, but extensive production compensated to some degree. While the diet was unvaried and was bereft of fresh fruits and vegetables for much of the year, there was no starvation in New England. The fact that conception declined dramatically in the early spring, when stocks of food were depleted, and while mothers were breast-feeding indicates low nutritional levels by modern Western standards, but not by those of early modern Europe or of much of the developing world today.

Housing and other creature comforts were crude, especially for the first generation. Staying warm was a major challenge in a region that was substantially colder in the seventeenth century than it is today. Rooms with low ceilings and few windows were testimonies to the difficulty of keeping warm, as were the large hearths and roaring fires. Historians have estimated that the average New England family burned three-fifths to three-quarters of an acre of timber per year. The settlers were fortunate to be living in a place where timber was so abundant that it was more often regarded as a nuisance than a resource. An advantage of the cold climate was that it was also a healthy climate. Water supplies were relatively clean, and low water temperatures impeded the development of typhoid and other bacterial diseases. Yellow fever and malaria, which added to the hazards of living farther south, did not appear in New England.

Sufficient food and a healthy climate were two of the factors that resulted in impressive population growth. Another was the fact that most settlers immigrated in families, providing more balanced sex ratios than obtained in the Chesapeake. Those who came to New England could expect to live what were for the time extraordinarily long lives—an average of about seventy years. They could look forward to having large families—an average of six live births for a first-generation woman—and they could anticipate that only one in ten children would die before the age of twenty. This survival rate—extraordinarily high for the seventeenth century—implies both that climate was salubrious and that mothers were healthy and well-nourished.

The low deathrate and high birthrate in early New England meant that the population exploded through natural increase. During the first thirty years of life in Andover, for example, there were 315 births and only 60 deaths. But the statistics meant much more in human terms. Husbands and wives could expect to spend most of their lives with one another, and young widows and widowers and blended families were not the norm. Children had the security of knowing that they would likely have living parents when they reached adulthood, and parents could anticipate seeing children and even grandchildren established in life as adults. Families and communities established a stability and permanence much more quickly than was the case in the Chesapeake.

There was also a downside to New England demographics. The potency and fertility of New England patriarchs and matriarchs and the high child-survival rate meant that what had seemed like a vast open land quickly became crowded. Because of the longevity of fathers and mothers, children sometimes waited a long time for land and thus for independence. While in the Chesapeake children inherited estates before adulthood, in New England many adults remained dependent on aged parents. When Andover's Daniel Poor died in 1689, his thirty-year-old son John, still unmarried, in-

36 herited his father's estate, finally becoming a landowner. Two years later he
was dead. While in one part of America childhood seemed too short, in another it must have seemed too long.

THE OTHER COLONIES

Virginia and the Massachusetts Bay Colony were the most important of the early colonies, and they developed into leaders in the South and New England respectively. During the century following the planting of Massachusetts Bay several other colonies were developed, so that by 1740 English settlements stretched from what is now southern Maine to northern Georgia.

Some settlement resulted from an expansion of existing colonies. Rapid population growth and religious disputation in the Massachusetts Bay Colony led to settlements in Rhode Island, Connecticut, New Hampshire, Long Island, and Maine, which was part of Massachusetts until 1820. North Carolina was settled mainly by small planters from Virginia.

South Carolina, the most important of the three colonies on the South Atlantic coast, was settled mainly by immigrants from the British sugar island of Barbados. After some difficult early decades in a region at least as unhealthy as the Chesapeake, South Carolinians developed a thriving commercial agriculture based on the production of rice, which was most successfully grown in coastal swamps where tidal action facilitated the flooding and draining of fields. The South Carolinians were also enthusiastic users of slave labor, and at the time of the Revolution theirs was the only colony in which a majority of the people were slaves. South of the Carolinas was the last British colony on the North American mainland, Georgia, founded in 1732 as a second-chance refuge for English debtors and paupers.

Much of the Middle Atlantic region came to the English through conquest. The Dutch had established an early presence there, setting up a fur-trading post at the present site of Albany, New York, in 1614. Eleven years later they founded a town called New Amsterdam—which became the capital of New Netherland and eventually New York City—on the southern part of Manhattan Island.

Initially the Dutch introduced the pattern of dispersed farm settlements in New Netherland. This was the method whereby the Dutch had settled marginal lands in the Netherlands, and the American wilderness apparently seemed analogous to those areas. Few small farmers immigrated, however, so the Dutch attempted to speed settlement by making huge land grants to wealthy patroons, who were supposed to bring tenants from Europe to work their lands. Some of these patroons enjoyed a modest success, but in general this method of settlement did not result in the level of immigration attained by neighboring English colonies.

In 1664 the English seized New Netherland from the Dutch during a war, thereby acquiring title to what they called New York, New Jersey, and Delaware. Delaware—founded as New Sweden by Swedes in 1638—had been conquered by the Dutch in 1655.

While New Sweden was not a major colony, pioneering methods introduced there by ethnic Finns under Swedish control significantly shaped the settlement of much of America. Girdling of trees (also practiced by many Indians), the log cabin, and worm fencing (fences consisting of sections of rails laid at ninety-degree angles to other sections, thus obviating the necessity of nails) were among the common frontier-settlement practices imported to America by these Finns, whose self-conscious independence and disrespect for authority also tended to be reflected in the stereotypical character of the American pioneers who replicated their methods.

The most important colony in the Middle Atlantic region was Pennsylvania, founded by William Penn in 1680 as a refuge for Protestant extremists called Quakers. It was Penn's goal to undertake settlement in an orderly fashion, similar to the way the Puritans in the Massachusetts Bay Colony had done half a century before. He wanted settlement centered in planned villages, surrounded by farmlands surveyed in a rational grid pattern, with ample common lands set aside for public use.

These plans collapsed almost immediately. Immigrants fanned out over the countryside ahead of surveyors, settling on choice land in individual farmsteads. Few of the planned towns got off the ground, as colonists preferred to scatter mills, stores, and taverns around the countryside where they were convenient. Moreover, settlers chose to enclose the land and to make little or no provision for commons.

The rapid collapse of Penn's vision was due in part to the enticements of a rich and abundant countryside. The character of the Quakers had something to do with it as well. They needed no lessons from local Finns in individualism and disrespect for authority; for them these traits were literally articles of faith. The English background also played a part. Most early Pennsylvanians came from the English Midlands, where settlement in small rural clusters rather than villages was the norm. Finally, by 1680, when Pennsylvania was founded, the commercialization of agriculture was well advanced and was increasingly accepted in the British Isles. Thinking and acting like agricultural capitalists, Pennsylvania Quakers shunned arrangements that implied the subordination of individual interests to those of the community. Their goal was individual success, and they were able to achieve it in the rich and fertile valleys of southeastern Pennsylvania.

By the middle of the eighteenth century an impressive string of British colonies stretched along the Atlantic Coast. These colonies were similar, in that they were all predominantly British and reflected that reality in their language, customs, laws, and political and economic systems. Yet they were all different, with varied settlement patterns, social organizations, and agricultural practices. These differences derived from the diverse origins, experiences, and goals of the settlers and the varied environments they encountered and were reflected in several distinct styles of rural living.

Most rural Americans, whatever sort of life they lived, confronted new opportunities and challenges in the eighteenth century. The opportunities came mainly as a result of growing economic prosperity. The challenges largely involved coping with a shrinking resource base and new labor systems. Together, these opportunities and challenges helped create a backdrop for the American Revolution.

THREE

Maturity

and Its Discontents

When Thomas Tuggle was organizing his farm and raising his family in Middlesex County, Virginia, in the 1660s the Chesapeake region was still a young and raw place. Dwellings were scattered in what was still largely a wilderness. Barely nine hundred people lived in the county. They were mostly young men—some landowners and some servants, as Tuggle had been—they were overwhelmingly of English birth, and most were unrelated to one another. The settlers fed themselves, but they depended on England to provide them with virtually all of the manufactures they consumed. Their tastes and standards were English, and their memories were of England.

In 1700, Thomas's son Henry worked the farm he had created, but much had changed. The population had nearly doubled, to about eighteen hundred people, contributing to a denser settlement pattern. More noteworthy than the change in number was the change in the structure of the population. There were still more men than women in Middlesex, but the county was approaching gender balance, and where it had once consisted mainly of young men, the community now included older people and children. Middlesex had become a place of families, most of whom were related to at least one other family in increasingly complex kinship networks. The population changed in other ways as well. At the end of the 1660s, 334 white servants and 65 African slaves lived in Middlesex. In 1700 there were only about a hundred white servants, but there were four hundred enslaved Africans. Free or enslaved, people in Middlesex lived in an increasingly self-sufficient world in 1700. They produced more of what they consumed, enjoyed well-developed social institutions, and governed themselves. They still considered themselves English, they still purchased English goods, and their traditions, language, institutions, and laws were English. But, like Henry Tuggle, they were increasingly of American birth and thought of Virginia as home. Middlesex was becoming a mature society.

The process of maturation Middlesex was undergoing was being repeated all along the English North American coast in the late seventeenth and eighteenth centuries. The process was uneven and incomplete, and its pace was dependent on the timing and progress of settlement. In general, the earliest places—the Chesapeake and southern New England, for example—achieved maturity by the early eighteenth century or even earlier, while such frontier areas as Maine, Georgia, and the Carolina backcountry were still in the maturation process when the American Revolution began.

Maturity could be measured in many ways, some of which were apparent to the naked eye. As the most attractive lands were taken up and cleared, as stumps were pulled and rocks removed, as milled lumber and brick buildings replaced rude huts and log cabins, the countryside simply looked more mature. Another indication of maturity was the development of local service businesses—taverns, mills, and stores—in convenient places. Governmental institutions, churches, and, in some places, schools were further signs of a maturing area.

Underlying the physical artifacts of maturity were economic and social realities. In mature economies, stable neighborhood and community relationships and interdependencies existed, farmers knew which crops to grow and how to grow them, and methods of and facilities for processing, importing, and exporting were firmly established. By 1750 these conditions existed in most places in British North America.

So, too, did a higher level of social maturity, as reflected in relatively even gender ratios, more balanced age distribution, and well-established families and kinship groups. Another sign of social maturity was a more complex class structure with wider separations between the rich, the middle class, and the poor. Social maturity could be seen in the development of local elites that served as self-conscious community leaders and had the ability to pass their status on to the next generation. And it could be seen in diminished social mobility, as fewer people went from servants to grandees in one generation and more replicated the status of their parents.

Maturity was a generally positive development in colonial America, because it carried a high level of security and self-confidence with it. But it was accompanied by a decline in the relatively high level of opportunity of the early years of settlement. Fertile land became an increasingly precious commodity, and people had greater difficulty securing it. As a result, the eighteenth century saw a heightened degree of rural conflict over land, conflict within and between families, between colonies, among colonists, Native Americans, and colonial governments, and between rich and poor. Early America promised land. But by 1750, increasing numbers of colonists were tenants or laborers on land owned by others.

Economic maturity thus saw the increased commodification of labor. While family labor continued to meet the needs of most farms, more people were placed in a situation where they needed to sell or barter all or part of their labor. And other people—especially in the South—were placed in a position where their labor was owned by others for life. Already in 1700 in Henry Tuggle's Middlesex nearly one in four people were slaves, uncontestable and horrible testimony to the way some colonists were turning others into commodities. Wage and slave labor also created strains in a mature society, the former by heightening class conflict and the latter by stimulating class and caste resentments and necessitating structures of social control.

The central event of early American history was the political and military struggle for independence. The process of securing independence—even of considering it—was inextricably related to economic and social maturation. Immature societies usually lack the sense of identity, self-confidence, and the established leadership to even contemplate, let alone successfully execute, such a step. But beyond that, the stresses of economic and social maturation in America created conflicts, anxieties, and yearnings that formed a backdrop for the Revolution.

On the other hand, the Revolution affected the maturation process, disrupting established economic and social patterns and, to some degree, offering the opportunities of immaturity again to Americans. In that sense, the Revolution was at once a result of maturation and a means of escaping the consequences of that process.

THE EARLY AMERICAN ECONOMY

The British mainland colonies achieved economic maturity in the late seventeenth and eighteenth centuries, and they enjoyed a remarkable level of economic prosperity. Their prosperity derived from a combination of factors, including their rich resource base, the energy and enterprise of their people, the wealth and power of the mother country, and an economic boom in the North Atlantic world in general.

By the early eighteenth century a rough differentiation of agricultural production had developed in the colonies. While colonial farm families—about 85 percent of the colonial population in 1750—were preoccupied with producing what they would consume, clear regional specialization appeared in agricultural marketing.

The New England and Middle Atlantic colonies produced foodstuffs and livestock for export. Meat, flour, and horses were prominent among the items they sold, and the British West Indian sugar islands were their major customers. Devoting virtually all of their precious land to their lucrative staple, sugar planters needed to import horses to power their mills and food to feed their slaves. Because of their relative proximity to the West Indies and the remarkable yields of their soils, Pennsylvanians were better able than New Englanders to profit from this trade.

The southern colonies produced foodstuffs for the West Indies as well, but their primary agricultural role was the production of specialty crops for the British and European markets. Tobacco from Virginia, Maryland, and North Carolina and rice and indigo from South Carolina were the major products of this portion of the Atlantic trade.

The commercial products of the colonial agricultural economy were determined in part by the environment and in part by the market, but the British mercantile system played a role as well. The economic theory of mercantilism held that colonies should benefit the mother country by helping her become self-sufficient and wealthy. Beginning in the 1650s, Parliament passed a series of laws relating to the colonies that were designed to advance those goals. Colonists were required to buy goods only from English merchants using English ships manned by English crews. Certain enumerated products, such as tobacco, rice, and indigo, could be sold only in England and nowhere else. On the other hand, colonial agricultural products that competed with those produced by English farmers, such as wheat or meat, could not be sold in England.

The mercantile system was designed to benefit the mother country—not the colonies—and Americans grumbled about some aspects of it and evaded some of its regulations. But on balance the colonies probably benefited from it. For one thing, it gave colonial producers of enumerated products a monopoly in the British market, and English economic energy and strength maintained a vigorous resale trade in American commodities on the European continent. Also, the producers of some commodities received the inducement of a cash subsidy, called a bounty, that profited them immensely. Finally, all American trade benefited from a strong British commercial and financial infrastructure and from the physical protection provided by the powerful British navy, which controlled the North Atlantic. The British connection was especially beneficial in the second third of the eighteenth century, when English and European prosperity and population growth led to increased demand for American products. The British even lowered their barriers to American foodstuffs, creating a new market for colonial farmers.

This prosperity had a generally positive, if uneven, effect on American standards of living. As productive people enjoying extensive use of a rich resource base and taking advantage of growing market opportunities, the colonists probably lived as well as any people anywhere. For the colonies as a whole, per capita wealth on the eve of the Revolution was only slightly lower than in England, and in some places—Pennsylvania, for example—was actually higher. Moreover, whatever the figures might show, observers agreed that the average American lived better than the average person anywhere else in the world.

As a consequence, Americans were progressively better fed, clothed, and housed. They drank coffee, tea, and rum, flavored their food with sugar and spices, and wore clothes constructed from imported textiles. They enjoyed luxuries their parents and grandparents had been unable to acquire, such as glass windows, crystal stemware, china, silver candlesticks, and lace. Especially attractive to colonial consumers were luxuries for the table, an indication that they were entertaining guests and perhaps that women were playing an important role in purchasing decisions.

Prosperity fueled expectations among colonists and prospective colonists. Immigrants poured in to share the American bounty, not only from England but from Ireland and Scotland and Germany as well. Farmers bought and cleared more land and hired labor. Planters bought slaves, speculated in western lands, and went into debt for luxuries, assuming that the upward economic trend minimized their risk.

The problem with discussing broad trends in economies or the economic behavior of people in the aggregate is that it leads us to lose sight of important qualifications and distinctions. The first and perhaps the most important qualification that must be made involves farmers' behavior and intent. Virtually all colonial farmers—including even most substantial planters—practiced a safety-first agriculture that was modified only slightly and imperfectly by burgeoning commercial opportunities. The essential goal of most farmers was not to fill a market demand but to provide a sufficiency for their families and dependents. It was their first priority to feed their own families from their own flocks and fields, clothe their families with thread spun and cloth woven at home, and warm their families from their own woodlots. Self-sufficiency is not the same as subsistence, however, and most farmers produced some sort of surplus for market most of the time. Market involvement was necessary because few farmers could produce enough of everything their families consumed. Hence, one might sell surplus wheat to purchase another's surplus apples or to buy a cooking pot. Moreover, farmers needed a surplus to generate profits to pay taxes, and they wanted a surplus in order to buy those luxuries that would make their lives more attractive. But it is important to remember that, while they participated in markets, eighteenth-century farmers were not market driven in the way their modern counterparts are.

Further diminishing the market orientation of colonial farmers was the persistent sense everywhere—stronger in some places and among some people than others—that relations among friends and neighbors should take place in the context of a moral, rather than a market, economy. This belief, which was an ingrained part of the peasant value system most colonists carried from Europe, emphasized that friends and neighbors had a moral obligation to share work and tools and food and even land, regardless of considerations of economic profit and loss. Even today the moral economy thrives in rural neighborliness, so it is not surprising that it was a more significant shaper of individual behavior and mitigator of market impulses in the less commercial age of the eighteenth century.

Finally, it is important to bear in mind that many farmers were not well circumstanced to take advantage of whatever market opportunities existed. Some farms were too small or had soil too infertile to produce enough even to maintain a family, let alone produce a marketable surplus. In order to fulfill their needs these farmers had to practice crafts or work for others. In these ways they benefited indirectly from market opportunities, but their farms were not part of the commercial world. Others found themselves too isolated to take full advantage of commercial opportunities. Especially in the backcountry, where navigable rivers were distant and roads were poor or nonexistent, farmers saw most of their potential profits eroded by transportation costs.

So the eighteenth century was a time of growing commercial opportunities and general prosperity, but it was also a time when traditional behaviors and habits of mind changed slowly and when opportunity did not come equally to all.

VIRGINIA AND THE SOUTH

By the end of the seventeenth century most of those areas in the Chesapeake, such as Middlesex County, that had been settled for a generation were achieving social maturity and stability. Increasing numbers of native Marylanders and Virginians, more balanced by age and gender ratios, and more intricate kinship networks were all signs that the early settlement days had passed.

Also indicative of maturity was the evolution of a complex and hierarchical class structure from the relatively undifferentiated small- and middling-planter society of the early years. Atop the new structure were substantial planters. In many cases these were the sons and grandsons of men who had been small planters or servants who, through industry or luck or even fortuitous marriages, had been able to build comfortable estates. Their heirs followed up on their initiative, adding land and servants and slaves and thus rising further above their neighbors. One of the early settlers in Middlesex, for example, was Oliver Seager, a former servant who acquired land in 1650. Forty years later his son Randolph was one of the important men in the county. Also at the top were English gentlemen or their descendants who began in the elite and stayed there. The leading man in Middlesex in 1700 was Ralph Wormley II, whose prominent father had patented over three thousand acres on the Rappahannock River half a century earlier.[1]

However modest or elevated their origins, by 1700 the elite of the Chesapeake conceived themselves as patriarchs with a responsibility to lead their families and communities alike. In the economy they maintained wharfs for the English tobacco ships, storehouses for tobacco, and commissaries filled with British goods. When Ralph Wormley died in 1701 his estate included two storehouses, a gristmill, and a wharf, in addition to sixty-four hundred acres of land. Thus they dominated local economies, handling and marketing the small planters' crops, retailing manufactured products back to them, and often extending credit to them. Socially, their leadership was reflected in their positions as vestrymen in the church and officers in the militia. They dominated government as well, serving as justices of the peace (positions in colonial Virginia that combined judicial and legislative functions) and in the colonial assemblies. Randolph Seager was a vestryman and a justice of the peace; Ralph Wormley was colonel of the militia and secretary of state for the colony.

Its growing social maturity in the late seventeenth century meant that the Chesapeake was a more stable place to live, but it remained a rough and primitive society. Small planters continued to live in small, crude cabins, hot and insect-ridden in the summer and cold in the winter. They continued to have monotonous diets, revolving around corn and meat, and to have few furnishings, tools, and utensils. And they continued to live in filth, infested with lice, putting dirty bodies into dirty clothes. Those conditions changed only gradually as the eighteenth century proceeded.

Even the elite lived primitive lives in a region a generation removed from wilderness. Substantial planters often worked in the fields with their servants and slaves and lived in houses that were only slightly larger and better furnished than those of their nonelite neighbors. Ralph Wormley's estate, Rosegill—named in the English fashion favored by the Virginia elite—featured a large frame farmhouse that fell far short of the elegance suggested by its name. Their diets, too, were unvaried, their standards of cleanliness low, and their tastes often crude. The Chesapeake plantation of our imagination—the stately mansion, formal gardens, polite leisure, and refined taste—was still off in the future, but its social and economic foundation was being laid in the last quarter of the seventeenth century.

The wealth of Chesapeake planters was based on tobacco, so the long depression in tobacco prices that began about 1680 and continued until about 1710 presented a major challenge. By definition, tobacco producers were commercial. The farmer who produced grain or meat could eat what he could not sell, but the tobacco planter's standard of living depended overwhelmingly on the market.

When tobacco prices turned downward planters sought to diminish risk through diversification. One way they diversified was by producing more of what they consumed at home. Women became increasingly responsible for spinning and weaving cloth and making clothes, for preserving meats and vegetables, and for making butter, cheese, cider, and beer. The result was homes that were more self-sufficient and neighborhoods in which local exchange partially replaced the importation of goods. Diversification also appeared in agricultural production patterns. Planters started to grow more wheat and to keep more animals, diminishing their concentration on tobacco.

Substantial planters were better able to diversify than were their small-planter neighbors. One reason was that they were more likely than their neighbors to be married and to be able to do without the labor of their wives in the fields, thus allowing them to develop household industries. And they were better able to buy livestock and the implements—such as plows—that allowed them to grow wheat and improved the efficiency of their corn production.

The depression in tobacco prices also led planters to consider how labor efficiency could be improved. Out of that consideration came an increased commitment to African slavery. By the last quarter of the seventeenth century, slavery was already a venerable institution in the Chesapeake. A Dutch trader had sold the first enslaved Africans at Jamestown in 1619. While there are some indications that these early Africans were treated as indentured servants and freed after a period of years, by the 1640s it is clear that imported Africans were being enslaved for life. While slavery eventually became the labor system that characterized Virginia and the rest of the South, its progress among planters was slow. Until the last quarter of the seventeenth century those who needed more labor than their families could provide most often purchased indentured servants from the British Isles.

Indentured servitude was a system in which a person sold his or her labor for a period of years—usually four to seven—through a middleman to an employer. Indentured servitude benefited laborers by making it possible for them to come to America, and the freedom dues people like Thomas Tuggle and Oliver Seager received upon completion of the indenture—or contract—allowed them to get a start in the New World. Freedom dues varied.

48 In the early years they usually included land, but by the late seventeenth century they commonly came in the form of clothing, seed, livestock, and sometimes firearms. Of the 120 thousand people who came to the Chesapeake from the British Isles in the seventeenth century, at least three-fourths were indentured servants.

For the planters, indentured servitude was a way to meet labor needs, but it was not without drawbacks. For one thing, substantial planters were constantly in the market for servants. The perils of seasoning for immigrants and the regular expiration of indentures meant that the planter's workforce had a high turnover rate. Exacerbating this problem was the fact that the supply of servants fluctuated. When times were bad in England servants were plentiful, but when times were good there they were few and expensive in the Chesapeake. Then there was the problem of quality. As one might expect, servants were drawn from the lower levels of English society, and included among them was a substantial number of rough and dangerous people. Nor did the danger end when indentures ended. Freed servants formed a seething underclass in Chesapeake society. They competed with their former masters for land and labor and were often resentful of the elite. Bacon's Rebellion against colonial authority in 1676 drew much of its power from disgruntled former servants, a fact not lost on those concerned with maintaining a stable social order.

As the problems connected with indentured servitude became clearer, planters turned increasingly to African slaves. Africans, however, were not a perfect solution to the labor problem. For one thing, they were expensive, usually costing half again to twice as much as an English servant. Compounding the risk represented by this price differential was the reality that unseasoned Africans, like Britons, died in large numbers in their early months in America. John Tuggle, the son of Henry and grandson of Thomas, lost an African girl and her toddler son within a year of one another, a blow from which his modest estate never fully recovered. While many Africans enjoyed a relative immunity to the summer maladies of the Chesapeake—and, indeed, contributed a new one of their own in a deadly strain of malaria—they seemed especially vulnerable to pneumonia and other respiratory conditions in the winter. It was also the case that Africans spoke no English and were very unhappy, and sometimes even desperate, in their bondage.

But the advantages of African labor increasingly came to seem more compelling than the disadvantages. Africans who survived were laborers for life, as were their descendants. In the early decades of slavery this capital-gain aspect of owned labor was minimal, because two men were imported for every woman and brutality and seasoning kept mortality high. By 1725, however, sex ratios had become less unbalanced, owners had become more careful not to destroy their laborers, and the African population was increasing naturally. In addition, there was the advantage of a large and seemingly inexhaustible supply of laborers in Africa, most of whom had had agricultural experience. At least as important in times of economic stringency was the fact that Africans could be worked harder and longer than English servants. English men and women demanded long breaks in the middle of the day and refused to labor on red letter days, as Sundays and holidays were designated on calendars. African slaves had no such expectations. Finally, though planters could hardly have foreseen it, black slaves diminished conflict in white society. Because they were laborers for life, slaves did not compete with masters for land. More importantly, the existence of blacks in the community gave whites a racial identification of sufficient strength largely to overcome their class differences. Underscored by multiplying neighborhood and kinship ties, this racial identity contributed to a growing sense of community in the rural Chesapeake.

Substantial planters were better able than their poorer neighbors to benefit from slave labor. Slaves were expensive, after all, and one needed a good deal of land to employ them efficiently. Consequently, slave ownership was concentrated in the upper strata of society, while small and middling planters often continued to employ servants. When Ralph Wormley died in 1701 he held eighty-five African slaves and only eight white servants.

Diversification and slaves helped planters survive the lean times between 1680 and 1710 and take advantage of the better times that followed. When prosperity returned to tobacco farming around 1710, the large planters were best positioned to enjoy it, and when a tobacco boom started about thirty years later they were able to live lives of comfort, gentility, and a high degree of leisure.

The planters did not forget how their estates had been built. They continued to strive for self-sufficiency and to acquire land and slaves. Half of the quarter-million slaves imported into the colonies and the later United States

50 came between 1740 and 1776. In 1776, when a Virginian wrote the Declaration of Independence, two in five of the people in his state and one in three people in neighboring Maryland were slaves of African birth or descent.

Slavery was even more important in South Carolina, which had become a heavily commercial agricultural colony very early in its history. The main commercial crops grown in South Carolina were rice and indigo, both of which called for substantial labor.

Rice culture in South Carolina underwent an evolution in the first fifty years of English settlement. The crop was initially produced on dry uplands, then in upland swamps, and finally in lowland swamps where the ebb and flow of tides allowed rice fields to be flooded with fresh water and drained frequently.

Lowland rice culture produced high yields, but it was hard and unpleasant work. Farmers labored in water and muck much of the time. Drainage ditches demanded regular dredging, and banks and floodgates had to be carefully maintained and monitored. Planting, weeding, harvesting, and milling to remove the husk from the rice kernel added further to the difficulty and tedium of the work. In addition to being hard and unpleasant, work in the rice swamps was unhealthy. Indeed, the seasoning process in South Carolina carried away a high proportion of English immigrants.

Africans met South Carolinians' labor needs and probably introduced many of the techniques of rice culture. Africans were available in abundant supply; unlike the English, they thrived in the swampy lowlands; and many had experience growing rice, a crop that was not produced in England. Indeed, South Carolinians so valued the agricultural experience of Africans that they attempted, whenever possible, to purchase slaves from such rice-growing regions as the Congo, Angola, the Senegal, and Gambia.

In the late-seventeenth and early-eighteenth centuries the African population grew only through importation, due to the same factors operating in the Chesapeake. Eventually, though, the African population began to increase naturally and, supplemented by continuing importation, came to dominate the South Carolina coast numerically. By the time of the American Revolution, the population of many South Carolina coastal areas and islands just off the coast was at least 90 percent black.

Like all immigrants, Africans attempted to recreate as much of their native culture as possible in their new surroundings. In most of the colonies, this was not easy, considering their diverse origins and the numerical pre-

*Onion Maidens, Wethersfield, Connecticut, circa 1700,
showing how market gardening in the northeast—unlike
staple-crop agriculture in the southern colonies—
could flourish by way of family labor alone.*
Courtesy of the Wethersfield Historical Society.

ponderance and ethnocentrism of the colonists who controlled them. The situation was different along South Carolina's rice coast, however. There, Africans' numbers and their origins in just a few locales allowed them to re-create Africa to a larger degree than was possible for slaves in the Chesapeake and elsewhere. Along the Carolina coast, slaves were able to reestablish African cultural forms in such areas as kinship patterns, courtship rituals, practices of naming and raising children, religious exercises, styles of music and dance, foodways, architecture, superstition and folklore, and even language, in their development of Gullah, which melded African and English words and grammatical forms together.

The partial recreation of Africa in America was undoubtedly comforting to the slaves, but it frightened the whites, who wanted to create an English society with Africans, not an African society. White South Carolinians became especially anxious about the implicit African threat after the Stono Rebellion, a slave uprising in 1739. They tightened the slave codes that controlled Africans' lives and increased their vigilance on slaves' activities.

Africans were the key figures in rice production because they did the work and because they introduced many of the techniques. They were the key figures in the culture of indigo—another crop raised in Africa and introduced in South Carolina in 1739—for the same reasons. Indigo is a member of the pea family, from which a rich blue dye can be extracted. It was a good companion crop to rice, because it grew well on uplands where rice did not thrive and was less labor intensive. Processing the plant, by boiling the leaves and extracting a paste that was dried into powder, was the most sensitive and demanding part of the production cycle. In an age before chemical dyes had been developed, indigo was a high-value crop, and the British government enhanced its attractiveness by paying a bounty to its producers. It was probably the most lucrative crop produced in the late-colonial period, on either a per worker or a per acre basis. One historian has estimated that a skilled slave could produce indigo worth $1,300–$1,950 a year.

The large planters who grew these valuable crops experienced a level of comfort and abundance unparalleled in the thirteen mainland colonies. They commonly maintained homes in Charleston, a relatively healthy summer refuge from the pestilential lowlands, leaving management of their estates to hired overseers during much of the growing season. In Charleston they enjoyed lives of luxury and cultivation, attending plays, balls, and galas, consuming fine foods and wines, purchasing English books, furniture, and luxuries, and sending their children to English schools. Like the ancient Greeks and Romans, they built a cultured civilization on the backs of slaves.

By the end of the colonial period the southern colonies were spectacular commercial successes. Annually, approximately 100 million pounds of tobacco, 60 million pounds of rice, and 1 million pounds of indigo flowed from the South to England and from there to the world beyond. Commercial success raised the living standards of many and the material expectations of most, but it also presented challenges to southerners.

One of the challenges involved the shortage of good land in long-settled areas. Population growth and the lure of the market conjoined to fill the countryside with people and drive up the cost of land. Small planters found it increasingly difficult to provide land for all of their sons. The imperatives of tobacco culture decreed that a farmer hold at least fifty acres per hand; when the land was subdivided too much it was overcropped, leading to a decline in fertility. In rice country the shortage of good land was compounded by the labor demands of the crop. Only a substantial slave owner could hope to establish himself as a South Carolina rice planter.

What were planters to do? One answer was primogeniture, the practice of passing on an estate intact to the eldest son. In Virginia, the popularity of primogeniture grew as land became less abundant. Primogeniture preserved the family estate and took care of one son, but what of the others? Some became tenants, renting land with the hope of becoming owners some day. Others moved to new lands. Sometimes large planters established their sons in new areas with land and slaves, while the sons of small planters were usually on their own, but in either case their movement was reflected in a spread of settlement inland.

On the southern frontier these migrants were joined by immigrants pushed out of Europe by economic hardship or religious persecution and drawn to the colonies by their relative prosperity and tolerance. Among these new colonists were substantial numbers of Germans, mainly from the western German states along the Rhine. Some of these people were Protestant Pietists fleeing persecution—the Amish are probably our most familiar enduring example—but most were peasants in search of a better life. Also important were Scots-Irish—ethnic Scots whom the English had settled in Ireland in the seventeenth century as part of their attempt to subdue that unhappy land. In the mid-eighteenth century, oppressive British commercial

54 regulations caused hardship in Ireland and induced many of the Scots-Irish to emigrate to America. They were a proud, tough, and independent people who contributed to the aggressive, rough-and-tumble nature of the southern backcountry.

Life in the southern colonial backcountry was fraught with challenges. Governmental and social institutions were weak, lawlessness was sometimes a problem, and high population turnover contributed to an atmosphere of impermanence and made it difficult to foster community loyalties. Nor did frontier farmers enjoy the degree of economic success achieved by their fellow colonists along the coast. While they could—and did—become fairly self-sufficient in the rich inland valleys, marketing was often a problem. The eighteenth-century southern frontier was mostly above the fall line, meaning that ocean-going ships were not locally available to carry off commercial commodities. Land transportation was prohibitively expensive, if facilities existed at all. As a result, southern frontier settlers concentrated on value-added products that were worth a lot relative to their volume—such as whiskey—and on products that could walk to market, such as cattle and hogs. Population increased so rapidly that what had been backcountry quickly became settled, intensifying pressures on the young and the poor. The experience of John Pulliam, the son of Scots-Irish immigrants who moved from the rapidly filling Shenandoah Valley to new lands along the North Carolina–Virginia border in the early 1770s, was repeated countless times in the expanding South.[2]

The anxieties and difficulties of life in the backcountry were sometimes reflected in violent political outbreaks. Unhappy with lawlessness, unresponsive local government, and unequal representation in colonial assemblies, North and South Carolina frontiersmen formed the Regulator Movement in the 1760s. The Regulators chased off tax collectors and other colonial officials, closed local courts, and executed or banished suspected criminals. The attempt by the royal governor of North Carolina to put down the Regulators and reestablish colonial authority resulted in a pitched battle in 1771. Clearly, the prosperity and comfort enjoyed by some southerners was not shared by all.

The peculiar nature of New England's settlement meant that it achieved social maturity much more rapidly than did regions to the south. Almost from the beginning the early New England towns enjoyed a high degree of social stability, well-established family and kinship groups, churches, and schools. And yet, these towns were not insulated from change, which began within the first few years after the planting of most communities.

Some significant changes in New England towns involved religious dissension, which frustrated the founders' goal of creating a community based on love for humankind and God. From the point of view of the rural historian, however, the most important changes in established New England towns came with increasing population pressures on the land.

When the original town grants were made, colonial authorities assumed they would be sufficient in size to provide for the original settlers and all of their progeny for many generations. This assumption was based on the colonists' experience with English farming and population growth. What the grantors had not reckoned with was the relative infertility of New England soils and the relative fertility and potency of New England women and men.

As indicated in the last chapter, New England towns began to face some land pressures within the first twenty years of settlement. Original settlers needed more land to provide for growing families, and when second-generation men came of age they demanded their own farms. Calls for new distributions frequently caused divisions in towns, as any issue involving property usually does. Disputation also arose because, as grants were made further from the town center, grantees desired to relocate, usually by forming new towns located more centrally for their purposes. Established towns were usually reluctant to divide themselves, leading to long and rancorous disputes. The same process often reappeared when the third generation came of age. By the time these grandsons of the original settlers had received grants, there was seldom much unallotted arable land left. At that point the established towns had to struggle with the consequences of maturity in a marginal agricultural environment.

By 1700, the shortage of land had become a problem in most long-settled New England towns. As the eighteenth century proceeded, that shortage became more acute. When William Ballard of Andover, Massachusetts, died in 1689, his three sons divided his estate of more than two hundred acres, a middling farm by first-generation New England standards.[3] Thirty years later, his son Joseph contemplated dividing a farm of less than one hundred acres among seven sons. Most New Englanders did not face the sobering prospects contemplated by Joseph Ballard's sons, but the land shortage was pinching all along the coast.

One historian has estimated that on the eve of the Revolution, thousands of Massachusetts farmers had fewer than forty acres of land, and the average farmer in long-settled Suffolk County had only forty-three acres. This was one-third as much land as the average first-generation Suffolk County settler controlled. Most historians agree that forty acres of New England land was usually enough to maintain family self-sufficiency. Moreover, market opportunities were greater for eighteenth-century New England husbandmen than for their fathers and grandfathers in the seventeenth century. Boston, Newport, New Haven, and other towns composed a growing local market, and farmers benefited as well from the same eighteenth-century economic boom that enriched their counterparts in the South. It is important to remember, however, that when forty acres was the average holding, many farmers controlled less than that. One historian has estimated that 40 to 50 percent of Massachusetts farmers at the time of the Revolution did not produce enough to provide for family self-sufficiency. For these people, market opportunities had little direct relevance.

The land shortage was rendered more acute by declining fertility in the region. New England soils were marginal at best, and yields began to decline very rapidly after settlement, all the more so because English cropping practices accelerated erosion. For a time, farmers compensated for declining yields by farming more extensively, but the land shortage eventually foreclosed that option. Agricultural reform was another answer. Farmers consolidated holdings and enclosed fields, usually without the rancor and bitterness that accompanied that process in England. Some confined livestock so as to manage manure more effectively, and those living near tidal rivers sometimes fertilized their fields with alewives, small, herring-like fish that entered the rivers to spawn in the spring.

Declining fertility also forced changes in cropping practices. Farmers devoted fewer acres to small grains and corn and more to forage for cattle and other livestock. Indeed, by the early eighteenth century, cereal production had fallen below consumption, forcing New Englanders to import grain for their bread. Apple orchards also became a more prominent feature of the

New England agricultural scene. While forty acres might maintain a family under a general farming regime, it would not be sufficient to do so if devoted to grazing and fruit.

The fact that increasing numbers of farms did not produce enough to achieve family self-sufficiency did not lead New Englanders to abandon that goal. It simply meant that they had to leave the farm to achieve it. Farmers supplemented their incomes by fishing, lumbering, trapping, and, especially, by working for neighbors. Hiring of labor in rural New England in the colonial period did not usually involve a cash exchange, in part because specie—gold and silver, which was the only legal money in America at the time—was in short supply for everyone. Instead, colonists worked for their neighbors in return for a few bushels of corn, some laying hens, a sow, or some other product that would help their families achieve self-sufficiency. Those in a position to exchange commodities for labor were owners of large farms that produced a surplus, some of which flowed into the channels of trade. Thus in New England, as in the Chesapeake and elsewhere, some were better able than others to take advantage of market opportunities and thereby rise in status and in material comfort, far above their less advantageously circumstanced fellows.

A more clearly articulated and widely separated class structure was not the only social effect of the land shortage. It had a marked impact on family dynamics as well. When towns granted no more land the burden lay on parents to provide farms for sons and dowries for daughters. Those with substantial farms could simply divide estates among children, but as farms shrank that became much more difficult. A family might scrape along on a forty-acre farm, but if it was divided among even two children it could no longer provide family self-sufficiency.

Families coped with this problem in several ways. They tried to acquire more land. That was difficult, in towns where there was little out-migration by landowners, and expensive, in a situation of low land supply and high land demand. Men and women had fewer children. For one thing, because they could not usually acquire farms as early as their ancestors had, they delayed marriage. Joseph Ballard married in his early twenties, as second-generation men in Andover commonly did, but his elder sons did not marry until their late twenties or early thirties. His eldest son, also a Joseph, married at thirty-one and inherited none of his father's land until he was fifty-two. When married, the colonists practiced family limitation. A rising infant-mortality rate, probably resulting from the progressive fouling of water supplies and the easier spread of epidemic diseases in a denser population, supplemented conscious family limitation.

Increasingly, parents found that they could not provide sufficiently even for the few children they had. Parents tended to pass their farms to one son, requiring him to provide for them in old age and perhaps to compensate his sisters and brothers. Opportunities were thus constricted for New England children. Sons labored for neighbors or in larger towns or became tenant farmers. Daughters with paltry dowries, or none at all, had difficulty securing husbands, leading to an increase in the number of spinsters, unmarried adult women living in dependency with parents or brothers. As parents lost the ability to favor children, they also lost the ability to control them. Sons moved away, and daughters married without permission, often using pregnancy to force parents' reluctant consent. In some New England towns, by the time of the Revolution, nearly half the brides were pregnant on their wedding days.

One answer to the problem of overcrowding that appealed to many eighteenth-century New Englanders was to move to newly opened lands in the hill country of Massachusetts and New Hampshire, in the upper Connecticut Valley of Vermont, in Maine, or in eastern Connecticut. Two of Joseph Ballard's sons relocated from Andover to Windham, Connecticut, and his nephew Jonathan moved to Billerica and then Oxford, new towns in southeastern Massachusetts.[4] In 1775, Jonathan's son Ephraim was among the early settlers in the Kennebec River region of Maine. As a rule, such movement was positive both for the people who left and for the communities they left, but life in the new towns did not guarantee success. Some migrants—such as those who settled in the fertile Connecticut River Valley—enjoyed the opportunity to create a much more abundant life than their parents lived. Others, in the rocky hills above the fall line, found agricultural conditions difficult and markets distant.

Whether they tried to acquire farms at home or moved to the frontier, New Englanders found themselves in need of ever larger amounts of capital. The land shortage drove prices higher in settled areas, and the practice of town grants had ended before the turn of the eighteenth century. Now colonial governments sold frontier land, often to substantial capitalists, and speculation in land in promising places like Springfield, Massachusetts, and Kent, Connecticut, was brisk.

Access to capital was a vexing problem for farmers who produced only a slight margin above what was necessary to maintain family self-sufficiency. Exacerbating the problem was the fact that there were no banks in colonial America. Debtors usually borrowed from local merchants or substantial farmers. These men usually recognized their obligation to their less fortunate neighbors, but they were also conscious of their need to ensure the security of their property. Hence, they extended credit for only a few years at a time and charged interest rates that compensated them for their risk.

The inadequacy of this credit system led to a number of debtor-relief measures, the most important of which was the Massachusetts Land Bank, created in the 1730s. The Land Bank was to print paper money, backed by the value of colonial lands, to be lent to borrowers. The Land Bank would provide a new source for capital, create a medium for the payment of taxes and discharge of debts in a specie-starved area, and, by increasing the money supply, inflate commodity prices, making it easier for farmers to meet their financial obligations. This last purpose caught the attention of the British government, which declared the law creating the Land Bank invalid in 1741. As a nation of shopkeepers, the British were especially wary of anything that might diminish the value of money debtors owed to creditors. The destruction of the Land Bank did not end the related capital and land shortages that had led to its creation. These remained acute problems in most of New England until after the Revolution.

The colonies in the Middle Atlantic region did not experience the population pressures that beset New England, at least not as early and not to the same degree. New York was the most heterogenous of the colonies, and the eighteenth century was characterized by the adjustment of disparate groups to one another. Particularly noteworthy was the adoption by predominantly Dutch farmers of new agricultural practices, such as the worm fencing introduced in the region by Finns and Swedes, and new cultural practices, such as traditional English methods of choosing surnames and naming children. Facilitating mutual adjustment was the increasingly commercial orientation of farmers in New York City's expanding hinterland.

Pennsylvania was almost certainly the most prosperous agricultural colony, at least from the perspective of the average farmer. The soils of southeastern Pennsylvania were rich, and the settlers were industrious, allowing a productivity increase of two- to three-tenths of 1 percent per year in the first three-quarters of the eighteenth century. This was a remarkable rate of increase, especially in light of the experience of New England, where productivity was static at best.

The productivity of Pennsylvania farmers was amply rewarded. Grain and meat flowed out of Philadelphia and into world trade, first mainly to the West Indies but later to the British Isles and New England as well, and Philadelphia itself—the largest city in British North America—formed a major market. One historian has estimated that four-fifths of Pennsylvania farmers produced a surplus and that, overall, 40 percent of the produce of Pennsylvania farms was marketed. This was an extraordinary level of market involvement for eighteenth-century farmers.

The relative prosperity and market participation by Pennsylvania farmers was reflected in their consumption of finished goods from England. Manufactured furniture, clocks, crystal, silver plate, fine china, lace, and such luxury utensils as forks appeared in the inventories of their estates with a frequency unmatched in other regions. So, too, did such advanced producer goods as plows and cradles (scythes with frameworks attached for catching cut grain as a means of reducing shattering). Still, even those farmers who participated in and benefited from the market strove to achieve the highest attainable amount of self-sufficiency. They were general farmers who grew a wide variety of crops and maintained a broad range of livestock.

As in other regions, women were primarily responsible for many of the activities aimed at maintaining family self-sufficiency, while men concentrated on commercial products. Women spun thread, wove cloth, and constructed homespun clothing. Women also planted and maintained vegetable gardens and preserved the produce thereof. Women commonly milked cattle and made butter and cheese, and they cared for poultry. As Philadelphia grew, these tasks originally meant to enhance family self-sufficiency often took on a commercial dimension. When that occurred, women and men sometimes cooperated to an extraordinary degree, and sometimes men displaced women from their traditional farm production roles.

Pennsylvania was undoubtedly "the best poor man's country" on the eve of the Revolution, but even it did not escape the stresses of a maturing society.[5] Rich lands close to markets filled rapidly, foreclosing opportunities for latecomers and some children. By the mid-eighteenth century, tenancy was becoming an increasingly common phenomenon in southeastern Pennsylvania, and larger numbers of cottagers (laborers provided a dwelling and the use of a small plot of land by their employers) and day laborers were appearing.

Population pressures in Pennsylvania were increased by extraordinary numbers of immigrants. German Pietists came, drawn by the tolerant attitude of the Quakers as well as by the agricultural possibilities of the region. Scots-Irish came as well. Moving to the west, where transportation to markets was more difficult and an enlightened colonial Indian policy left Native Americans in possession of substantial amounts of land, some Scots-Irish settlers seethed against the Quaker oligarchy. In 1764, a group of them called the Paxton Boys massacred a band of peaceful Indians and marched on Philadelphia, threatening to overthrow the government. Clearly, as the American Revolution approached nearly every colony was coping with the social and economic strains of maturation.

THE REVOLUTION AND RURAL AMERICA

It would be misleading and overly simplistic to suggest that the maturation process sketched above somehow caused the American Revolution. The nation's founders were people of wisdom, vision, and idealism. They were free moral agents, and to reduce their actions to mechanistic responses determined by larger social and economic forces would be to seriously misunderstand their motives and diminish their accomplishment.

But the actions of American revolutionaries did not take place in a vacuum. Only a mature society has the leadership and the confidence to make a revolution. Moreover, both the benefits and the problems of maturity contributed to the background of the Revolution. Planters whose rising expectations led them to go deeply into debt to British merchants and small farmers who fed their families in part by working for neighbors both had an acute understanding of the meanings of dependence and independence. In addition, concrete British actions heightened the anxieties of people coping with the negative consequences of maturation. The Proclamation of 1763, banning American settlement west of the Appalachian mountains, raised the anger of substantial land speculators and land-hungry farmers alike. The specter of British taxes disturbed those struggling with a specie-scarce economy, especially if they were in debt. And the threat to land titles, embodied in the Massachusetts Government Act of 1774, struck at the core of farmers' identity and independence. In short, while maturity is not in itself a sufficient explanation for the American Revolution, it is a necessary part of the explanation.

The physical struggle that secured American independence was shaped by the rural nature of the country. The reality that most farmers devoted most of their energy to producing for family consumption had a major impact on the war effort. First, it limited the number of men who could be freed for extended military service. Rural America—then and through most of its history—harbored a fair number of underemployed people, and the ranks of the Continental Army were filled with agricultural laborers and younger sons of small farmers. But most rural males were needed on the farms most of the time to maintain family self-sufficiency. Second, the self-sufficiency orientation of most American farmers limited the size of the permanent force that could be supported. Armies and their horses consumed large amounts of food and fodder, and uniforms, weapons, tents, and blankets all had to be paid for with money raised, in some way, through the sale of surpluses. Rural America's ability to support a large army in the field was distinctly limited.

This is not meant to suggest that rural America's contribution to the war effort was minimal. Virtually all farmers served in the colonial and, after 1776, the state militias. Amateur military organizations that functioned mainly to protect local citizens from Indians and other threats, the militias were no match for the professional European troops the British dispatched to America. But the militias could fight a pesky, irritating, guerrilla style of warfare that made it hard for the British army to hold rural areas. And, as the United States learned in Vietnam, an army that cannot secure the countryside in a predominantly rural country is doomed to defeat. The militias also provided a labor pool from which the Continental Army could draw, supplemented the regular army with regiments when it was in the area, and maintained local control, suppressing those who might remain loyal to the mother country. Finally, the militia was the living embodiment of the spirit of American independence. It *was* the American people, and as long as it was true to the cause of independence there was no way Great Britain could regain American allegiance.

Militia service was not the only way in which the Revolutionary War affected rural Americans. It disrupted their established market relationships, making it harder for them to serve the needs of such traditional customers as the West Indians but providing them with new markets in the large armies operating on the continent. Military action did not usually disturb production, but the flight of many slaves to British lines in Virginia and South Carolina had a disruptive effect locally.

Enhanced local commercial activity helped debtors, who benefited from other developments as well. The profligate printing of paper money by Congress and the states dramatically inflated prices and, when it was made legal tender, allowed the easy discharge of debts. Moreover debtors, conscious of the power of the people in a republic, sometimes frustrated creditors by securing legislative enactment of stay laws (statutes preventing creditors from collecting debts or foreclosing for a specified amount of time) or by closing courts (foreclosure, as a judicial procedure, cannot be undertaken if courts are closed).

The war also unblocked narrowing channels of opportunity by increasing the amount of available land and enhancing the access of some Americans to it. The suspension of the Proclamation of 1763 by the Continental Congress opened the West to settlement. By 1783, when the Treaty of Paris ended the war, 100 thousand Americans already lived beyond the mountains, including such romantic pioneers as Daniel Boone, who participated in the opening of Kentucky, and John Pulliam, who moved his family through the Cumberland Gap when his service in the militia ended. The confiscation and sale of the estates of loyalists opened new lands in the East, as did the rapid liquidation of unsold colonial lands by many of the new states. And the land grants made by states and Congress to veterans—all Continental Army soldiers, for example, received land warrants at the end of the war—gave poor men the opportunity to own land.

Perhaps most important, the war altered rural horizons and habits of mind. Rural people came in contact with many others, and their isolation and insular ways of thinking were thereby eroded. Armies of people from all over America and from several places in Europe moved through the country. Soldiers from isolated farms and country villages served with men from many places and moved up and down the Atlantic seaboard, gaining fresh perspectives and observing different lifestyles. Men who survived the war were less timid and more adventurous than they had been previous to their military experience.

There was in general a spirit of improvement abroad in the land. As citizens of a new country with a new and exciting political system, Americans looked at all of their institutions in new ways. Practices that seemed to vio-

64   late the republican principles of liberty and equality, such as quitrents (token money payments to colonial proprietors, such as the Penn family in Pennsylvania, representing feudal dues owed by vassals to lords), primogeniture, and entail (a device to keep large estates intact by preventing them from being sold piecemeal) were abolished, the deference lower- and middle-class people paid to the elite declined, and farmers grew friendlier to new ideas, such as reforms in agricultural practices.

That such changes occurred does not mean that rural practices and behaviors were revolutionized. That rural Americans now were guided by a commitment to liberty and equality did not mean that most of them considered freeing their slaves. Nor, despite rhetoric about a republican womanhood, did it mean that they were ready to modify a patriarchal family system that placed wives in a position of dependency and inequality. But, within the firm limits set by the realities of environment, tradition, and human nature, the war had a freshening and quickening effect on rural America, creating new outlooks and possibilities and allowing people to loosen some of the confines of a maturing society.

FOUR

Agriculture and Economic Growth
in the New Republic

If there was ever an age of the farmer in the United States, the period between the conclusion of the Revolution and the onset of the Civil War was it.
Agrarians, represented most eloquently by Thomas Jefferson and his fellow
Virginian, planter-philosopher John Taylor, celebrated farmers extrava-
gantly for their supposed centrality in a good society, their political virtue,
and their superior morality. And virtually all policy makers, whether they
subscribed to the tenets of Jeffersonian agrarianism or not, recognized agriculture as the key component of the American economy. Consequently, government at all levels worked to encourage farmers as a social group and agriculture as an economic enterprise.

State and national governments developed transportation infrastructure,
building canals, roads, bridges, and railroads, deepening harbors, and removing obstructions from navigable streams. The federal government imported plant and animal varieties and launched exploring expeditions into
prospective farmlands in the West, while states conducted exhaustive surveys of their potential agricultural resources. Presidents and congresses ex-
tinguished Indian claims, surveyed lands for settlement, and made terms for
the acquisition of those lands progressively easier. And trade policies facilitated the exportation of agricultural products.

66 For their part, farmers seemed to meet the social expectations agrarian philosophers had for them, as their broader horizons and greater self-respect, both partially products of the Revolution, were reflected to some degree in their behavior. Farmers seemed to become more scientific, joining agricultural societies and reading the farm newspapers that sprang up throughout the country. They began using improved implements, tried new crops and pure animal breeds, and became more receptive to modern theories of soil improvement.

They also responded to inducements by state and national governments. Farmers streamed to the West, filling frontier lands with stunning rapidity. By 1820 they had spread agriculture from the Appalachians to the Mississippi and were gazing beyond, to Texas, the Great Plains, Oregon, and California. But farmers responded less to agrarians' expectations and government inducements than they did to growing market opportunities. European demand for American food and fiber seemed insatiable. First the Napoleonic Wars, and then European industrialization and urbanization, kept demand high.

American cities grew as they handled the goods farmers bought and sold, but agricultural commerce was not their only occupation. Businesses rose to process agricultural products, and even industries not directly related to farming thrived because of the market, capital, and labor provided by that key enterprise. Growing commercial and industrial cities in turn shaped local agriculture through their own demand. While farmers tended to see cities as parasitic, the relationship between cities and agriculture was more symbiotic. Cities lived on the countryside, and the countryside thrived because of the cities. But as cities grew they achieved a degree of cultural dominance that Jeffersonians abhorred. Ironically, a dynamic agriculture facilitated the development of an urban culture that increasingly defined America and an industrial sector that would eventually dwarf it.

AGRICULTURE, AGRARIANISM, AND PUBLIC POLICY

In the early decades of the United States, the farmer was society's hero. In the hands of agrarian thinkers and writers, the farmer was transformed into the purest representative of the finest people on earth and a person on whose well-being the health of the Republic depended.

American agrarians contended that agriculture and rural life were superior to all other occupations and styles of living and that farm people were better, in every way, than others. As Thomas Jefferson put it in his *Notes on the State of Virginia*, "those who labor in the earth are the chosen people of God, if ever he had a chosen people, whose breasts he has made his peculiar deposit for substantial and genuine virtue."[1]

Agrarians argued that farmers were superior in part because their occupation was the most legitimate. Farmers produced the commodities that met the most basic human needs to be fed and clothed, and they did so through hard work. Nonfarmers were inferior because many of them—lawyers, bankers, and merchants, for example—produced nothing at all, while craftspeople produced to fulfill human wants but seldom human needs. Farming was thus the most basic, necessary, and legitimate occupation.

Also contributing to the superiority of farmers, in the eyes of their agrarian champions, was their contact with nature. Living in natural surroundings and coaxing forth nature's bounty made rural people purer, more moral, and more respectful of God than their urban counterparts. Rural living also contributed to the simplicity of farmers, in the most positive sense of the word. Rural people, agrarians argued, had simple tastes, abhorred artificiality, luxury, and ostentation, and were honest and straightforward.

Property ownership also presumably contributed to rural superiority. Owning farms made people self-sufficient and independent, responsible and mature, conservative and jealous of their liberties. Farmers' love of their land translated easily into love of country, making them the most patriotic members of society.

None of these popular ideas—of which we still hear echoes—was very fresh or new in the young United States. They stretched back into ancient Rome, to Cato and Cicero and Cincinnatus. And they were popular in contemporary Europe, as well. The Enlightenment—the philosophical fashion of the Western world in the late eighteenth century—extolled the benefits of nature and a natural life. English ruralists praised farmers for their simplicity and virtue, and French Physiocrats blended laissez-faire economics with Enlightenment philosophy in their contention that agriculture was the basis for a nation's wealth and morality.

Jefferson was well aware of these traditions, but his strident agrarianism, and that of other American policy makers and thinkers, was not the product of an attempt to copy intellectual fashions created elsewhere. Americans were attracted to agrarianism because it addressed some of the most acute needs of the young republic.

68   At the end of the American Revolution the United States was the world's only important republic. Every major nation was a monarchy, and most political theorists argued that human selfishness in an environment of insufficient governmental authority made republics dangerously fragile and unstable forms of government. By arguing that the lifestyle of 80 percent of the citizens of the United States made them independent, virtuous, and patriotic, agrarians were able to claim for their country a degree of immunity to the problems suffered by many republics.

Agrarianism also helped Americans fulfill their need to assert cultural independence and superiority. When they were colonials in a great empire, Americans were viewed—and viewed themselves—as culturally deficient. England was the metropolis, the seat of wisdom, learning, and culture, while America was a hinterland. By turning American defects such as simplicity and ruralism into virtues, agrarians were able to set the new nation apart from the Old World and fashion an independent and superior identity for it. Agrarianism thus played an important role in the development of an American national consciousness.

Agrarianism certainly had an effect on the cultural life of the young republic. Transcendentalism, the romantic philosophical position associated with such figures as Ralph Waldo Emerson and Henry David Thoreau, reflected its reverence for nature. And it is noteworthy that the hundreds of communitarian experiments that sprang up in the forty years before the Civil War were virtually all rural in nature. Where better than the countryside to attempt to perfect human nature?

Agrarianism was reflected as well in the popularity of gentleman farming among merchants, lawyers, and other professionals. The eagerness of such people to buy and work farms embodied a concession to the superiority of rural life. Members of the Boston elite who became gentleman farmers, for example, did so largely to insulate themselves from the materialism and spiritual corruptions that they feared accompanied the commerce in which they were mainly engaged.

Another indication that agrarian theory influenced rural reality was the growing interest farmers showed in enhancing and professionalizing their occupations. There had long been farmers who searched for scientific principles in their endeavors—Jefferson and George Washington are famous examples—but the early nineteenth century witnessed the creation of dozens of local and state agricultural societies dedicated to conducting experiments and sponsoring county fairs to share information and display results of improved practices. Innovative farmers planted new crops, such as Jerusalem artichokes, or imported purebred animals, such as Merino sheep. The early nineteenth century saw the birth and rapid expansion of agricultural journalism, as numerous farm papers were started and found avid readerships. Farmers tinkered with machinery and looked to improve their soils. Virginia farmer Edmund Ruffin, who was disturbed by the agricultural decline of coastal Virginia and the Carolinas, developed and disseminated important information on the use of calcereous manures to restore the fertility of acidic soils.[2] Many of these efforts had an economic purpose, at least to some degree, and they never engaged more than a small minority of the agricultural population. But efforts at agricultural improvement—and self-improvement—indicated a new respect for farmers and their potential, both within and outside of the rural community.

Agrarians stressed the cultural, political, and social importance of farmers, but the centrality of agriculture in the economy of the young republic provided another compelling reason for nurturing it. In 1800, approximately four of every five Americans were engaged primarily in agricultural production. Farmers consumed most imports, and agriculture provided the bulk of exports in a debtor nation that had to sell on world markets to survive. Nearly all merchants lived by handling farmers' crops and selling goods to farmers, and most industry either processed agricultural products or manufactured for the rural market. Most available investment capital went into the factors of agricultural production, especially land and slaves. In short, agriculture made the whole economy go.

Every policy maker in the young republic recognized the primacy of agriculture to the nation and the necessity of keeping it healthy. Jefferson's praise of farmers' moral and political virtues did not blind him to their economic importance. Alexander Hamilton, Jefferson's great rival, dreamed of an industrial and commercial empire in America's future, but he, too, recognized the centrality of agriculture in the country's economic present. This universal agreement led to the development of an agricultural policy designed to encourage the growth and prosperity of the nation's premier economic enterprise.

First, the new nation sought to encourage a vibrant trade in agricultural products. While tariff rates fluctuated throughout the early decades of our existence, they were generally low enough to discourage customers from retaliating against American agricultural exports. The federal government further encouraged agricultural marketing by negotiating commercial treaties, dredging harbors, building breakwaters, and clearing rivers of snags and sandbars. States and municipalities developed marketing infrastructures by building roads, canals, bridges, and, later, railroads.

Second, the government sought to acquire lands for potential agricultural settlement. One part of this effort involved bringing new territories under American sovereignty, such as Louisiana (including much of the area west of the Mississippi River and east of the Rocky Mountains) in 1803, West and East Florida in 1812 and 1819, Texas in 1845, the Oregon country, including all of the Pacific Northwest, in 1846, and California and the Southwest in 1848.

Another part of this effort involved the extinguishment of Indians' titles to lands in the path of settlement and their removal to less coveted places. In 1795, under the Treaty of Greenville, Indians in Ohio relinquished most of that territory to the government. Over the ensuing twenty years northwestern Indians were forced to surrender most of the rest of the territory between the Ohio River and the Great Lakes. South of the Ohio the major Indian cessions came during the first three decades of the nineteenth century, when the Cherokees, Creeks, Choctaws, Chickasaws, and Seminoles were forced to relinquish major portions of Georgia, Alabama, Mississippi, North Carolina, and Florida and to move to what later became Oklahoma.

The third major way in which the federal government encouraged agriculture was by providing for the orderly disposal of the public domain, beginning with congressional passage of the Basic Land Ordinance in 1785. This legislation dealt with lands in what was at the time called the Northwest—the area occupied today by Ohio, Michigan, Indiana, Illinois, and Wisconsin—which Congress acquired when Virginia and other states surrendered their claims to the region. The ordinance stipulated that the public lands in the Northwest be divided into square townships of six miles on each side. These would in turn be divided into thirty-six one-mile-square (640-acre) sections, to be sold at public auction for a minimum price of one dollar per acre. Congress sought to ensure an educated citizenry for the republic by reserving one section in every township for the support of public schools.

The Basic Land Ordinance was more reflective of Congress's desire to profit from the land—the only real asset it had in 1785—than of a commitment to fill the Northwest with settlers. The minimum purchase of 640 acres was eight or ten times as much as a farm family could reasonably hope to handle, and the minimum purchase price of $640 (the government did not extend credit) effectively limited sales to speculators. Congress's receptivity to speculators was underscored soon after passage of the ordinance, when it sold 7.5 million acres of unsurveyed land in Ohio to land companies for less than a dime an acre.

There were other problems as well. The method of survey, as anyone flying over the Midwest or the Great Plains today recognizes, imposed a rigid order on the land. However, it was an order that ignored natural features and even the curvature of the earth, a stubborn reality that forced regular surveyors' adjustments. More problematic than the survey itself was the reality that Americans chose to ignore the prescribed process of land disposal. Survey crews entering new areas usually found squatters already on the land. A final problem with the ordinance was that one section per township proved woefully inadequate to support public education.

As a result of its many problems, the Basic Land Ordinance proved to be a first, rather than a last, step. Over time, its terms were modified in such a way as to make it easier for settlers to acquire farms. In 1820 Congress made it possible for buyers to acquire farms as small as eighty acres for a minimum price of $1.25 per acre, and in 1832 the minimum purchase was cut to forty acres. In 1854 the Graduation Act lowered prices on unsold land and, finally, in 1862 the Homestead Act made it possible for a settler to acquire 160 acres of land in return for making stipulated improvements and paying a filing fee of ten dollars.

The land policy of the United States thus became progressively more liberal, but it was never liberal enough to ensure everyone a farm. Beyond the cost of the land itself, settlers paid substantial sums to make a farm. Moving to the land, purchasing implements, and feeding families while waiting for crops to come in were all expensive propositions. Two investigators who have done a careful study of settlement in the Midwest have concluded that it cost more than seventeen hundred dollars to make an eighty-acre farm in that region in 1860.[3] That was about three times as much as the average wage earner made in a year and was enough to put such a farm beyond the reach of most midwesterners. Even a forty-acre farm was too expensive for two-fifths of the rural residents of the Midwest in 1860. Compounding the problem was the difficulty of securing credit, which was often scarce and usually expensive in new regions.

Farmer plowing his field under the approving gaze of the female figure of Columbia
(symbol for the Philadelphia Society for Promoting Agriculture).
Courtesy of the Library of Congress.

The costs of farm making assured that land speculators would play a prominent role in American rural history, and they indeed dominated the history of some places, such as California. Land speculators are sinister figures in American history and folklore, and often for good reason. They frequently used their political connections and corrupted legislators in order to engross huge parcels of choice land at cheap prices. In 1795, for example, land companies bribed Georgia legislators in order to receive thirty-five million acres of what became Alabama and Mississippi for pennies an acre. Some speculators also stood accused of impeding development by holding onto unimproved tracts in anticipation of rising prices, as in California, where massive parcels of promising land in the Central Valley and other areas were held unbroken for decades. On the other hand, speculators often made farms available to tenants, allowing them potentially to climb the agricultural ladder to ownership, and they frequently provided credit to farmers purchasing their lands. Good or bad, speculators were inevitable in a society in which wealth was unevenly distributed and land was a commodity.

Farmers could avoid buying land from either government or speculators by squatting—occupying lands they did not own. Squatters hoped to profit in a couple of ways. If they were able to harvest and market a few crops before the owners of land put them off it, they might be able to raise the money to make a farm or even to buy the land on which they were squatting. And if they made improvements on the land, by clearing fields and erecting buildings and fences, these could be sold to those who bought the land. Squatters persistently pressured Congress for a more permissive land policy, and in 1841 that body responded with the Preemption Act, which gave squatters the right to purchase 160 acres of public land, if they could prove they had occupied and improved it, for $1.25 an acre. Speculators were less accommodating, frequently using force to remove squatters, who in turn sometimes responded with violence. Squatters were often the majority of the population in newly opened lands, and for some people squatting became a way of life, whether by choice or by necessity. John Pulliam, for example, squatted in Kentucky, Illinois, and Missouri for better than a quarter of a century, never owning a farm of his own.

AGRICULTURAL EXPANSION

The conclusion of the Revolution was challenging to American farmers, because with independence they ceased to be part of the British mercantile system. On the positive side, the end of British mercantilism meant that Americans could sell all commodities directly to any European nation and could, indeed, trade wherever they chose, outside of the British Empire. Americans pursued this opportunity with some imagination, even developing a vigorous trade in New England–grown ginseng, which the Chinese used as an aphrodisiac. On the negative side, the end of British mercantilism meant the end of familiar commercial patterns and favorable trade terms. No longer did Americans enjoy special advantages in British markets, such as the West Indies or the mother country itself. Also gone were bounties, such as that on indigo, which was immediately reduced to the status of a minor crop and then disappeared altogether.

The disruptions caused by the end of mercantilism, the loss of markets provided by the armies, and a dramatic outflow of specie brought on by an American buying binge of British goods resulted in an agricultural depression after the Peace of Paris concluded the war in 1783. This depression resulted in no little hardship and some disorder, represented especially by Shays' Rebellion, an uprising by debt-ridden Massachusetts farmers against their state government in 1786.

The mid-1790s, however, saw the onset of a period of agricultural prosperity that, though interrupted by several sharp economic downturns, gen-

74 erally continued until the Civil War. In its early years, this period of agricultural prosperity was tied to European warfare. The wars of the French Revolution and Napoleon, beginning in 1793 and running more-or-less continuously until 1815, quickened the demand for American agricultural products, especially from England. After the conclusion of the wars, demand remained brisk, as American farmers were called on to help meet the food and fiber needs of a rapidly expanding—and urbanizing and industrializing—European population.

Most American foodstuffs were in demand on the European market, but the vast bulk of meat and grain was consumed in the United States, with the growing cities providing a rapidly expanding market. By far the most important American export product was cotton, preferred by the European textile industry over flax or wool because it was easy to process and soft to the touch. Mechanization of spinning and weaving allowed dramatic centralization and expansion in the textile industry, and the demand for cotton surged.

American producers were able to meet this demand largely because of the invention of the cotton gin by Eli Whitney in 1793. Cotton could be grown throughout the South, but separating the fiber—or lint—from the seed was an arduous process. Sea island cotton was relatively easy to process by hand, because its fibers were long and seeds were concentrated at the base of the flower, but it demanded a long growing season, available only along the coast. Short-staple cotton required a much shorter growing season, but the shortness of the fibers and their mixture with seeds meant that a worker could hand-process only about one pound per day. Whitney's gin was a hand-powered machine with revolving drums and metal teeth to pull cotton fibers away from seeds. Using the gin, a worker could produce up to fifty pounds of lint in a day. The later development of larger gins, powered by horses, water, or steam, multiplied productivity further.

The dynamic, mutually reinforcing interaction of improved processing and high demand led to the rapid spread of cotton cultivation and to a surge in production. In 1790, three thousand bales of cotton were produced in the United States (today a bale is a standard measure of cotton weighing five hundred pounds; before the Civil War bales could weigh anywhere from four hundred to five hundred pounds). Ten years later 73 thousand bales were produced; in 1820 production reached 732 thousand bales; and in 1860,

3.841 million bales were produced. Ominously, the slave-labor system received a new lease on life from cotton, spreading westward with the crop.

Cotton became the main American export, dwarfing all others. In 1802, cotton composed 14 percent of total American exports by value. Cotton had a 36 percent share by 1810 and over a 50 percent share in 1830. In 1860, 61 percent of the value of American exports was represented by cotton. In contrast, wheat and wheat flour composed only 6 percent of the value of American exports in that year. Clearly, cotton was king in the trade of the young republic.

The growing market for cotton and other American agricultural products led to an unprecedented expansion of agricultural settlement, mostly west of the Appalachians and east of the Mississippi. Between 1791 and 1821 eleven new states were admitted to the Union, and another nine joined between 1836 and 1859. Of these twenty states, only California was not primarily agricultural at the time of its admission.

The population of the new western states grew dramatically. The population of Kentucky tripled between 1790 and 1800, then nearly doubled again between 1800 and 1810. Tennessee claimed 36 thousand people in 1790 and 262 thousand twenty years later. Ohio went from 45 thousand in 1800 to 231 thousand in 1810 and then to 581 thousand in 1820. That represented a population increase in just twenty years of nearly 1,300 percent. The defeat of the Creek Indians in the War of 1812 and the opening of rich cotton lands pushed Alabama's population from 9 thousand to 128 thousand in the decade of the 1810s alone. That same decade Indiana's population jumped from 25 thousand to 147 thousand. As older states filled, the process was repeated farther west. Illinois's population tripled in both the 1820s and 1830s. By 1840, 476 thousand people lived there. Arkansas, with 30 thousand people in 1830, expanded to 436 thousand in the space of thirty years.

The growth of the West was tied to increasing market opportunities, which became more compelling as transportation improved. Markets cannot affect the behavior of people if people lack access to them. In the years after the Revolution, water provided the most feasible mode of agricultural transportation, effectively confining settlement to the valleys of the Ohio and Mississippi Rivers and to major tributaries thereof. Merchants or groups of farmers built and filled flatboats, to be floated down the river system to New Orleans. Flatboats were usually twelve to fourteen feet wide and forty to fifty feet long and could carry up to one hundred tons—or four hundred to five hundred barrels—of produce. In order to maximize the value of the cargo, shippers usually sent processed agricultural products, such as flour, pork, and corn whiskey, instead of live animals or bulk grain. At New Orleans they sold their cargo—which was subsequently shipped elsewhere, usually to the East—broke up their flatboats, sold the lumber for firewood, and returned home.

Flatboating was a common Midwestern experience (Abraham Lincoln was among the many midwesterners who rode a flatboat to New Orleans), but it was arduous, especially in the early years. Snags, rapids, and bars in the rivers all presented potential hazards. Before 1803, the Spanish controlled New Orleans, and they were capricious about giving Americans the right to navigate the river and land their cargoes in the Crescent City. That imparted a high level of instability to the marketing system. Returning home was often an adventure. Flatboatmen commonly walked home over the Natchez Trace through Mississippi, Tennessee, and Kentucky. Especially at the southern end, the Natchez Trace was infested with bandits and cutthroats.

Some of these problems were solved, making river marketing more attractive. The purchase of New Orleans and the rest of Louisiana eliminated the problem of the Spanish, and the steamboat vastly improved the transportation situation. Steamboats were well suited to western waters, especially because of their shallow draft, which allowed them to operate far up streams. In 1815 steamboat tonnage operating in the West was only 10 thousand; by 1845, that figure had reached 188 thousand. Farmers continued to market with flatboats, but steamboats provided a faster, safer, and more comfortable return trip.

Settlement outside of the river system was retarded by the difficulty and expense of land transportation. It was estimated that shipping by wagon from northern Ohio to New York City in 1820 under optimum road conditions would cost twenty-five dollars a ton, a prohibitive price for high volume, low-value agricultural products. Marketing became much easier with the completion of the Erie Canal, linking Lake Erie, at Buffalo, New York, to the Hudson River, at Albany, in 1825. The completion of the canal dropped the price of sending a ton of produce from Ohio to New York City to three dollars, facilitating settlement there and throughout the Great Lakes region. The canal also made New York City (at the mouth of the Hudson) the major commercial and agricultural marketing center of the United States. Eager to duplicate New York's success, other states and cities undertook canal projects. Before 1815, less than one hundred miles of canals had been built in the United States. During the next quarter century, more than three thousand miles of canals were constructed.

Water transportation was cheap, but it had its drawbacks. Obviously, but significantly, it only worked where there was water, and the water had to be unfrozen and to have a certain minimum depth. Before the Civil War, railroads came to play an increasingly important role in supplementing and, in some places, replacing water transportation. Already in 1840 the country had 33 hundred miles of track, nearly twice as much as all of the nations of Europe combined. By 1860 the United States had nearly 31 thousand miles of track, most of it between the Appalachians and the Mississippi.

The rapid spread of agriculture from the Appalachians to the Mississippi and beyond meant that the settlement process was carried out in thousands of locations by hundreds of thousands of people. The first priority of early settlers in an area was to produce a crop, and as a consequence they lived in very primitive conditions, sometimes in wagons, lean-tos, dugouts in slopes, or even brush huts. When John Pulliam's son Robert came to Sugar Creek in central Illinois in 1819, he housed his family in a sugarhouse he had constructed on a maple syrup-gathering expedition two years before. At least Pulliam's dwelling had four walls; some early huts consisted of just three walls and a roof, with a roaring fire on the open side. Pioneers quickly cleared a few acres, either by girdling and burning or by the more laborious process of felling trees with axes, and enclosed their cleared fields, usually with worm fences, to protect crops from the hogs and cattle they grazed in the woods. They usually put in a crop of corn initially, to provide for family food needs and take the fat out of new lands.

Early settlers commonly built a more substantial dwelling, usually a log house, in their second year on the land. For some, the first-year agricultural system continued for a long time. In the southern piney woods and hill country regions, for example, many farmers pursued a subsistence agriculture based on grazing and corn growing long after the early settlement years had passed. But most farmers expanded their fields, and by their second or third years on the land were planting such cash crops as cotton or wheat along with corn.

The early stage of settlement fascinated Americans in the young republic. The frontier and the stereotypical frontier settler became cultural icons, representing to Americans and Europeans as well what was unique about the United States, and such western figures as Daniel Boone, Davy Crockett, and Andrew Jackson were fashioned into larger-than-life heroes in their own times. To a substantial degree, the mythological pioneer shaped American popular culture and continues to shape it to some degree even today. In the American imagination, the frontier settler was a male, living by his courage and his wits, self-sufficient and in splendid isolation from corrupting civilization. He was a natural man, the prototypical American, freed of the social, economic, and cultural restraints that confined others.

Like most stereotypes, that of the pioneer was rooted in half-truth. While people migrated to the frontier with families and even with their slaves, frontier areas did tend to be dominated by young males in their first few years. Robert Pulliam left his family at home when he first visited Sugar Creek, and his first neighbors in nearby Drennan's Prairie were four men and six of their sons. In addition, the decision to move families to the new country was usually made by men, with little consultation with their wives. How wives responded to decisions affecting their fate so dramatically and to the privations of early frontier life, bereft as it often was of schools, churches, and neighborhoods, depended on a complex variety of cultural factors. Robert Pulliam's wife Mary, from a squatter family like her husband's, probably did not particularly resent it when her husband moved her and their five children into that tiny sugarhouse in 1819. On the other hand, the wives of southwestern planters were often bitter about being uprooted from supportive kin networks on the seaboard and transplanted in the rough new cotton country of Alabama or Mississippi, where they sometimes lived in tents or crude cabins of the sort one claimed "looked as dismal as a prison."[4] Personal factors also played a role. Joanna Townes found life in early Perry County, Alabama, exhilarating, but her sister-in-law Eliza Blassingame, sixteen miles from her nearest kin and tyrannized by a brutal and neglectful husband, longed to return to her South Carolina home.

The good news for those living at the edge of settlement was that primitive conditions usually did not last for long, nor did separation from friends and family. Those who succeeded on the frontier were more likely to have come with friends or kin than alone. As was the case in the colonial backcountry, kinship groups provided support for individuals and laid the groundwork for further migration to the area from more settled regions. Among the first four families to settle the Drennan's Prairie neighborhood in Sugar Creek were two led by brothers and a third led by their brother-in-law, Job Fletcher, who located nearby in 1819.[5] Fletcher was followed within a dozen years by the family of his brother James, the family of his sister-in-law Elizabeth Fletcher, and two families related to James's wife Jane. Shortly after Dave Wood relocated in Trempealeau County, Wisconsin, from Oneida County, New York, in 1856, he was followed by his father, Alvah.[6] Western communities experienced a good deal of physical mobility, with as many as three-fourths of the names appearing in one census gone by the time the next was taken a decade later. But those who stayed and prospered and provided the basis for stable communities and institutions were usually part of tightly knit kinship groups.

Likewise, the agricultural frontier was far removed from the self-sufficient utopia of popular imagination. Late-eighteenth- and early-nineteenth-century Americans were part of a modern material world. At the very least, they needed things that only others could supply—guns, powder and shot, nails, horseshoes, pots, harness, salt, and so forth. And they wanted the goods that symbolized modern material comfort. One historian has found that, even on the early Kentucky frontier in the 1790s, settlers desired—and acquired—English textiles, ceramics, glassware, and kitchen utensils, and they commonly copied, in their clothing and eating and behavior, what they perceived as civilized eastern and European styles.[7] People came west not to escape or recreate civilization but to improve their material circumstances. But in their dependence on kinship groups, their continuing fealty to accepted material and behavioral standards, and their desire to make a strange and sometimes frightening environment more familiar to themselves, they created a western lifestyle similar to that they had left in the East.

The material needs and wants of westerners symbolized their involvement in a market economy of increasing complexity. They produced commodities that flowed into the channels of international trade. They found their behavior shaped by the preferences and demands of others and their living standards influenced by factors beyond their control. Fewer of their commercial relationships were personal. In the early years of settlement, westerners often sold or bartered their products to local merchants who sometimes also functioned as processors. As time went on, they were more likely to sell their products through middlemen, such as drovers and commission merchants, who in turn sold them to millers or packers or brokers in distant places like Chicago or Cincinnati or New Orleans.

Credit also diminished face-to-face relationships and farmers' control of their fates. In colonial times the farmer needing a loan went to a local grandee who was familiar with his character. Now he borrowed from a local merchant, who in turn received credit from a wholesale house in St. Louis that had its own credit relations with commercial firms in Philadelphia or New Orleans. Or he borrowed from one of the local banks that sprang up in the West, a bank that itself borrowed from a financial institution in Chicago, which in turn derived credit from banks in New York. Or he borrowed from a local loan agent, usually a realtor or lawyer, who sold farm mortgages, through various intermediaries, to Boston investors.

Extended lines of credit helped finance western agriculture, but they also made that enterprise more treacherous. Personal relationships no longer softened lenders' demands, and borrowers could be jeopardized by adverse financial developments beyond their ability to control. Merchants and banks failed regularly, carrying their debtors down with them. Financial panics in 1819, 1837, and 1857 led to plunging commodity prices and widespread farm foreclosures in the West.

It was ironic that, at the very time farmers were being praised by agrarians for their independence, they were becoming more dependent on a variety of other people. Fluctuating prices and capricious credit made farmers ambivalent about the market system in which they were enmeshed. They expressed distrust of merchants and brokers, who they thought manipulated prices and the money supply to the detriment of farmers. Sometimes they even opposed transportation improvements that they thought might increase their exposure to the vagaries of the market or alter the social character of their communities. Unpredictable market conditions also confirmed the wisdom of minimizing risk. The more self-sufficient they were, farmers reasoned, the less vulnerable they would be to economic forces beyond their control.

Farmers' ambivalence about the market and their unwillingness to let it dominate all of their relationships was reflected in other ways as well. The farm remained a home, based on intimate relationships, even as it became more of a business. Moreover, a moral economy continued to exist among neighbors and kin. Neighbors shared tools and work and food with one another. Barn raisings, husking bees, and other communal activities continued, unaffected by market factors. While historians perceive a contradiction between the traditional moral economy and its rising market counterpart, rural people were quite able to practice elements of both without an apparent sense of conflict. As a German immigrant working on an Illinois farm in 1851 shrewdly noted, "the Americans living around us are thoroughly good neighbors, ready and willing to be of help. But in business they are just as crafty as all their countrymen. When doing business they have no conscience at all."[8]

AGRICULTURAL EXPANSION AND NATIONAL DEVELOPMENT

In the 1830s Cincinnati was the pork-packing capital of the West. Every fall, drovers herded swine to the Queen City's slaughterhouses from miles around, creating for a few weeks what one English visitor called a "city of pigs" in which "swine, lean, gaunt, and vicious-looking, riot through [the] streets."[9] If they repelled some visitors, Cincinnati's pigs attracted packers, as well as farm laborers who could earn a dollar and a half a day during hog-killing season. Cincinnati's hogs indirectly attracted others, such as British immigrants William Proctor, a candlemaker, and James Gamble, a soap-maker, both of whom found lard an essential component of their products. In 1837 these two entrepreneurs formed a partnership to manufacture soap, which was retailed mainly to farmers in the Mississippi Valley, and a great American consumer products company was born.

Proctor and Gamble provides a noteworthy example of the relationship between agriculture and industry prior to the Civil War, but not a unique one. American industry drew its strength from the thriving agricultural sector in both direct and indirect ways. Such industries as flour milling, meat-packing, and tanning (the processing of animal hides into leather) were dependent on agricultural abundance, and others, such as brewing and distilling and the manufacturing of soap and leathergoods, were benefited by it. The farm implement industry depended on prosperous customers in agriculture, but most consumer goods were marketed heavily to farmers as well. Rhode Island textiles and Massachusetts shoes clothed rural bodies, and Connecticut clocks and Pennsylvania furniture adorned rural homes.

By providing raw materials for successful processing industries and markets for manufacturers' products, a prosperous agriculture helped American industry acquire capital. But that was not the only way. Trade in agricultural products enriched insurers, shippers, brokers, and commission merchants, all of whom poured capital back into industrial development. And by providing most of what the country sold abroad, agriculture made it possible for Americans to acquire specie to pay the interest on funds borrowed from overseas, thereby encouraging further foreign investment in American enterprises.

In addition to supporting industry and facilitating capital accumulation, agriculture also served industrial development by freeing labor. Before the Civil War the average farmworker produced enough to feed himself or herself and three others. Some portion of these others were thus available for industrial employment. Moreover, farm families themselves labored in industry. People working on farms provided a pool of winter workers for the lumber and packing industries, among others. In New England, where farms were marginal and labor was bartered even before the Revolution, many families took in winter outwork—contract finishing of manufactured products, especially items of apparel—in their homes. In such cases, manufacturing work was less a jarring transition from agriculture to industry than an extension of the Revolution-era emphasis on home manufacturing and labor exchange.

Outwork was the salvation of many New England farm families, but its day as a labor system was relatively short in a number of industries. The development of large, highly mechanized textile and shoe factories in the early nineteenth century dramatically limited certain types of outwork. For a time, the factories seemed to offer another means of advancing family self-sufficiency. During the 1820s and 1830s the large textile mills at Waltham and Lowell, Massachusetts, hired unmarried farm girls, who often sent a portion of their wages home, but this system only lasted until a new labor force appeared in the form of Irish immigrants. The decline of some types of outwork made it difficult for many New England farm families to remain on the land under familiar terms. They faced the choice of expanding their farms into commercial operations, relocating to western lands, or abandoning agriculture and working in commerce or industry.

Many chose the last of those options. The dynamic commercial activity in agricultural products and the growth in manufacturing led to a surge in the urban population in the early republic. In 1790, only 5 percent of the American people lived in cities—defined by the census as places with twenty-five hundred or more people—and as late as 1820 only 7 percent lived in such places. In 1840, about 11 percent of the people were urban, and by

1860 American cities—fueled by commerce, manufacturing, and large-scale immigration from Europe—claimed nearly 20 percent of the nation's population.

Established cities grew, and new ones sprang up everywhere. Existing eastern commercial centers such as New York, Philadelphia, and Boston flourished and added manufacturing to their economic bases, while new ones like Baltimore appeared. Meanwhile new manufacturing centers, such as the Erie Canal towns of Buffalo, Rochester, and Syracuse, became important cities almost overnight. The result was a surge in the urban population of the East, especially between 1840 and 1860. Between those census years the urban proportion of the population of Massachusetts advanced from 38 to 60 percent, while that of New York went from 19 to 39 percent. In Connecticut, the percentage of people living in cities leaped from 13 to 27 percent between 1840 and 1860.

In the West, cities thrived on agricultural commerce. In the early nineteenth century, such river cities as Pittsburgh, Cincinnati, Louisville, St. Louis, and New Orleans became major places. Later, as Great Lakes commerce quickened, such places as Cleveland, Detroit, and Chicago—destined to be the great metropolis of the West—surged. The West remained primarily agricultural, but already in 1860 Ohio's urban population was 17 percent of her total, and 14 percent of Illinoisans lived in cities.

Even before the urban surge of the 1820–60 period, towns and agricultural hinterlands had close and even symbiotic relationships, but the scale of those relationships changed dramatically. Larger cities had much more extensive agricultural hinterlands. Eighteenth-century New York maintained a commercial relationship with farmers on Long Island and in the Hudson Valley. With the development of the transportation network centered on the Erie Canal and an extensive rail system, most of the region north of the Ohio, east of the Mississippi, and south of the Great Lakes became New York's commercial hinterland. New York's financial power provided another tie that bound these areas, as well as much of the South, to America's premier city.

Farmers living in northern Illinois or southern Michigan in 1840 probably did not think much about being part of New York's hinterland, because the impact of that great metropolis was not readily apparent in their day-to-day lives. But farmers living in the East could hardly avoid the conclusion that cities were shaping their lives. Eastern farmers who were flexible and inno-

84 vative enough to do so shifted their production to fill the needs of nearby urbanites. Truck farming—the production of fresh fruits and vegetables for market—and dairy farming became dominant in areas around growing cities. Producing such items often demanded agricultural reforms, including increased fertilization. It was an indication of urban dominance that farmers often met their fertilization needs by purchasing city waste.

The growth of cities and towns affected eastern farmers in other ways as well. The value of real estate on the urban fringe rose dramatically, benefiting farm sellers but making it harder for others to provide locally for sons. Urban growth also affected labor markets as the wages of hired hands rose when rural people went to towns for part-time work or moved there permanently.

The difficulty of providing land to pass on to children contributed to declines in human fertility in most areas of the East. Declining fertility and the movement of young people to nearby cities or to the West conjoined to bring drops in population in some rural areas and population stagnation in others. This had a psychological impact, as many rural easterners concluded that their communities were in retreat and their lifestyles were doomed.

Adding to this loss of morale was the increasing cultural dominance of cities. It was not simply that young people from the countryside went to the cities, it was that the best and the brightest seemed to be drawn to the excitement and opportunity there. Moreover, urban control over media allowed cities increasingly to define tastes and values and cultural standards, even for rural people.

The rise of cities was not the only development in the decades prior to the Civil War that affected the morale and the fortunes of eastern farmers. The growth of the West also played a major role. Western farmers, enjoying the advantage of soils that were richer and were usually more easily worked than those of their eastern counterparts, were much more productive. Indeed, two students of agricultural productivity before the Civil War have concluded that the average midwestern farm was twice as productive as the average farm in the Northeast and nearly nine times as productive as the average New England farm.[10] A substantial differential existed in the South as well, where the productivity of new cotton lands in the West was often double that of lands in the Southeast.

This differential in productivity led to population shifts from East to West, and it also eroded eastern incomes. Though they enjoyed greater proximity to markets, northeastern farmers found that they could not compete with the western wheat that flowed in to feed urbanites. Southerners, as well, were pushed by western competition to diversify or to reform their agricultural practices.

As a result of all this, agriculture in much of New England and the Middle Atlantic region was transformed in the first half of the nineteenth century. Between 1770 and 1860 in Franklin County, Massachusetts, for example, farm units were expanded, land was more intensively farmed, farmers concentrated on agriculture more exclusively, they were more commercial and innovative, and they focused on the production of specialty products for regional urban markets. Those who desired to continue to live by agriculture had to adjust in the face of new competition and new opportunities. It would not be the last time farmers would have to adjust.

The decades between the end of the American Revolution and the beginning of the Civil War were fraught with irony for American agriculture. While agriculture expanded dramatically and markets for food and fiber grew, some farmers found it increasingly difficult to survive. Agricultural prosperity raised farmers' living standards, while feeding an industrial economy that would dwarf agriculture and swelling cities that would dominate the nation economically, culturally, and socially. Jeffersonian agrarians continued to praise the independence of people who were, in fact, increasingly dependent on others to lend them money, carry and consume what they produced, and manufacture for them.

Small wonder that farmers were ambivalent about change. They grasped commercial opportunities but often in a timid and tentative way. They remained as self-sufficient as they could be, pursuing traditional family-survival strategies and depending on supportive networks of neighbors and kin. They enjoyed the material advantages industry offered, while clinging to the land. Two observers have judged farmers "irrational" for their commitment to an investment that returned only half the yield of an investment in industrial enterprise.[11] But there was no shortage of people who wanted to acquire farms. Whatever its shortcomings, farming still promised a higher degree of individual independence and family security than urban occupations offered. And the farmer was still celebrated as the prototypical American and the most perfect representative of all that was good about the country.

FIVE

Rural Life
in the Young Nation

As agricultural settlement spread across the North American continent, the potential shock and social disruption of dislocation and mobility was minimized by the presence of remarkably adaptable rural institutions. Rural people brought to new areas strong families, a durable sense of community, and a tradition of neighborliness reinforced by kinship ties. Also buttressing the rural community were churches and schools, institutions that moved with settlers and imparted a sense of familiarity and stability in newly settled areas.

Lending further stability to rural America in this time of dynamic growth and expansion was the undeviating rhythm of rural life. Work continued to be governed by the seasons and the day, not by the clock, and the material realities of rural life changed slowly, if at all. Despite their increasing commercialization, rural people continued to live lives of hard physical labor, mitigated only slightly by modern creature comforts.

There was a remarkable similarity between rural living in the North and in the South, with the significant exception of the presence of slavery in the South. Slavery as an institution complicated life in the rural South. Because of slavery, there were three rural communities in the South, rather than one—a biracial community, a white community, and a slave community.

The cohesion of the biracial rural community was seriously compromised by two other communities based on racial identification and racial antipathy. Whites formed a community in which blacks played no role. And slaves formed a community that sustained them, emotionally, psychologically, and, to some degree, physically and helped them survive a destructive institution.

THE INSTITUTIONAL STRUCTURE OF RURAL AMERICA

The foundation of rural America was the nuclear family. It was the key institution in other rural societies as well, of course, but the American practice of family settlement on individual farmsteads seemed to give it a special centrality here. The farm family served most of the functions families historically served and more. The family was, first, a means of controlling sexual behavior and a standard venue for bearing and raising children. It served a psychological function, providing love and care for its members. In nineteenth-century America it was society's premier welfare institution, providing supervision and sustenance for those unable to function independently. And it was also an educational institution that dwarfed the school. Not only was the family primarily responsible for socializing children, it also provided a setting in which boys and girls learned to play the roles they would likely fill throughout their lives.

The nineteenth-century farm family was most remarkable for its economic function. While urbanites increasingly separated their work from their homes, the family farm remained both a social and an economic institution, a business as well as a home. It was very much a cooperative economic endeavor. Men and boys mainly worked in the fields, producing crops and livestock for sale. Women and girls mainly maintained homes and produced food and household manufactures that advanced family self-sufficiency. In the Hallowell, Maine, home of Ephraim and Martha Ballard, Ephraim and his boys grew crops, raised animals, and milled lumber, while Martha and her girls carried on household manufacturing, preserved food, and produced vegetables, herbs, poultry, and dairy products for sale. Martha and Ephraim maintained strict financial accounts of their endeavors; otherwise, they were quite typical of rural couples.

It was not simply a convenience or an advantage to have a family in rural America a century and a half ago, it was a virtual necessity. Men experienced great difficulty making a success at farming without wives to advance self-sufficiency and children to provide labor. For women there were few alternatives to marriage in rural America, and those that existed were generally unpalatable, though leaving the countryside for cities was an option women exercised with increasing frequency.

Rural women lived in a patriarchal world in the years between the Revolution and the Civil War. Legally, their economic subordination to men was assured by laws defining them as minors incapable of making contracts of most types, by the requirement that their property become their husband's upon marriage, and by inheritance statutes that guaranteed support for widows without giving them the means to achieve independence. Laws reflected the community's sense that men were farmers and women were farmwives, that men should represent families in public by participating in commerce and politics while women stayed home, and that men should make decisions regarding moving, purchasing land, implements, or livestock, and growing crops, while women should obey. These beliefs were rooted in ancient traditions that changed only very slowly, despite talk of republican motherhood and other concepts that might conceivably widen the sphere of female activity and authority.

Patriarchalism seems undemocratic and even oppressive to most Americans today, but it is important to understand it in the context of the times. First, patriarchalism generally reflected the sense of the whole community, women as well as men, regarding how families should operate and spouses should relate to one another. Few people conceived of alternatives. It is also important to remember that patriarchalism placed obligations on men to provide leadership and care for families, even while it gave them authority. The wives of southwestern planters who damned their husbands did so on the grounds that men were avoiding their responsibility to assure the emotional and physical well-being of their families by moving to the raw cotton frontier. Finally, like any cultural construct, patriarchalism described an ideal that was not always real. Men frequently did consult with wives on all sorts of issues and did view them as partners and equals, and women did sometimes play roles that were considered inappropriate for them by the community at large.

Certainly, while women were not usually deeply involved in the commercial side of agriculture, they did undertake activities that enhanced family self-sufficiency and thus contributed mightily to the economic success of the farm. Women were commonly engaged in the production of fruits, vegetables, eggs, cheese, butter, cider, beer, and so forth. They frequently manufactured cloth, clothing, soap, and candles, they provided putting-out labor for manufacturers, and when extra hands were needed in the fields women usually provided them. Only the rare farm would have survived without the efforts of women.

The role of rural women and the social conception of what that role should be changed only slowly, but change it did. In the years before the Civil War, changes derived from developments in the agricultural and industrial economies and from the challenge of new, urban-born conceptions of the proper social and familial function of women.

The commercialization of agriculture had some impact on the role of women on the farm. As a general rule, men's activities were concentrated on production for the market, while those of women focused on the maintenance of family self-sufficiency. When such traditional areas of female production as poultry and dairy became more lucrative, as they did in the urbanizing Northeast, men tended to replace women in such endeavors.

The industrial development that was intertwined with agricultural commercialization also affected the work of farm women. Commercial butter and cheese factories provided stiff competition to home producers, and farm families with disposable income often found manufactured soap or textiles to be preferable to similar products made at home. The decline of the putting-out system that resulted from the advance of the factory system further diminished the importance of home manufacturing.

In urban America, economic changes had contributed to a new conception of the proper social role of women. In towns and cities work was increasingly being separated from the home, rendering it less of an economic institution and removing men from it for much of the time. To authors on domestic relations, like Catharine Beecher, and to such middle-class women's magazines as *Godey's Lady's Book*, this was quite desirable. Champions of domesticity argued that the home was the proper sphere of women, due to their elevated moral sensibilities and their innate nurturing qualities, and that they should concentrate their energies on raising and instructing children and on making pleasant homes for husbands. Urban America increasingly set cultural standards for the whole country, so it is not surprising that the domestic ideal filtered down to the countryside, often with farm newspapers as conduits.

The domestic ideal had some impact on rural people. Farm women were increasingly attentive to urban standards regarding child rearing, the plan-

90

ning and arrangement of domestic space, home furnishings and decoration, and cooking in the years before the Civil War. But a strict separation of men's and women's spheres, like that envisioned by Catharine Beecher, was simply impossible on the farm, where the home remained the center of the business.[1] Nor was it necessarily desirable. While the farm work women did was frequently oppressive, tedious, and even brutal, some women found that it gave them a sense of self-worth and independence that domestic labors alone could not provide. It is hard to imagine a woman like Martha Ballard, busy supervising a range of home-centered enterprises and conducting a thriving trade as a midwife, being happy confining herself to baking, mending, and reading children's stories.

The lives of farm children, as well as those of women, were defined largely by a combination of economic necessity and patriarchal ideology. The romantic popular image of barefoot boys and apple-cheeked girls frolicking through meadows has little relation to reality. While there were some farmers—substantial southern planters, for example—who indulged their children, and while there was a good deal of affection between parents and children everywhere, farm children usually functioned as an economic resource. Children began helping with chores by the age of five or six, and eleven- or twelve-year-old boys and girls were expected to do the same things their parents did. While this seemed natural, normal, and necessary to parents, children sometimes remembered it as brutal and cruel. John Muir, the environmentalist and naturalist, who was put to the plow by his immigrant father at the age of twelve, remembered a life of tedious and unremitting toil: "In winter father came to the foot of the stairs and called us at six o'clock to feed the horses and cattle, grind axes, bring in wood, and do any other chores required, then breakfast, and out to work . . . by daybreak, chopping, fencing, etc. . . . no matter what the weather, there was always something to do."[2] Nineteenth-century farm life did not put a premium on childhood.

If the family was the most important visible institution in rural America, the neighborhood was the preeminent invisible one. While there were political units in rural America—counties, townships, and so forth—neighborhoods had little to do with legal units of government. Sometimes rural neighborhoods were bound by a geographic feature, sometimes they included families related to one another, as in the case of Drennan's Prairie in Sugar Creek, sometimes they were centered on a school, a church, a mill, or a store, and sometimes their people shared a common ethnic heritage or place of origin. Some or all of these factors might help define a neighborhood, but the essential characteristic all neighbors shared everywhere was a sense of identity and mutuality—a sense of neighborliness.

Neighborliness played a role in the rural community that was both unifying and necessary. Differences in class, politics, or religion could be mitigated by neighborliness. Neighborliness gave people a sense of comfort, security, and belonging. It was—and is—an essential characteristic of rural life that is difficult to duplicate in other settings.

Neighbors provided a good deal of emotional sustenance and support to one another. They helped with births, weddings, illnesses, and deaths. They were confidants with whom one could share troubles and joys, and they served as strands in the social safety net in a society with little in the way of formal welfare institutions. Neighbors provided recreation. They were people with whom one hunted, fished, visited, and quilted. They provided help when grain was to be threshed or houses or barns needed to be raised. One borrowed tools from them and exchanged labor with them. The reciprocity of life in the rural neighborhood was generally a positive thing, but it could have its negative aspects. People sometimes imposed on one's neighborliness, demanding more than their due or receiving more than they could return. But the ancient tradition of mutuality, underscored in many places, such as the South, by a strong sense of individual and family honor, kept the ideal and the reality of neighborliness alive.

It was good to live among people who cared for and about one's life, but it could be oppressive. Neighbors pried into one's affairs, making it difficult to maintain much of a private life in the countryside. Neighbors set standards to which individuals were expected to conform, with ostracism as the penalty for those who did not. Neighbors could be judgmental, and they gossiped. Retaining the good opinion of one's neighbors held one to strict conformity with social and moral standards and limited the expression of individuality.

Also upholding community social and moral standards was the church. At the beginning of the nineteenth century, the settled areas east of the Appalachians were adequately served by churches, but denominational leaders worried that westerners were going through life without the consolation of organized religion. Shortly after 1800, the evangelical denominations—especially the Baptists, the Methodists, and the Presbyterians—launched a series of revivals in the West. One result of that enterprise was to make revivalism enduringly popular in rural America. Another was that soon the West was, if anything, overchurched.

Overchurching meant that most rural congregations were too small to afford full-time ministers and were thus compelled to share circuit-riding clergymen with other congregations. Rural ministers were often bereft of formal education, but they made great strides in giving churches an aura of sanctity in the early nineteenth century that had not been customary. Hymnals and organs standardized and imparted majesty to the musical component of services; glass windows, stoves, and paint improved the physical environment; and the prohibition of tobacco chewing and the banishment of dogs lent greater dignity to services.

Churches provided consolation, celebration, and explanation, just as they do today, but they were also major recreational centers in rural America. Services, weddings, christenings, funerals, oyster suppers, and other activities provided important opportunities for socializing. The church was an especially significant social outlet for women, because it was the only public institution in which it was usually acceptable for them to play an active role.

The effect of the church on community cohesion was mixed. In some places, religious disputation was the main wedge dividing neighbors from one another. In others, churches provided a tie binding neighbors together. Churches everywhere underscored neighborhood efforts to regulate behavior by disciplining members for such offenses as adultery, drunkenness, and fornication.

In some places, schools also served as important community institutions. Free—that is, taxpayer-supported—public schools were not universal in rural America before the Civil War. The New England colonies had required towns to support public schools and, while education statutes were not always strictly observed, most did. By the time of the Revolution common schools (institutions covering grades one through eight) were available in most of New England and much of the Middle Atlantic region. In the Northwest, public education received a boost under the Basic Land Ordinance (see chapter 4) whereby Congress set aside one section in every township for its support. Unfortunately, revenues from these lands were insufficient to support public schools, requiring people who wanted them to tax themselves or to donate funds for that purpose. No southern state required free public education, and no lands were set aside for its support. Planters sometimes hired tutors for their children, and smaller farmers frequently banded together to support subscription schools, wherein patrons paid a per-pupil fee to maintain a facility and hire a teacher.

In whatever form they existed, common schools reflected the priorities of the family and the neighborhood. Districts were very small (in some midwestern counties there were as many as two hundred of them) and were often coincidental with neighborhoods. District boards, made up of local farmers, kept schools under close scrutiny and tight control. Terms were short and were timed to interfere as little as necessary with the agricultural year. Teachers were frequently older siblings of pupils, curricula focused narrowly on a handful of subjects that could not easily be taught at home, standardized textbooks were not required, and schools were expected to reinforce the moral and cultural standards of the neighborhood. In many places, the school was more significant as a social than an educational institution. Buildings frequently served as community centers, hosting potluck suppers, lodge meetings, and political gatherings. And school activities, such as declamations and spelling matches, focused community pride and loyalty.

The kinship networks, the tradition of neighborliness, and locally controlled and oriented churches and schools that characterized rural America made the settlement process relatively easy and comfortable. People moving west fit into communities like those they had left with institutions that were familiar to them. The localistic traditions of rural America also made it a reasonably congenial place for the hundreds of thousands of immigrants who settled there, coming in large numbers from the 1840s until after the turn of the twentieth century.

Immigrants were similar to native migrants in important ways. They tended to practice chain migration, settling near kin or fellow villagers who had come earlier and urged them to follow. Dave Wood's father had followed him to Trempealeau County, where they were joined by Norwegians and later Poles who came in a similar manner and for similar reasons.[3] Immigrants were also like other migrants in that they tended to be risk takers, more adventurous and alive to the possibilities of a wider world than were those who remained behind. In other ways, immigrants faced challenges that native migrants did not confront. Although the United States had a temperate climate similar to that in those parts of Europe from which most immigrants came, American soils tended to be heavier and more difficult to work. Moreover, while some of the same crops were grown on both continents, corn, the premier American cultivar, was not grown in most places in northern and central Europe. Different cropping methods in America forced changes in European ways, and the American practice of individual settlement meant a much heavier reliance on family labor than was the case in the Old World. There were some enduring differences between immigrant and native farmers—Germans, for example, were more likely to use wives and daughters in field labor and were more committed to dairy farming than were Americans of older stock. Immigrant and native alike fastened on such differences in disparaging each other, as did the German immigrant in Ohio who wrote of American women in 1836 that "there's nothing they'd rather do than ride around a bit and go to the stores . . . and to sleep late in the morning."[4] American farm women were less likely than Germans to perform field labor, but such a characterization scarcely fit their lives!

In matters of culture and tradition, Europeans were generally able to transplant their ways to the New World. More often than not, they lived in close proximity to kin and friends from the same cultural background. They built ethnic churches that, ironically, became more important in the New World than in the Old, because here they were an important component of ethnic identity. And they effectively controlled their local schools, even to the point of having instruction in their native language. All of this meant that it was possible, in a limited way, to recreate Germany or Norway or Sweden in America.

It is also important, even in matters of culture and social behavior and standards, not to overemphasize the differences between the Old World and the New. Farmers in both places operated in what was increasingly a market economy. In both the United States and Europe, farmers found themselves mediating between traditions of mutuality and market demands. Immigrants and natives alike were part of a Western cultural, philosophical, and religious tradition; in large matters, they thought alike. In both places, cultural standards were being set to an ever-greater degree in cities. The urban ideal of female domesticity that met Norwegian immigrants in Iowa or Wisconsin, for example, was not all that different from the ideal they had encountered in Norway. Immigration was inevitably a jarring experience, but it was softened by the cultural similarity of the giving and receiving societies and by the wide latitude for self-definition and institutional self-control people enjoyed in rural America.

DAILY LIFE IN RURAL AMERICA

The daily lives of most rural Americans were dominated by work, as families struggled to maintain maximum self-sufficiency and to achieve commercial success. Agricultural labor was governed by the day and the season. Families rose with, or before, first light and worked until darkness curtailed their labors. The agricultural year governed men's tasks. Spring was devoted to planting, summer to cultivating, and fall to harvesting, which could extend into the winter. Corn could be picked almost anytime, as long as the weather was dry. And cotton producers were still picking when Christmas approached in most areas. Animals demanded more attention just when crop work intensified. Cows calved (gave birth) and freshened (began lactating) in the spring, demanding attention and initiating dairy production. Sheep, important animals in the North, were sheared in the spring, the season in which they, too, gave birth. Hogs were commonly slaughtered in the fall.

During the winter the character of work changed, as farmers flailed grain, shelled corn, and cured tobacco. In winter farmers repaired fences, tools, and harness. They cut wood, pulled stumps, and, in the early spring, removed rocks from their fields. In the North farmers cut ice in the winter for sale or for summer use. Home manufacturing, either for family use or under contract to a local manufacturer, intensified in the winter, and farmers and their sons sometimes took jobs in town or worked for lumbermen or packers.

The work of women was less seasonal. While fall tended to direct more of their attention to food preservation and spring initiated the planting of vegetable gardens and the intensification of dairy work, most women's tasks continued the year around. People ate every day, regardless of the season; floors had to be swept, clothes washed, cows and chickens tended, and children cared for in winter and summer alike.

While the lives of farmers were characterized by toil, they were lightened by some recreation. There was usually time in some evenings and on Sundays for reading, playing games, and, especially, visiting neighbors, the most common rural recreation. School spelling matches, weddings and funerals, dances and frolics, and holidays such as the Fourth of July presented further recreational opportunities. Rural people had a facility for combining work with leisure. Barn raisings and quilting bees, for example, were as much recreational as functional. And such common male activities as hunting, fishing, and trapping replenished the family larder and purse even as they provided pleasant diversions.

Further diminishing the arduousness of farm labor was the fact that it was task, rather than time, oriented. The worker set the pace of his or her work. A field had to be plowed or a dinner prepared regardless of the time it took, and the worker had some control over how rapidly the task was completed. Rural labor was not done under the tyranny of the clock. Indeed, it was the uncommon farm home that even had a clock in the years before the Civil War.

From the standpoint of modern rural people, farmers in the early nineteenth century lived crude and primitive lives. Housing was rudimentary, especially in the early stages of settlement. While farmers usually attempted to build permanent dwellings as soon as it was feasible to do so, commercial success always came first. Consequently, one northern visitor to Alabama in the 1850s was stunned to find that "much the larger proportion of the planters of the State live in loghouses . . . frequently rude in construction, un-*chinked*, with windows unglazed, and wanting in many of the commonest conveniences."[5]

When they could, southern farmers replaced such houses. The stately plantation mansion comes readily to mind when we think of antebellum rural southern housing, but it was the exception rather than the rule. Much more common was the spacious one-story frame farmhouse including a large room for eating, entertaining visitors, and sleeping, with a loft above for further sleeping space. It was common, especially in the lower South where hot weather was the rule for much of the year, to cook in a lean-to or in a building separate from the house.

Southerners commonly expanded houses of this type by building an annex a few feet away and extending the roof over the space between. It was said that the breezeway or dogtrot between the buildings was constructed because southerners were so considerate of their dogs that they didn't want to require them to run all the way around the house to reach the other side. But the dogtrot had important human functions as well. It provided a place where items could be stored out of the rain and a relatively cool place where the family could sit, eat, or even sleep during hot summer nights.

In the North, the most common successor to the log cabin was the two-story frame house. The first floor consisted of a kitchen, a parlor or sitting room, and sometimes a dining room. The second usually included three

New-Year's Eve in the Country.
Harper's Weekly, *January 5, 1861.*

bedrooms, one for parents, one for boys, and one for girls. Family life tended to revolve around the kitchen, especially in the winter, when it was the warmest room in houses that were usually uninsulated and lacked central heating. Further enhancing the relative comfort of the kitchen was the fact that by 1850 most families had replaced fireplaces with iron stoves.

There were certain realities with which rural people in every section lived. Very few families before the Civil War had water in the house. Women drew water from streams and wells for use in cooking, cleaning, and bathing. This was one of the most demanding of the constant tasks women performed. The absence of water in the house made plumbing impossible, of course. When it was inconvenient to go outside people relieved themselves in chamberpots to be emptied later. Farmers commonly had privies in their yards, but these were far from universal. While outhouses were the norm in the North, where the weather was cold for much of the year, they were a rarity in the lower South. Southerners did not usually have privies, but they always had the woods.

Most rural people had limited wardrobes. Men and women usually had one or two sets of day-to-day clothes, shirts and pants for men and simple, one-piece dresses for women. Often, but not always, people had a set of finer clothes for church and special occasions. Children's wardrobes were certainly no more elaborate and were usually more limited. Younger children wore hand-me-downs, and toddlers of both sexes were commonly put in simple shifts. Rural people did not approach modern standards of cleanliness in regard to clothing. Hard labor in dirty surroundings made clothing filthy, and the many demands on farmwives and farmers' daughters, in addition to the rigors of hauling and heating water, probably meant that clothing was not washed more than once a week at the most.

Many of the items of apparel essential to us were absent from rural wardrobes. Underwear, for example, was seldom worn. In its place, men and women wore shirts or petticoats that reached to midthigh or below. Likewise, shoes and boots were not worn by all people all of the time. Before the Civil War, shoe manufacturers produced one men's size, one women's size, and one children's size. As a result, few people could buy cheap shoes that were comfortable. Cobblers made shoes and boots to fit, but these were too expensive for average people to afford. As a consequence of these realities, many northerners wore boots or shoes only in cold weather, and a substantial portion of rural southerners did not wear them at all.

The standard rural diet was rudimentary and relatively unvaried. At most meals, one could expect to see meat and meal in some form. The meat was usually pork, and the meal was usually corn. The meat would commonly be fried, and the grease would be turned into gravy. People used a lot of salt. For sweetening they sometimes used refined sugar, maple syrup, or honey; southerners commonly used homemade cane or sorghum syrups. Beans, sweet or Irish potatoes, apples, and eggs also appeared on rural tables with some regularity, as did butter and cheese. Fresh fish and game were also common rural fare. People drank water, coffee, cider, or beer. The rural diet was less remarkable, perhaps, for what it did contain than for what it did not. Usually absent from the farm table were fresh vegetables, especially of the leafy green variety, and fresh fruits. Also absent was fresh milk; what was not turned into butter or cheese was commonly fed to the hogs.

This high-fat, high-starch diet provided the calories that hardworking farm people needed. Unfortunately, it was short on some of the vitamins and nutrients essential for good health. Calcium deficiency was reflected in poor dental health and such childhood conditions as rickets. Too little consumption of fresh fruits and vegetables resulted in serious skin conditions, such as pellagra, scurvy, and the mysterious "big itch" that Andrew Jackson suffered as a boy.[6] Another result of this diet was more-or-less chronic constipation, a condition one historian has referred to as a "national curse" in the young republic.[7]

Diet was a major contributor to rural health problems, but it was not the only one. Hard physical labor and the rigors of life in ill-heated, poorly ventilated, and smokey houses had an adverse impact on physical well-being. So, too, did some rural behaviors. Included among these were tobacco use, almost universal among men and not rare among women, and the abuse of alcohol. Misuse of alcohol was a serious problem in rural America, especially, but by no means exclusively, in the South. Most men imbibed throughout the day, and private visits and ceremonies and public gatherings usually witnessed heavy drinking. Alcohol played a central role in male bonding, but its social and health effects were serious. Eliza Townes Blassingame's alcoholic husband abused and neglected his family and eventually died of the effects of drink. Unfortunately, his story was not a rare one in rural America before the Civil War.

Probably the most serious threat to rural health was the lack of cleanliness. People lived at the center of a world of germs. The concept of screening doors and windows still lay in the future, with the result that houseflies—so ubiquitous as to be worthy of declaration as the national bird in the nineteenth century—moved freely between human and animal waste in the yard and food on the table. People drew water from streams and wells contaminated by human and animal feces, making typhoid fever a common summer problem. Hookworm, a parasite that afflicted as many as half of white southerners, passed from human feces into the body through the soles of bare feet. Add epidemics of such diseases as yellow fever, exacerbated by standing water, and cholera, and the sum is an unhealthy rural life.

Because rural Americans did not understand the causes of disease, they failed to follow commonsense preventative procedures. They were not careful about protecting their bodies, food, or water supplies from germs. Consequently, large numbers of women continued to die from puerperal fever, an infection introduced in the body during childbirth from dirty hands or instruments, as they had for centuries. Nor was it surprising that children playing in farmyards often fell victim to tetanus or that even minor cuts frequently led to gangrene.

When they suffered health problems, rural people commonly fell back on traditional treatments, conveyed either by home medical books or by word-of-mouth, or on midwives such as Martha Ballard or other neighborhood healers. Hospitals were unavailable, and doctors were expensive and usually not very helpful; indeed, before the Civil War the average physician was as likely to do one harm as good. Consequently, self-treatment was a wise course of action.

In light of the many threats to health in rural America, it is remarkable that life expectancy in the countryside was higher than in the cities. Indeed, the urban population, often ill-nourished, crowded closely together, and consuming contaminated food and water, could not have sustained itself through most of the nineteenth century without the continual influx of migrants from Europe and the American countryside. Nineteenth-century country living was healthy relative to city living, but rural well-being was hardly impressive.

SLAVERY

The rural community in the South was largely shaped by the institution of slavery. Many southern whites lived in communities very similar to those in which rural northerners lived. But others lived in plantation communities, which were biracial and relatively self-sufficient and self-contained. Blacks also lived in these communities, but they formed a slave community with its own practices, institutions, traditions, and values.

Slavery had been introduced into the British North American colonies in the seventeenth century as a means of coping with the chronic labor shortage in those rapidly expanding economies (see chapter 3). The institution existed everywhere at the time of the Revolution, but it was most important in places, like Virginia and South Carolina, that concentrated on labor-intensive crops for the export market. In part because of its relative social and economic insignificance and in part because of revolutionary idealism, slavery was set on a path to abolition in every state north of Maryland and Delaware by 1800.

While slavery was fading away in the North, it was revitalized in the South with the development of short-staple cotton, a labor-intensive crop (see chapter 4). By 1860, four million slaves—or about one-eighth of the American population—lived in the fifteen states, stretching from Delaware and Maryland in the northeast to Missouri, Arkansas, and Texas in the west, that still permitted slavery.

Slaves were not evenly distributed throughout the South. In some places—such as the southern Appalachians—there were virtually none, while along the South Carolina coast, in the Yazoo River delta region of Mississippi, and in some of the sugar parishes of Louisiana, slaves composed 90 percent or more of the population. As a general rule, the slave population tended to be most heavily concentrated in the black belt, a band of rich cotton land spreading from South Carolina through central Georgia, Alabama, Mississippi, Louisiana, and into eastern Texas. There, and elsewhere, slaves lived under diverse social and economic situations, but the vast majority were agricultural laborers, and three-fifths of them lived on plantations employing twenty or more slaves.

Like any other institution, slavery evolved over time, but in its essence it was the same in 1850 as it had been in 1750 or, for that matter, in 1650. At bottom, slavery was a labor system in a world capitalist economy, in which capital was invested in the purchase of human beings by people who hoped to profit from the work slaves did. Indeed, the very act of buying a slave committed one to market activity and to at least some level of commercial success. Slaves were property under the law, who could generally be treated as any other type of property could be treated. They could be bought and sold, deeded and willed, put up as collateral for loans, and seized for nonpayment of debts. Masters had the right to all of the wealth slaves produced by their labor and to ownership of all children produced by slave mothers. As property, slaves had no legal or civil rights, could not themselves own property, and could make no contracts, including the contract of marriage.

Still, slaves were a special, or "peculiar" type of property, as whites in the Old South liked to say. Because they were assumed to have moral sense—the human ability to distinguish right from wrong—they were held responsible when they committed criminal acts. Moreover, they were legally protected against murder or severe mistreatment and neglect by masters, whereas other living property was not. Legal protections for slaves were of little practical value, however, given the fact that blacks could not testify against whites and other whites were reluctant to do so.

More effective than the law in protecting slaves was the fact that they were valuable property. Presumably, rational masters would not behave toward their slaves in such a way as to harm their own economic interest. This was usually the case, but exceptions were frequent and sometimes extreme. The working assumption of classical economists notwithstanding, slave owners were not always rational. By all appearances Samuel Townes was a rational, profit-maximizing planter, but he so abused his slave Phillis that he apparently drove her mad.[8] Perhaps Townes was a rational man who simply lost his temper. In a society in which some enjoyed massive power over others, such self-indulgence by the powerful could be disastrous for the powerless.

The fact that slaves were valuable property was probably the main reason they were adequately maintained. Slaves were generally fed, clothed, and housed well enough to keep them healthy, and when they got sick most planters secured medical care for them. Some historians have concluded that slaves lived at least as well as poor whites in the South, but the fact that only one of every four dollars they produced for the master came back to them for maintenance is eloquent testimony to the fact that they did not enjoy lives of abundance.

Returns such as masters received on the labor of slaves clearly indicate the slaves worked hard. Women as well as men were worked from dawn to dusk, with only a few breaks during the day, and at busy times, such as harvest in the sugarcane fields, they worked well into the night as well. When slaves did not work in the fields, masters kept them busy at tasks to enhance plantation self-sufficiency, such as home manufacturing. Constant labor sometimes had a harmful effect on the health of slaves. For example, historians believe that low infant birth weights and high infant mortality rates among slaves were due mainly to the planters' tendency to work women in the fields late into pregnancy and to compel their rapid return to field labor, resulting in an early cessation of breast-feeding.

One of the biggest challenges confronting profit-maximizing slave owners was that of compelling slaves to work. The most common positive and negative incentives effective with free labor did not work with slaves, who received no pay and could not be fired. Imaginative planters developed a variety of positive incentives, such as extra holidays, better food and clothing, or a small plot of land for one's own use. Some planters used a task system that rewarded slaves finishing jobs quickly with leisure time. But positive incentives were seldom sufficient even when they were used, meaning that negative incentives to compel labor were a prominent part of the slave-labor regime. Negative incentives almost always involved corporal punishment, usually whipping, and frequently extended to the threat of sale of recalcitrant slaves.

The institution of slavery was complicated by the fact that, while it was mainly a labor system in which some derived profits from the compulsory labor of others, it was a human institution in a way most other labor systems were not. Slaves and masters lived with one another day and night, year after year, through their lifespans. With lives often so intricately intertwined, it was not uncommon for black and white families to develop genuine care and affection for one another.

Further humanizing the institution of slavery were expectations and responsibilities placed on masters. Southern churches emphasized that masters must be Christian stewards for those in their care, and the patriarchal ideal extended from the master's biological family to his slave family as well. Many masters conceived themselves as fathers to their slaves. When Andrew Jackson addressed the slaves gathered around his deathbed as his children, he was expressing what apologists for the institution considered to be the correct relationship between masters and bondspeople.[9] But if patriarchalism was an ambiguous ideal in relations between men and their wives and children, it was much more so in relations between masters and slaves. A father in a healthy family does not live off the labor of his children, and he does not whip them, rape them, or sell them to another. More often than not, what passed for patriarchal concern on the part of masters was no more than a cynical manipulation of slaves to compel loyalty and labor, and what passed for filial devotion on the part of slaves was no more than a device to shame or trick masters into providing better treatment.

Much more sustaining to most slaves than their relationships with masters were their relationships with one another in the slave community. The accomplishment of slaves in creating a community that was in some ways independent and self-directive is a tribute to the indomitability of the human spirit. Coming from societies more diverse than those from which the European settlers came and owned by ethnocentric masters, their opportunity to sustain independent cultural elements was much less than that enjoyed by Germans or Swedes or other free immigrants to rural America. But sustain they did, carrying African cultural forms, language patterns, kinship relationships, musical styles, superstitions, folktales, and many other nonmaterial artifacts from generation to generation by means of a vital oral tradition. African-American culture helped slaves retain a sense of identity and psychological independence in an oppressive institution.

The family, defined both in narrow nuclear terms and in the broader sense of a kinship network, also helped sustain slaves and imparted a sense of meaning and value to their lives. But maintaining slave families was a difficult proposition. Though masters often encouraged monogamy and staged marriage ceremonies, slave unions were not legal. Sometimes couples had different owners, and all slaves faced the constant danger of having a spouse or children sold away. Slave families confronted other special problems also. The option of domesticity was not open to female slaves, who were responsible for field labor as well as housework. Husbands could not protect wives from punishment or sexual abuse, and parents' ability to discipline children was compromised by the authority of masters. Slaves were able to compensate partially for the instability of nuclear families with supportive kinship groups composed of grandparents, aunts, uncles, cousins, nieces, and nephews, but these were fragile, too, when one could be sold and moved without notice. One effect of the fragility of the family was to make it especially precious to slaves: after emancipation, southern roads were filled with former slaves searching for husbands, wives, children, and kin from whom they had been separated.

Nearly as important in the slave community as the family was the church. While slaves were invited to attend services with their masters, and usually did, they retained their own, less formal religious organizations. Sometimes masters or white ministers provided some instruction to slave preachers, who were unordained and were often illiterate. But it was their depth of religious feeling and spirituality that gave them positions of respect among their fellow bondspeople. Slave services were sometimes public events in which the entire plantation participated, but they were usually restricted to bondspeople, and because it was illegal for slaves to meet unless supervised by whites, the services were commonly held in secret and at night. Services tended to be emotional, enthusiastic, and interactive, and sermons and music emphasized the pain of bondage and God's love and forgiveness. The slave church provided communicants with a sphere of independent action, as well as explanation, consolation, and hope for the future. When freedom came, the underground slave church transformed itself into the leading public institution in the black community.

The realities of bondage shaped the white community as well as the slave community. Slavery potentially divided rich and poor, because wealth and social status were closely related to the ownership of slaves. Southern concerns about class divisions over slavery crested in the decade prior to the Civil War, when surging slave prices made it unlikely that most rural whites would ever become slave owners. But slavery probably served to unify whites to a greater extent than it divided them. The presence of blacks gave all whites a degree of equality. No matter how low on the social scale a southerner might be, he was equal to the highest planter in the sense that he enjoyed freedom, and his race made him the superior of every black. Slavery thus tied whites who feared that its end would imperil their status to those who had an economic stake in its perpetuation. In more practical, day-to-day terms, all whites were responsible for cooperating to uphold the institution of slavery by serving on the slave patrols that maintained order among the bondspeople and by helping enforce the slave codes, laws controlling slaves' behavior.

The existence of slavery shaped the agricultural economy as surely as it shaped southern rural society. The impact of slavery on southern economic well-being is one of the many issues regarding the peculiar institution that historians dispute. When we look at southern per capita agricultural wealth and income it appears that the South was as prosperous as the North in general and probably better off than the Midwest in 1860. Southern staples were highly profitable crops. When we look at income distribution, however, a much different picture emerges. The lion's share of southern agricultural income went to large planters, who returned only a small portion of it to their slaves. Small farmers could achieve a high degree of self-sufficiency and could participate in the market to a limited extent, but their competitive disadvantages with their slave-owning neighbors put a low ceiling on their commercial opportunities.

Slavery affected the way in which farming was conducted. Slave owners were necessarily committed to the market, but they also produced food crops, both because food production increased plantation self-sufficiency and diminished risk and because production of food gave slaves, who had to be fed and clothed whether or not there was work for them to do, more labor to occupy their time. The main food crop produced on plantations was corn. Corn is a versatile crop, and its labor requirements conflicted with those of cotton only when both had to be weeded. Winter wheat was a crop that could have been grown in many areas of the South, but wheat would have to be sown when cotton was being picked and cut when cotton was being chopped (thinned and weeded). Thus slavery dictated that commercial crops be grown, and those in turn dictated the subsistence crops that would be produced.

Another way in which slavery affected farming was by impeding mechanization. In the North, where free (as distinct from slave) labor prevailed, farmers invested capital in machinery in order to diminish their labor costs. But in the South, where the planter's labor was owned, no savings could be captured by mechanization; the people displaced by machinery would still have to be maintained. Indeed, mechanization would have diminished planters' wealth by lowering the value of the slaves they owned. The value of the planters' labor—which, under slavery, was part of their capital—could be maintained only if farming remained labor intensive. One result was that, in 1860, the value of implements per farmworker was only thirty-eight dollars in the South, far below the sixty-six dollars per capita in the North.

This is not quite as simple as it has been made to appear. Wheat is different from tobacco or cotton, and the differences made mechanization of wheat production easier. The uniform ripening of winter wheat, its durability, the evenness of the stands, and the concentration of the grain and the top of the stalk made wheat especially appropriate for mechanical harvesting, while cotton and tobacco were not. But the reality is that, as long as farmers had a financial interest in the value of labor, as southerners did before the Civil

War, or as long as labor was cheap, as southern labor was after the war, planters had no incentive to look for ways to save labor. Their unwillingness to look stifled mechanical innovation and mechanization well into the twentieth century.

Slavery thus impeded the development of the southern implement industry, but other industries as well were retarded by slavery in three main ways. First, available southern capital flowed overwhelmingly into slaves and land. Because they did not own labor, northerners had more liquid capital for other investments. Second, while a free labor force could move in response to economic opportunities, even if only for a few weeks per year, a slave labor force was normally confined to one place. Northern farmers and farm laborers provided temporary help for industry, and some left farms permanently for industrial employment. But unfree southern laborers were commonly kept on the plantations, where they were unable to supplement local industries. The way those slaves were used impeded industrial development in a third way. During the slow weeks of the year, slaves were set to work doing the things that would make the plantation more self-sufficient. Slave smiths might make nails, carpenters fashion tools, and weavers turn homespun into cloth. They were not as efficient as workers in iron foundries, tool works, and textile mills, but the owner was less interested in the sorts of measures of efficiency an employer of free labor would use than he was in minimizing the cost of maintaining his human capital assets while a cash crop was not being produced. In using his slaves for plantation manufactures, the owner unconsciously stultified local industry by shrinking the market for manufactured products.

In addition to minimizing the capital, labor, and market necessary for the encouragement of manufacturing, slavery fostered a habit of mind that stifled industrial development. Planters, because they were committed to an institution that seemed to be doomed by the progressive march of civilization, tended to be very conservative people, wary and even fearful of the future. But while slavery was at the heart of the conservative persuasion, that attitude affected many areas of economic and social life that were unrelated to the peculiar institution. Planters dimly perceived industrialization as part of a threatening modernity, and as a consequence they were disinclined to invest in local industry, patronize it, or support public policies meant to encourage it.

All of this is not to say that the South was industrially primitive. Southern towns had their factories and skilled workers, and railroads crisscrossed the region. On a per capita basis, southern manufacturing was respectable, and certainly ahead of such places as Russia, Spain, and Italy. But relative to the North, the South was backward and in 1860 was falling further behind. The nature of the agricultural system had much to do with that condition, a condition that would cause serious problems for a South fighting a Civil War.

The Unmaking and Remaking
of the Rural South

The Civil War is the central event in the history of the republic, and its impact on rural America was immense. In some ways, the war highlighted the essentially rural and agricultural character of the country. The men who served in the contending armies, especially those who fought for the Confederacy, were overwhelmingly farm boys. Serving in units drawn from local communities, men fought and died with neighbors and kin just as they had worked and lived with them at home. Drennans, Fletchers, and Pulliams went off together from Sugar Creek to Shiloh, Vicksburg, and Chickamauga. As farm boys they were well prepared for a war that rewarded those who were comfortable in the out-of-doors and were familiar with horses and firearms, but they were not assured they would come home whole, or even return at all, and many did not.

Much about the Civil War reflected rural manners, ways, and backgrounds, but it also demonstrated the industrialization and the growing technological sophistication of both the Union and the Confederacy. This was a war of mass-produced weapons, iron ships, and rifled small arms and artillery; it was a war as well in which railroads moved armies from front to front and in which commanders depended on the telegraph for information.

Technological sophistication affected rural people not directly touched by

110 the war in addition to those in the armies and in the paths of the armies. Northern farmers were able to feed their region and hold export markets in part because they substituted machinery for labor and could rely on a strong and dependable transportation infrastructure. Because they were committed to labor-intensive methods and depended on a weak transportation system, southern farmers were less successful in meeting the needs of their region.

The war was mainly about slavery, and the Union victory doomed that institution that had made the rural South unique. But in freeing four million people, most of them agricultural laborers, the war raised many questions. Was there a future for southern agriculture? What labor system would be devised to replace slavery? What role would the freedpeople (the former slaves) play in rural society? What shape would the southern rural community assume? The death of the institution that, more than any other, had defined the rural South meant that the freed and the defeated had to struggle together—and separately—to redefine their lives, their work, and their relationship.

Within fifteen years of the end of the war, the questions it raised were being answered. There was a future for southern agriculture, but it was not as bright as the past. A free labor system replaced slavery, but those operating in it coped with severe social and economic constraints. The freedpeople would be free and would benefit from that freedom in many ways; but their class and race would doom them to the status of a degraded and oppressed caste in their native region. And the rural community of the South would continue to be three communities as it had been under slavery—one biracial, one black, and one white. Well into the twentieth century, rural southerners would live with the legacy of an institution that died in 1865.

THE CIVIL WAR AND THE RURAL NORTH

The Civil War presented northern farmers with a challenge. They had to continue to maintain a high level of self-sufficiency while meeting the heightened food needs of a country at war, and they had to fulfill these production demands with a sharply diminished labor force. Eventually, over two million men served in the armed forces of the United States, or about 40 percent of all the males in the North between the ages of eighteen and thirty-five. A disproportionate number of those who served were farmers and farmers' sons.

The absence of men from farms placed new and unwelcome burdens on farm women. Accustomed to managing homes and undertaking mainly gender-specific agricultural tasks, women found themselves responsible for entire farm operations. Adding to the difficulty of these burdens was the reluctance of local males to accept women outside of their traditional subordinate and private roles. Women complained to distant husbands of the difficulties of running farms and husbands sometimes tried to manage from a distance, but that was not really possible to do. Many were reduced to impotent complaints, such as that of Iowan Thomas Ball that a neighbor had taken his wife's only milk cow to satisfy a debt. "If I was George I would not take the last cow that a woman and children has if I was at home and her man in the army," he fumed, but Ball could do little beyond urging his wife Serilda to appeal to the sympathy of others and rely on kin for help.[1]

To a significant degree, northern farmers were able to compensate for labor shortages through mechanization. For a generation, inventors and on-farm tinkerers had been turning out improved plows and harrows, seed drills, cultivators, mowers, reapers, and horse-powered threshers. Some improvements—steel moldboard plows, for example—were adopted rapidly and almost universally. Others became part of the productive arsenals of only the most progressive farmers.

Because it created a combination of high crop prices and scarce and expensive labor, the Civil War made increasing numbers of farmers consider the advantages of any innovations that promised to increase productivity. Of the available mechanical innovations, none was more important than the reaper, patented by Virginian Cyrus McCormick in 1834 and mass-produced in Chicago beginning in the late 1840s.

The reaper was an implement designed for the crucial harvest stage in the production of wheat and other small grains, during which only about ten days is available in which to cut the crop. Historically, the small-grain harvest had been a labor-intensive operation. By the mid-nineteenth century, most farmers cut grain with a cradle, but some still used short-handled sickles. A worker with a sickle could cut about an acre of grain a day, while one using a cradle could cut two or three acres. Using a reaper, a farmer could cut twelve to fifteen acres per day. Counting the workers who followed the cutter, raking up the grain and binding it into sheaves, a farmer using a reaper needed a crew of eight a day for a fifteen-acre field, as opposed to a crew of fourteen cutting the same field in a day with cradles.

By dramatically simplifying, cheapening, and accelerating the harvest, the reaper facilitated an impressive expansion of wheat production. It also encouraged mechanization of other stages of grain production. Now that they could cut more acres, farmers came to see the advantages of improved riding plows, harrows, and grain drills that allowed expanded planting and of horse-powered threshers that helped them handle a greater volume of wheat. The use of reapers also contributed to a shift from oxen to horses for motive power. Horses were more nimble than oxen, were faster, and moved at a steadier pace, all factors that made them especially appropriate for machinery. Taken together, these innovations resulted in a decline in the number of worker-hours required to produce an acre of wheat from thirty-five in 1840 to twenty in 1880.

In the long run, mechanization proved a mixed blessing for farmers. It allowed them to raise their incomes and standards of living, but it cost them some self-sufficiency and increased their risk. It minimized their labor demands but also contributed to rural depopulation. In the short run, though, mechanization was mostly positive. Farmers were able to meet domestic needs and also satisfy a surge in foreign demand. Between 1861 and 1865, the United States exported an average of over twenty-seven million bushels of wheat per year, a dramatic jump over the average of under eight million bushels per year between 1856 and 1860.

Wheat producers were not the only northern farmers who benefited from wartime economic conditions. Demands for wool, flax, corn, and meat were high. Producers of perishable crops benefited from advances in food-preservation technology spurred by the effort of the War Department to better feed the troops. New canning machinery made it cost efficient to put up vegetables and fruits, extending the season for those crops to the whole year. And Gail Borden's perfection of the method of preserving milk through condensation expanded the market for dairy farmers.

Government actions during the war indicated both an appreciation for the significance of agriculture and a recognition of its potential as a technically sophisticated enterprise. In 1862 Congress made the United States Department of Agriculture (USDA), which had been a division of the Patent Office, an independent government department. This action symbolized the economic and social status of agriculture and reflected the potential of agricultural science. Indeed, the USDA quickly became what it remains today—

the most important locus of scientific expertise in agriculture in the United States.

The increasing commercialization and technological advancement of agriculture was further reflected in other legislation approved by the Civil War Congress, especially in the Morrill Land-Grant College Act, passed in 1862. The Morrill Act provided thirty thousand acres of federal land for each of a state's senators and representatives, to be used to create and support at least one college specializing in instruction in "agriculture and the mechanic arts." Vermont Senator Justin Morrill's remark that his legislation was necessary to provide the children of "the industrial classes" with a "liberal and practical" education suggested the complexity of motivations for the act.[2] In one sense, it was an expression of agrarian and free-labor idealism and faith that ordinary people with opportunity could do great things. In another sense it reflected the reality that agriculture was becoming more economically and technologically sophisticated and the hope that it could be based on scientific principles. Finally, it also indicated dissatisfaction with existing colleges that did not seem to address the practical needs of ambitious individuals and a dynamic nation. Eventually nearly seventy land-grant colleges were created or enhanced under the Morrill Act and an 1890 supplement of the same name, including such leading American universities as Illinois, Wisconsin, and Cornell.

The Morrill bill had appeared in previous Congresses. Its passage in 1862 was due to the voluntary absence of obstructionist southerners. Also benefiting from that fortuitous circumstance was legislation providing federal aid for construction of transcontinental railroads. In 1862 Congress passed the Pacific Railroad Act, authorizing the building of a railroad between Council Bluffs, Iowa, and Sacramento, California, and provided loans and land grants for that purpose. Two years later a second Pacific Railroad Act provided even more generous encouragement for construction of a line between Duluth, Minnesota, and Portland, Oregon. These railroads, and the others that joined them, were essential to the agricultural settlement of the Great Plains.

The last great piece of land legislation, the Homestead Act, was also passed in 1862. This act allowed any head of household, male or female, who was a citizen or intended to become one to receive 160 acres of public land virtually for free. If the claimant paid a ten-dollar filing fee, made specified

114 improvements on the land and built a dwelling on it, and lived on it for five years, he or she would receive clear title. The homesteader unwilling to meet these conditions could pay a commutation fee of $1.25 per acre and take possession immediately.

The Homestead Act holds a cherished place in the American imagination, but it was flawed in its operation and did not appeal to everyone. In many of the areas where it operated, 160 acres was insufficient to support a family. It was also marked—as was most other land legislation—by a good deal of fraud and unscrupulous speculation. Moreover, only about 10 percent of the available public domain was disposed of through the homestead process. Not all federal lands were available for entry, and many settlers preferred to purchase railroad lands because of their proximity to transportation or to buy public lands and thus receive title immediately. Finally, farm-making costs meant that even free land was too expensive for many poor people. The Homestead Act did, however, reflect an American commitment to individual opportunity and to the rapid agricultural settlement of the country.

Taken together, the creation of the USDA and the Morrill, Pacific Railroad, and Homestead Acts embodied an agricultural vision somewhat different from Jeffersonian agrarianism. These actions foresaw a dynamic, rapidly expanding, and increasingly commercial, scientific, and technologically complex agriculture in the nation's future. By envisioning that sort of agriculture, these measures helped bring it to life.

THE RURAL SOUTH DURING THE CIVIL WAR

What were some of the best of times for the rural North were some of the worst for the rural South. Making war to defend the institution of slavery, without which they did not believe their society or their economy could survive, white southerners ironically accelerated the realization of the emancipation they had feared. And in the process they lost their foreign markets, struggled with diminishing success to serve their domestic market, watched their financial and transportation infrastructure collapse, and even saw their agriculture deteriorate to the point where observers questioned whether it could be rebuilt.

At the beginning of the war, southern farmers faced a task similar to that confronting their northern counterparts. They, too, were required to feed themselves, their army, and the off-farm population of the Confederacy and to continue to serve European export markets. But in some ways, their task was easier than that of northern farmers. The South was overwhelmingly rural and agricultural and could shift production out of inedible staples into food crops as the need arose. Moreover, the southern agricultural labor force was largely unfree, so military recruitment was less disruptive in its effects.

In the early part of the war, southern farmers rose to the challenge before them, but by 1863 they were facing serious difficulties that intensified over time and contributed materially to the Confederate collapse. One problem that bedeviled southern agriculture was a decline in productivity traceable mainly to the decreasing efficiency of slave labor. Slaves were difficult to manage even for people accustomed to doing so, but when slave owners and their sons went off to fight, as many did, normal labor-control problems were magnified. Old men, boys, and women frequently found themselves responsible for supervising slaves. Women, especially, were thrust into unfamiliar and unrequested roles, as were many of their sisters in the North. The difference was that they lived in a society that was even more paternalistic and less tolerant of women in public roles, and their responsibility consisted largely of inducing unhappy and unwilling people to work. Southern women did their best, but they complained frequently, and often bitterly, that their husbands were breaking their half of the patriarchal bargain to lead and care for families and family enterprises.

The normal difficulties of managing slave labor, for managers of both genders, were exacerbated by the war itself. The slaves were well aware that the outcome of the war would likely have a dramatic impact on their lives and that a Union victory was more likely to be positive for them than a Confederate one. Hence, owners found slaves more reluctant and resistant than usual, further diminishing the efficiency of slave labor. The tendency of slaves to escape to Union lines, especially after the issuance of the Emancipation Proclamation on January 1, 1863, deprived some masters of labor and led others to move their bondspeople far from the battlefront. That tactic allowed owners temporarily to keep their slaves, but it left their fields untended. The decreasing efficiency of slave labor was an especially serious matter for the South because, unlike the North, it could not easily substitute machinery for people. Slave owners' resistance to innovation and the fact that the nature of many southern crops made mechanization difficult meant that the tools simply were not available to do much of what the slaves did.

Even when southern farmers maintained production levels, it was increasingly difficult for them to get their crops to market. Northern naval

116 power made trade on the rivers and along the coast risky. The deterioration of the rail system, weak even before the war, under the pressure of increased usage and insufficient replacement parts made marketing more problematical. Taken as a whole, the South never ran out food, but getting it from where it was grown to where it was needed became a major problem. While housewives in Richmond rioted for bread and soldiers subsisted on partial rations, tons of bacon and meal spoiled and moldered in warehouses and on sidings throughout the Confederacy.

Increasingly unable to meet domestic demand, southern farmers were even harder pressed to satisfy foreign buyers. The shift of many farmers from cotton to food crops, the Union blockade, the fall of New Orleans and other cotton-marketing centers, and the Confederate effort to restrict the exportation of cotton as a means of inducing England and France to extend diplomatic recognition all sharply limited trade in the South's leading staple. The Europeans responded in part by developing sources of supply in India, Latin America, and Egypt and other parts of Africa. Never again would American cotton dominate the European market to the degree it had before the Civil War.

The Confederate surrender in the spring of 1865 found southern agriculture on the verge of collapse. Freedom for the slaves resulted in a capital loss estimated conservatively at $1.5 billion in 1860 dollars. To put that amount in perspective, consider that the total federal budget in 1860 was under $70 million. This loss of capital in the form of labor was accompanied by a dramatic decrease in the value of land. The per-acre value of southern farms in 1865 was less than 60 percent what it had been in 1860. Some of this decline was due to real decreases in fertility, largely as a result of the wartime inability to import nitrogen-rich guano for fertilizer. But the decline was mainly due to an absence of capital at the end of the war and genuine uncertainty regarding whether southern agriculture would ever be profitable again under whatever labor system succeeded slavery. Southern agriculture suffered further from the loss of domesticated animals. Military demands for meat and draft animals and the general disorder at the end of the war meant that there were only two-thirds as many cattle, horses, mules, and swine on southern farms in 1865 as there had been five years earlier.

Finally, in the last year of the war there had been substantial damage to the transportation and processing infrastructure on which southern farmers depended. The devastating military campaigns of William Tecumseh Sherman in Georgia and the Carolinas, Philip Sheridan in the Shenandoah Valley of Virginia, and Henry Wilson in Alabama, along with the more random violence done by thousands of bummers, deserters, and outlaws, resulted in the destruction of hundreds of miles of railroads, dozens of bridges, and hundreds of cotton warehouses, gins, grain elevators, flour mills, and so forth. This was not a propitious situation for reconstructing the rural South, but southerners had no choice but to undertake that task.

THE REMAKING OF THE RURAL SOUTH

The task of creating new social and economic institutions for the rural South fell mainly to the people of the region. While the North had a keen interest in the process of reconstruction in general, and while it was concerned about the futures of both the former rebels and the former slaves in particular, Americans in 1865 were not believers in federal governmental activism. They did not think that it was the place of government to help determine or shape the social arrangements under which people lived. Nor did most Americans think that government should right economic wrongs, interfere in the operation of markets, or involve itself in the relationship between capital and labor. As a result, black and white southerners worked out their own social and economic relationships with little outside interference but under the constraints of a severely disrupted agricultural system, financial hardship, a heritage of racial antipathy, and the continuing reality of inequality in power and resources.

The racist assumption underlying slavery—that blacks were incapable of controlling their own lives—was poor training for freedom, but the former slaves behaved in remarkably responsible ways. Freedom provided them with the opportunity to stabilize their families, create sustaining public institutions, and achieve economic independence. All of that made freedom exciting, but there was also a frightening side to liberation for people who were usually penniless and illiterate and were wholly unused to making contracts, bargaining, or making economic decisions for themselves.

Rather than being paralyzed by freedom, as many of their former owners believed they would be, the freedpeople were energized by it. Indeed, the first few months after the end of the war witnessed a whirlwind of activity by newly free men and women anxious to create satisfying lives for themselves. The family was the first priority under slavery, and it remained such in freedom. The first aim for many former slaves was to reunite with husbands, wives, children, and parents who had been sold away or otherwise separated from them. Slave couples flocked to ministers, especially Union Army chaplains, to have their marriages legalized and solemnized. And they abandoned the plantations, intent on living their family lives without the interference of former masters.

Family dynamics among the former slaves paralleled those of other free people in the rural South. Families were patriarchal, with men asserting and exercising authority over women and children, who were expected to obey. Whereas women had been compelled to labor in the fields under the slave regime, the freedpeople tended to divide labor along gender lines, with women responsible mainly for maintaining homes and raising children and men responsible mainly for commercial economic activities. Women seemed to find this arrangement attractive and found domesticity to be less stultifying and degrading than field labor under the slave regime.

Other social institutions also came alive quickly under freedom. The black church, so often an underground institution under slavery, rapidly became a key component of the black community, as people withdrew from the churches of their former masters to form their own congregations, usually as Baptists or as members of the all-black African Methodist Episcopal Church. Ministers commonly played a leading role in the black community, and churches often were affiliated with other supportive institutions, such as mutual benefit societies, that undertook a variety of social welfare functions.

The freedpeople had a need and a desire for learning, but schools came slowly. The Freedmen's Bureau, a temporary agency within the Union Army created to ease the transition from slavery to freedom, and northern philanthropic organizations cooperated to provide schools to give the former slaves the rudiments of literacy and numeracy. There were never enough of these schools, though, and unsympathetic whites frequently terrorized teachers or burned buildings of those that existed. During Radical Reconstruction, a brief period in which Republicans controlled southern state governments, state constitutions guaranteed free public education for the children of both races. Even during the best of times, though, these schools were woefully underfunded and overcrowded, and they faced the chronic hostility of the white community. Despite these problems, schools became important community centers, and teachers became significant community leaders and role models.

The freedpeople and their children also enjoyed some opportunities for higher education. Northern philanthropists founded several black colleges in the South in the years just after the Civil War. In 1890 the second Morrill Act provided funds for black colleges to instruct students in agriculture and the mechanic arts. The institutions created or supplemented under this legislation—such as Tuskegee Institute, Alcorn A&M, and Florida A&M—offered agriculture and home-economics classes but concentrated their efforts on teacher training.

It was the goal of most of the freedpeople to become landowning farmers, and they were given cause to believe that such a status was in their future. In some places—on the South Carolina Sea Islands and along the Georgia coast, for example—Union commanders had divided the estates of absent masters among the former slaves. The freedpeople had created farms similar to those of white small farmers, concentrating on achieving self-sufficiency and producing only a slight surplus for market.

There was some sentiment in Washington for extending this system throughout the former Confederacy. Thaddeus Stevens and other Radical Republican congressmen believed that large southern estates should be confiscated and divided among the freedpeople in order to punish the rebels, compensate former slaves for their years of involuntary labor, and ensure them the means of self-support. Another potential door to land acquisition was opened by the Southern Homestead Act of 1866, which made over forty million acres available for entry by the former slaves. In meetings and conventions throughout the South, freedpeople expressed their enthusiasm for these and other measures that would make it possible for every family to acquire "forty acres and a mule."

Unfortunately for the freedpeople, the promise embodied in these measures went unrealized. President Andrew Johnson ordered the army to return confiscated lands to original owners making valid claims. Stevens's confiscation plan represented too much of a violation of traditional property rights and constitutional protections for most representatives in Congress—even most Republicans—to accept. And the Southern Homestead Act was minimally effective due to white hostility, black poverty, and inferior land. Some former slaves did overcome substantial obstacles to become farm owners, but it was clear that the immediate future for most of the freedpeople would not be characterized by independent land ownership. What it would be characterized by remained in doubt.

The people who owned the land before the war continued to own it after-

A white overseer supervising black cotton pickers, 1928.
Courtesy of the National Archives.

ward. Indeed, there was remarkably little turnover among the owners of large plantations in most areas between 1860 and 1870, and some even increased their holdings. But the people who owned the land no longer owned the labor. The big question in the postwar South was how—and even whether—the land and labor that had been put asunder could be rejoined. This problem was rendered especially difficult by the fact that neither the freedpeople nor the former masters had any experience with free labor. The former slaves, unaccustomed to owning their labor, were unsure of how to sell it, what to demand for it, or how to relate to those who purchased it. The former masters were unused to associating with labor on a consensual basis. They were used to commanding and compelling, not negotiating with those who might refuse to carry out tasks or who might walk away from jobs.

In the months after the end of the Civil War, the planters tried to create a free-labor system that was only minimally different from the slave-labor system with which they were familiar. Backed by state law and sometimes aided by sympathetic Union Army officers and Freedmen's Bureau officials, planters required laborers to agree to year-long contracts, with wages deferred until completion of the contract. Laborers breaking contracts received no pay, and in some states their contracts, and thus their labor, could even be sold by the courts to other employers. States helped planters not only by passing and enforcing onerous contract and vagrancy laws but by making it difficult for the landless freedpeople to survive. Laws prohibiting fishing and hunting on private property and herd laws requiring livestock owners to confine animals that had previously roamed freely in the neighborhood dramatically diminished the practical independence of those with little or no land.

Employers believed that a harsh system was necessary because they needed to ensure the presence of an adequate number of laborers at chopping and harvest time, and they lacked cash to pay workers until the crop was sold. Also understandable, given their experience, but even less justifiable, was the desire of landowners to work their laborers in gangs and to inflict physical punishment on workers they judged to be recalcitrant.

The freedpeople did not know much about free labor, but the system the former slave owners were trying to put in place looked a lot like slavery to them. They rebelled by refusing to work, fleeing employers, and joining organizations such as the Union League, which promised to make them secure in their freedom. The southern free-labor system also looked a lot like slavery to Radical Republicans in the North, and their determination to alter it

122

was one of the things that led them to impose a demanding policy of political reconstruction on the South.

Thus, the first attempt to bring land and labor together failed, but different people still owned land and labor and still had to be brought together under some arrangement. The laborers refused to work under a system resembling slavery, and they lacked the money to buy the land, even had they been able to find whites willing to sell to them. Some sort of rental arrangement seemed to make sense, but cash rental was out of the question because few freedpeople had implements or mules, let alone liquid capital to rent land.

By 1870, tenure arrangements in which laborers and landlords split the harvest were becoming increasingly popular means of joining the labor owned by freedpeople with the land owned by planters. The nature of the split depended in part on the local supply of and demand for labor. Now that labor was free to move, planters had to compete for it, not only with neighbors but also with labor contractors from outside the community who tried to induce freedpeople to pursue other opportunities. More important in determining the split was the relative contribution the owner and the laborer made to production. If the laborer had his own implements and draft animals and if he could contribute to the purchase of seed and fertilizer, he would commonly receive two-thirds to three-fourths of the harvest. Such farmers were usually called share tenants and had a property right in the crop under southern law. Unfortunately, relatively few of the freedpeople owned tools or draft animals or had money for seed and fertilizer. When the landlord provided production goods, the laborer's share of the crop was seldom more than half. These sharecroppers who brought nothing but their labor to this arrangement were defined as laborers under southern law and did not have the legal guarantees to their portion of the crop that share tenants enjoyed. The sharecropper had to feed and clothe his family out of his share of a crop that would not be harvested and sold for several months. In order to get furnish—necessities for daily living—he sometimes borrowed from a merchant, putting up his share of the prospective crop as collateral. More often his landlord provided him with furnish, charging it against his share of the crop.

Sharecropping was in part a means of sharing risk, and as such it was a positive arrangement for owners and laborers alike. Beyond the risk-sharing aspect, though, the benefits of sharecropping were uneven. Owners tolerated sharecropping because it assured that the work would get done, it allowed them to profit from their land, and it relieved them of the task of closely supervising their labor, as had been necessary under slavery. On the other hand, their ability to command and compel labor was seriously diminished, as were their profits, both because free laborers claimed a much larger share of the pie than had gone to slaves and because the pie was smaller, for reasons that are elaborated later. The freedpeople tolerated sharecropping because it allowed them to live more independently. Instead of dwelling in quarters close to a master's house, they now lived in cabins scattered over the plantation, which had been subdivided into farms, commonly of about forty acres each. Croppers now could live and work on the land for themselves, without the constant supervision of the landlord. Sharecropping gave the freedpeople some choices. They could work when and as hard and as long as they chose, they had some discretionary income and some choice of what to consume, and they could choose to move if they were dissatisfied with the landlord, a choice exercised frequently.

It is important to recognize, though, that sharecropping was a good choice only in comparison with slavery, or with day or seasonal labor, a status in which many of the former slaves found themselves. While croppers enjoyed a modicum of independence, the law viewed them as laborers without property rights. They could be put off the land at any time. Landlords could cheat them with impunity at the settle in December, when planters informed croppers of profits and losses for the year, and for a black person to protest mistreatment by a white in the South of the late-nineteenth and early-twentieth centuries was to risk severe sanctions, including death. Nor could croppers act politically to change the situation under which they lived. By the mid-1870s in most places, blacks who voted did so under the supervision of powerful whites, and by 1900 most did not enjoy the right to vote at all.

These shortcomings might have been less severe had sharecropping led to something better, but for the vast majority of croppers it was a dead end. Croppers lived a hand-to-mouth existence, subsisting on credit, moving from place to place, seldom seeing more than a few dollars cash at any time. Improving their status was so unlikely that few pursued strategies that had that object. While the children of landowning farmers sometimes delayed marriage in order to acquire the means to independence, children of croppers married early, because all one needed to work on shares was a spouse and children to help with the labor. Cropper families tended to be large, because children were valuable in a labor-intensive system and parents were not expected to provide an economic start for them in life. Subservience to landlords meant that croppers did not develop entrepreneurial and managerial skills appropriate to landownership or other business enterprises. And such behaviors as hard work and thrift, which many Americans in a dynamic economy found functional, seemed pointless in the stagnant world of the sharecropper.

Sharecropping was not the preferred system for either freedpeople or landowners. The former would have preferred to have their own farms, but federal conservatism and their own poverty prevented that. The latter would have preferred slavery—after all, they had fought a war to preserve it—but the United States government and the Union Army had doomed that institution. Sharecropping turned out to be the best available option, but it was not an option anyone liked very much, and in the end it cannot be said to have served either the freedpeople or the South very well.

The problem of joining landless labor with laborless land was not the only one confronting the postbellum South. The South also faced the challenge of rebuilding a shattered marketing structure and creating a credit system to finance agricultural production. Before the Civil War, commission merchants and professional brokers handled planters' crops and extended them credit. Small farmers usually marketed their crops, for a fee, with those of their planter neighbors or through local storekeepers. The war disrupted this system severely, and peace found farmers in need of credit and new marketing relationships.

Local merchants largely filled the credit and marketing vacuums. Their connections with northern wholesale houses allowed them to buy goods on credit, which they in turn retailed to local farmers. But farmers usually lacked cash and had to borrow the food, clothing, and other necessities that merchants had to offer. Merchants were reluctant to advance credit without collateral, and the collateral they preferred was the crop the farmer was going to produce. Hence, merchants developed the crop-lien system, under which planters, small landowners, tenants, sharecroppers—indeed, whoever wanted to borrow—put up their prospective crop as a guarantee to satisfy their creditors. When the crop was harvested, it was brought to the lienholder, who marketed it and used the proceeds to satisfy the farmer's debts. The merchant thus profited both as a lender and as a crop broker.

The crop lien system of the postbellum South, like sharecropping, has been blamed for a multitude of evils. From any perspective, interest rates were high, often above 40 percent and as high as 60 percent a year on goods that were already marked up substantially in price. Merchants in the postwar South did assume a substantial risk, and they, in turn, paid high rates to the firms from which they borrowed, but it is clear that they frequently took advantage of farmers who had no other sources of credit. Credit was so hard to get in the postbellum South and depended so heavily on the reputation of the borrower that the crossroads merchants could effectively monopolize it in most areas. They saw their opportunities and took them, often ruthlessly.

Some historians have argued that interest rates were so high and crop prices so low that many farmers never satisfied the merchant-creditor and fell into debt peonage, a condition in which they were tied to a creditor for life, working to pay debts that continued to grow and were never retired. While many farmers were compelled to take out crop liens nearly every year, true debt peonage was probably rare. Rational creditors—and crossroads merchants were rational with a vengeance—want debtors to relieve their debts, and the high level of physical mobility in the rural South is indicative of a degree of freedom that contradicts the notion of widespread debt peonage.

This is not to say that the crop lien system was in any way positive for the South. High interest rates were one of the factors that kept southern agriculture impoverished for most of the late nineteenth and early twentieth centuries. By encouraging farmers to plant cash crops almost exclusively, moreover, the crop lien system exacerbated the insecurities of a relatively undiversified agriculture. The crop lien system also had a substantial impact on the rural power structure. Their control of credit and marketing made merchants the equals of planters atop the social scale. Indeed, they often became substantial planters themselves on lands they bought cheaply or acquired from debtors who could not meet obligations. The crop-lien system solved a credit problem, perhaps in the only way possible, but its consequences were far from benign.

Despite their negative social and economic consequences, sharecropping and the crop lien system contributed to the recovery of southern agriculture, if cotton production is any indication. Between 1870 and 1900 the production of the leading southern staple rose by an impressive 170 percent.

Several factors beyond the new labor and credit arrangements explained this dramatic increase. First, new cotton lands were opened throughout the

South but especially in the Southwest. Much Texas land was broken and put in cotton in the late nineteenth century. The same was true in Arkansas, where drainage of the swampy Arkansas River delta and reclamation of the sunken lands submerged by Mississippi River waters during the New Madrid earthquakes of 1811 and 1812 opened cotton lands as rich as any in the region. A second reason for the dramatic increase in cotton production involved its more exclusive culture on traditional cotton lands. Whereas antebellum plantations had been general farms, the tenant farms that succeeded them emphasized cotton at the expense of food crops and livestock at the behest of landlords and lien holders. The last major factor contributing to the dramatic increase in cotton production was the entrance of large numbers of white small farmers into that enterprise. Before the Civil War, farmers without slaves usually produced small quantities of cotton or tobacco for market, but they concentrated their efforts on production of food items that would enhance family self-sufficiency. After the war, economic and social conditions created a mixture of carrots and sticks that induced many small farmers to emphasize cash crops.

One of the carrots was high cotton prices in the years immediately after the end of the war. Another inducement to greater cash crop production was the end of the institution of slavery that, ironically, most whites who did not own slaves had fought to preserve. Many small farmers perceived that they would have fuller commercial opportunities now that they no longer had to compete with slave labor. The postwar boom in railroad building was also an inducement, because movement of crops to market had always been a problem for those farmers who lived in such areas as the Carolina Piedmont and the hill country of Alabama and Mississippi, where water transportation was not convenient. Finally, by accelerating plant growth, new phosphate fertilizers shortened the growing season, making cotton feasible in areas where it had once been threatened by frost.

Mixed with these carrots were some sticks. Providing family self-sufficiency was much more difficult in the South after 1865. Restrictive herd and game laws created hardships for marginal whites, as they did for freedpeople. Moreover, the tax burden on the property owner increased dramatically during Reconstruction. State governments provided more services and mandated free public schools. States and communities directly or indirectly subsidized entering businesses, especially railroads, further increasing tax burdens. Taxes had to be paid in cash, requiring that the taxpayer produce something that would generate money. Finally, like most southerners, small farmers frequently needed credit to get back on their feet after the war. Their credit came from local merchants who put liens on their crops and demanded payment in cotton.

Once they started down the cotton road, small farmers found it hard to turn back. When prices were low, as they were for most of the late nineteenth century, they found themselves working harder and getting less from it. In their anger and frustration they frequently turned on blacks, always the South's favorite scapegoats, supporting restrictive racial laws and engaging in such violent acts as lynching and whitecapping (mob destruction of property). Sometimes they turned on planters, merchants, and middlemen, joining agrarian reform movements that promised to get them out of a situation that was, in its own way, nearly as hopeless as sharecropping. White small farmers truly were, as one historian has characterized them, "the defeated generation."[3]

RECONSTRUCTED SOUTHERN AGRICULTURE AND RURAL LIFE

Before the Civil War, cotton had been king. Afterward, it was a cruel tyrant. Southerners knew that cotton's comeback had not been paralleled by a return to regional prosperity, and the figures bear them out. Before the Civil War, per-capita income in the South was comparable to that in the North and exceeded per-capita income in the largely agricultural Midwest. In 1900, per-capita income in the South was barely half the northern average.

Observers of the southern economy understandably regarded the Civil War as the source of the income problem. The conflict had obliterated concentrations of capital, disrupted the labor system, and severely damaged agriculture and its economic infrastructure. But the more fundamental problem with cotton, as well as with rice, another major southern staple, was that world supply had come into balance with—and even exceeded—world demand. In the first half of the nineteenth century, the dramatic growth of the textile industry worldwide brought substantial and generally growing profits to cotton producers. Their land and their slaves appreciated steadily in value, and their investment probably returned more than any alternative investment would have. But an imbalance between supply and demand cannot continue indefinitely in a free market system. Supply will eventually rise to meet demand, and that is what happened with cotton. When it fully reentered world markets after 1865, the South found that its premier staple competed with cotton produced by Latin Americans, Africans, and Asians. Certainly, this development was accelerated by the Civil War, but it is unrealistic to think that it would not have happened anyway, given the supply-and-demand imbalance.

Southern leaders in business and agriculture recognized that dependence on a single crop was harmful, and they urged diversification. Farmers should become more self-sufficient, they argued, and should develop market alternatives to cotton. Diversification was easier to preach than to practice, however. Soil and climate conditions made it difficult to produce some crops and animals. In the hot, wet climate enjoyed by much of the deep South, humus (organic matter in the soil, such as dead leaves or stalks of plants) tended to break down quickly, and the nitrogen and other nutrients created by that process leached rapidly away. The hot, wet climate was not conducive to the growth of small grains, which need cool and dry weather in order to impede the development of funguses and to allow plants to head out properly. Likewise, cattle production was difficult in many parts of the South, given the prevalence of such parasitic diseases as babesiosis and anaplasmosis, introduced by ticks.

That is not to say that no diversification was possible or that none was practiced. Some truck farming was certainly feasible, and with the introduction of refrigerated railcars in the 1870s southern winter vegetables, strawberries, peaches, and citrus fruits began to appear in northern markets. The growth of truck farming was stunted, however, by the absence of local markets for produce, and even at best fruit and vegetable culture could offer an escape from cotton for only a relative handful of farmers.

Diversification was impeded by more than just environment and climate. Landlords and lien holders preferred cotton, because it was nonperishable and easy to handle and could be marketed quickly through existing channels of trade. As well, southern farmers *knew* cotton and were equipped to produce it. Other crops required knowledge and tools that they did not necessarily have.

There were reasons to grow cotton, there just was not much money in it. The price for cotton was low, and most farms were small. In what historian Gilbert Fite has succinctly referred to as "the agricultural trap in the South," most farm units were too small to provide a decent standard of living for a family, and most farmers could not earn or borrow enough capital to expand to the point where a decent standard of living could be obtained.[4] The absence of capital kept farm sizes down in still another way. While northern agriculture was mechanizing, southern farmers were still using walking plows and hoes to plant and cultivate and were picking cotton by hand. They remained tied to labor-intensive methods in a nation in which fossil fuels and animal power were increasing the amount of work people could do and the acreage individual farmers could work. Part of the reason for retarded mechanization in southern agriculture lay in the nature of the crops produced, but other factors also played a role. The ability of landlords to hold a semicaptive labor force on the land by limiting other options and the absence of the kinds of farming profits and accumulations of capital that would attract the attention of inventors and implement manufacturers clearly helped keep southern agriculture labor intensive.

The related problems of lack of capital and a labor-intensive agricultural system unquestionably kept southern farms small and unremunerative. In 1910, only Virginia and Texas, of the states of the Old Confederacy, had an average farm size of at least 100 acres. The average farm size in Alabama, South Carolina, and Mississippi was 79, 77, and 68 acres, respectively. Even that is misleading, in light of the fact that a large majority of farms were not more than 50 acres in size. One historian has estimated that the average cotton farmer could count on making about three hundred dollars for his normal production of five or six bales when cotton sold for a dime a pound, which it seldom did. When cotton dropped to seven cents, or a nickel a pound, even that marginal income was constricted.

Exacerbating the problem of low incomes and living standards and inadequate capital was the fact that the rural South was overpopulated. In 1900 the rural population in Wisconsin was twenty-three per square mile and fifteen per square mile in Minnesota, while over thirty people lived on the average square mile of rural Alabama, Georgia, and Mississippi. Overpopulation was intimately related to underemployment. While there was always plenty of work when the crop was to be chopped and picked—indeed, planters liked to keep lots of families on the land to assure adequate numbers of hands at these busy times—farmers were idle for substantial portions of the year.

It would seem that underemployed people with low incomes would move to places where there was work and good pay. The United States was industrializing in the decades following the Civil War and was generally prosperous. While the average cotton farmer in the late nineteenth century was making $300 or less a year, unskilled workers in northern cities were earning at least $450 a year, and semiskilled machine tenders in manufacturing were averaging more than $600.

Certainly, some southerners did migrate, to the West—especially Texas and Oklahoma—to southern and northern cities, or to the Appalachian coalfields, where the organization of work and credit resembled the sharecropping and crop lien arrangements with which they were familiar. In the 1870s and 1880s thousands of blacks, hungry for land and angry with the racism of southern whites, fled the region, especially for Kansas but for many other places as well, including Africa.

But most southerners, blacks and whites alike, stayed in the countryside. One reason was the relative lack of opportunities for them in the South. Most southern staples did not have the forward or backward linkages that encouraged industrial development, and the self-sufficiency of plantations had stunted industrial development before the war. That situation did not change dramatically after the war. The South's proportion of the nation's manufacturing establishments and the value of its manufactures was no higher in 1900 than it had been in 1860. There was industrial development—tobacco in Virginia and North Carolina, textiles in the Georgia and Carolina Piedmont, iron and steel in Alabama, and lumber and mining in many places—but most desirable, high-wage industries shunned a region where potential workers lacked education and skills and potential consumers were poor.

This meant that most rural southerners seeking opportunity would have to consider moving to the industrial North. That involved going far from home, away from kin, to places where they knew no one. Long moves were expensive moves, especially for people with families, and many rural southerners were too poor to contemplate such a step. Finally, there was the problem of ignorance. Rural southerners knew little about the North, and their southern employers took advantage of their ignorance with horror stories about Chicago or New York. All of this began to change during World War I, when labor agents came South with tales of high wages in northern factories, even for unskilled labor. The establishment of southern communities and families in northern cities made life easier for future migrants. And government programs during the 1930s raised southern wage levels and encouraged rural-to-urban migration. But these developments lay in the future and were of little relevance to postbellum southerners. Their lives were defined by a dreary and apparently unbreakable circle of poverty formed by over-population, undercapitalization, and labor-intensive production of commodity crops on farms too small to provide decent living standards.

The poverty of the rural South was much more than just a statistical abstraction; it affected the lives of most people every day in many ways. Marginal incomes meant fewer of the little luxuries that enriched living and fewer even of the material necessities that sustained life. Poverty could be measured in higher infant-mortality rates, lower life expectancies, and endemic chronic health conditions such as hookworm and pellagra. Economic hardship was reflected in an inability adequately to support community institutions. The effects of low income could be seen in poor schools and in ignorant and illiterate people; some historians have estimated that as few as one in four rural black children were learning to write in 1880.[5] Poor people are frequently isolated people with limited horizons. A trip to the county seat was a rare treat; a journey to Atlanta or New Orleans an impossible dream. Men had a public life that softened isolation, but women's lives were closely constricted. Typical, perhaps, was Nannie Johnson, an Arkansas farm woman at the turn of the century, whose social circle consisted of about twenty neighborhood women, whom she visited when rains did not turn dirt tracks to mud and swell streams to the point where crossing logs were no longer safe.[6]

All of this is not to suggest that life in the postwar South was hopeless or totally without satisfactions. For the freedpeople, even a life of poverty and prejudice was far superior to life under slavery. Now the former slaves could form and control their own families, develop sustaining social institutions, and have some minimal degree of control over their economic fortunes. But in general it was true throughout the late nineteenth and early twentieth centuries that the rural South was what Franklin Roosevelt called it in 1938—the number one economic problem in the nation.[7]

SEVEN

Rural America
in the Age of Industrialization

The years between 1870 and 1900 were a time of dramatic expansion for American agriculture. By virtually every measure, agriculture doubled in size during that remarkable period. The number of farms increased from 2.66 million to 5.74 million. Acres of land in farms jumped from 407.735 million to 841.202 million. And the total value of farm property rose from $9.4 billion to $20.4 billion.

Crop production surged as more farms were developed and more acres were brought under the plow. The production of wheat went from 254 million to 599 million bushels. Corn production rose from 1.125 billion to 2.662 billion bushels. In 1870, 4.352 million bales of cotton were produced; in thirty years, production hit 10.124 million bales. Cattle numbers rose from under 24 million to nearly 68 million, and the swine population went from a little over 25 million head to nearly 63 million.

Part of this expansion was due to the opening of the Great Plains, the last major American agricultural frontier. In 1870 it was still mostly covered with grass on which buffalo grazed. By 1900 the Plains had become the wheat belt and millions of cattle lived on its ranges. In 1870 there were barely 50 thousand farms in Kansas, Nebraska, and the Dakotas. By 1900 those four states contained nearly 400 thousand farms. But the Plains was only the most spectacular scene of expansion. The number of farms and the amount of land in farms increased in every area of the country between 1870 and 1900, even including New England, which agricultural commentators had doomed to inevitable decline years before.

The expansion of American agriculture was stimulated mainly by industrialization and urbanization in the United States and Europe. While the farm population was doubling between 1870 and 1900, the urban population of the United States was tripling. In 1870 there were twenty-five places in the country with a population exceeding fifty thousand people; in 1900 there were seventy-eight such places. While the value of agricultural products a little more than doubled, the value of manufactured products quadrupled, and in 1890, for the first time in American history, the total value of manufactured goods exceeded the total value of agricultural products.

Industrialization and urbanization affected farmers in several ways. First, these developments provided them with growing numbers of prosperous customers. Second, related improvements in transportation such as railroads and steamships ensured that their products would reach markets in a timely fashion, and innovations in agricultural processing diminished the likelihood that their crops and animal products would spoil. But industrial development did not only affect the farmers' markets and the way they marketed, it also changed their lives. Farm families found a swelling cornucopia of factory-made goods available to them, either in the local towns or by mail order. Farmers could buy ready-to-wear clothing, furniture, carpets, art works, musical instruments, toys, draperies, and hundreds of other items. They no longer needed to construct their fences from hand-wrought rails, when barbed wire could be purchased, or to build homes, when Sears, Roebuck offered prefabricated models, or even to produce their own food, when Armour, Heinz, and Pillsbury were quite willing to undertake that responsibility—for a price.

All of these goods that appeared in the local stores or in the farm papers, town magazines, and mail-order catalogs that found their way into the farmer's home were seductive. They presented farm people who could generate income through market participation with the opportunity to enrich and enhance their material standards of living, which most wanted to do. But consuming urban products, often in ways suggested by urban advertisers and merchandisers, inevitably meant at least some rural conformity to urban standards of culture, taste, and value.

Rural conservatism impeded greater farmer commitment to the market. Farming remained a high-risk enterprise, without government safety nets. Drought or insects could wipe out a crop, and commodity prices fluctuated wildly and unpredictably. The unfortunate farmer did not face starvation, as his European peasant forbearers had, but he could lose his farm. Prudence dictated the continuation of the traditional safety-first strategy that had always tempered market involvement. Hence, while farmers grasped market opportunities, they did so in a tentative, gingerly manner. As late as 1900 the United States Department of Agriculture estimated that fully 60 percent of what the average farm family consumed was produced on the farm.

Farmers might choose to be in the market a lot or a little, but they could not choose to be out of it completely. They needed income just to remain farmers. Land was expensive, and the cost of money was high, especially considering the deflationary trend in the economy in general and in the price of farm products in particular. Taxes rose, as well, especially in states and localities upgrading institutions and encouraging economic development. It had never been possible for American farmers to do without some income, but after the Civil War it was more difficult than ever.

Enthusiastically or reluctantly commercial, late-nineteenth-century farmers were increasingly vulnerable to forces beyond their control. In particular, they struggled with the three Ms—markets, middlemen, and money. The three Ms were so vexing that in times of particular hardship they spawned agrarian political movements. The Grange in the seventies, the Farmers' Alliance in the eighties, and the Populist party in the nineties all attempted to lead farmers out of the problems commercialization entailed. None was successful, but each was eloquent testimony to the stresses on agriculture in this time of challenge and change.

Farmers were ambivalent about the future at the turn of the twentieth century. While they enjoyed lives of greater material abundance than their parents or grandparents had, they felt themselves at the mercy of an economic system whose rules they could not influence. More and more they felt like strangers in their own country. They no longer controlled the government, if they ever had, and they saw the standards and values of their country defined increasingly by others, often at their expense. To live in the countryside in 1900 was to have the sense that the nation was passing you by, leaving you behind, ignoring you at best and derogating you at worst.

One of the major national enterprises of the last third of the nineteenth century was the settlement of the Great Plains, that vast region of grass stretching from the western edge of Minnesota, Iowa, Missouri, Arkansas, and Louisiana on the east to the Rocky Mountains on the west and from the northeastern states of Mexico northward through Canada's prairie provinces. Settlement of the Plains presented a challenge that sobered even the normally optimistic American pioneers.

Between the end of the Revolutionary War and 1820, American settlers scrambled over most of the area between the Appalachians and the Great Plains like so many army ants, unstopping and seemingly unstoppable. But they did stop at the Plains. By the beginning of the Civil War they had leaped over the Plains, to Oregon in the 1830s, Utah and California in the 1840s, and Colorado in the 1850s, but their penetration of the great grasslands was tentative and incomplete.

What held them back? First, there was the problem of transportation. How could people living on the Plains move bulky commodities vast distances? Ground transportation was prohibitively expensive, and few rivers were navigable. Railroads ultimately provided the solution to the transportation problem, but only when technical advances and government encouragement made them feasible in the vast region.

Then there was the threat of powerful Native American groups. The Sioux, the Comanche, the Arapaho, the Cheyenne, and others moved across the Plains following vast herds of bison. They were as well adapted to the ecology of the Plains as any people before or since. They were skilled, brave, and frequently hostile, and their nomadic lifestyle made them more difficult to control than the settled village Indians of the East.

Another factor that inhibited settlement of the Plains was the strangeness of the region to people from farther east. It was, for example, generally treeless except for the few river bottoms that snaked shallowly through the grasslands. To people from forested regions the grasslands were alien, so alien that they compared the waving grass more often to waves at sea than to anything they had seen on land. Standing on windswept hills, contemplating unbroken horizons in every direction, they felt uncomfortable, exposed—even naked—to a hostile and uncontrollable nature. Until the late ante-

136 bellum period, many Americans associated trees with fertility and assumed that plains and prairies were barren, a further deterrent to potential settlers.

But it was not just that trees made people comfortable. Timber was a practical necessity to American farmers. The nineteenth century was the age of wood. Housing and fencing were constructed of wood, as were furniture and tools. Wood was the fuel of choice. Not until 1887 did the total energy derived from burning coal exceed the energy derived from burning wood in this country. Small wonder that people contemplating life on the Plains questioned how they would shelter and warm themselves and protect their crops.

Another practical problem on the Plains was the relative absence of water. Median precipitation in most of the Plains is under twenty inches per year, and much of the region receives less than fifteen. Twenty inches might well be enough to produce decent crops if rainfall is timely, soils hold water well, and evaporation is not rapid, but when twenty inches is the median, in roughly half the years less precipitation will be available. Americans used to producing crops and using methods appropriate in more humid areas did not view farming on the Plains with eager anticipation.

Then there was the weather. Because most of the Great Plains is far distant from potentially moderating bodies of water, it enjoys a continental climate characterized by cold winters and hot summers. Steele, North Dakota, to cite a remarkable but telling example, has recorded temperature extremes of 121°F in the summer and −50°F in the winter, for a range of 171 degrees. To those from more temperate climates, Plains summers must have seemed like hell and winters like hell frozen over. The wind, unchecked by mountains or trees, seemed a constant companion and contributed to the discomfort caused by temperature extremes. Violent thunderstorms and hailstorms, tornadoes, and blizzards further enhanced the region's reputation for natural undesirability.

Other factors, while less imposing, gave potential settlers pause. Could the tough sod of the Plains, held together by the matted roots of countless generations of grass, be broken economically? Would Rocky Mountain locusts—grasshoppers—consume the crops, as they had in eastern Nebraska and Dakota and western Minnesota in the 1870s? Tales of locomotives that could not get traction on rails covered with grasshoppers and of the Kansas woman who found her house filled with hoppers that had shredded her cur-

tains and eaten three loaves of freshly baked bread were not reassuring.
Could farmers coexist with the millions of bison on the Plains in 1860?
Would the buffalo respect crops? Would they even respect fences?[1]

It took such new and difficult questions, and such a frightening and forbidding land, to slow the westward march of a rapacious and energetic
people. But their progress, as it turned out, could only be slowed, not
stopped. Eventually they answered the questions and solved the problems,
seldom in a complete or satisfactory manner but well enough for thousands
of hardy—sometimes foolhardy—pioneers.

The problem of transportation was most easily solved. As early as the
1840s the railroad had been seen as the most viable form of transportation
for the region. There were technical difficulties with antebellum railroads,
but the most serious problem was the circular one that investors were reluctant to build roads where there were no people and people were reluctant to
live where there was no transportation. The federal government solved the
problem indirectly, beginning with the Pacific Railroad Act of 1862. This
legislation financed railroad building through liberal loans and grants of
land. The first land-grant road, which became the Union Pacific, was followed by other subsidized transcontinentals, the Northern Pacific, the Atchison, Topeka, and Santa Fe, and the Southern Pacific. A nonsubsidized railroad, the Great Northern, joined the land-grant four in spanning the Plains.

These great railroads, along with later entrants, branches, and feeders,
provided transportation for the Plains and even shaped urban development.
Because they preceded settlement, the railroads were free to create towns
wherever they chose, to impose street plans on them, and even to name those
streets. Sales of town lots to eastern businesspeople contributed mightily to
railroads' profits in the early decades of Plains' development. The railroads
vigorously promoted agricultural settlement as well. The land-grant roads
offered their properties for sale at attractive prices and reasonable terms and
maintained departments of immigration in the East and in Europe. The
roads encouraged those looking for solutions to the agricultural problems of
the Plains and boosted the region as enthusiastically—and shamelessly—as
any boomer. The Great Plains has always maintained a love-hate relationship with the railroads, but two things are certain: appreciable farming and
ranching would not have developed on the Plains without the transportation
the railroads provided, and no entities were more fervent than the railroads
in their wish for a vital and prosperous agriculture in the region.

Overcoming the resistance of Native Americans on the Plains was a slower and more difficult process. Congress could—and did—throw money at the problem, but to less immediate or satisfying effect than was the case with transportation. By the postbellum period the government had concluded that most Native Americans should be confined to limited reservations, opening most of their historic territory to non-Indian settlement. The government preferred to pursue this goal deliberately, but pressures from actual or would-be settlers sometimes forced an acceleration of the process. Such was the case on the Plains, where agricultural settlement on the eastern edge and mining settlement in Colorado, Montana, and the Black Hills of South Dakota at once aroused Native American resistance and compelled federal action. For their parts, the prominent Indian groups on the Plains had no inclination to relinquish either their country or their lifestyle. And the United States Army, which usually had the job of forcing that relinquishment, was ill prepared to control the Plains Indians efficiently. Slow, weighted down by equipment, and often arrogant and tactically deficient, the army confronted a brave, imaginative, and highly mobile foe.

Eventually the army was successful. Part of its success derived from its dogged persistence. Officers willing to throw hundreds of men at entrenched Confederates at places like Antietam and Cold Harbor would just as stoically pursue Arapaho and Sioux all over the Plains. Backed by an advanced industrial and agricultural economy, the army could afford to devote all of its time to plodding around the Plains. Living closer to the margin, Plains Indians had to spend much of their time getting food.

Getting food was increasingly difficult. At the end of the Civil War the destruction of the great bison herds began in earnest. In the early nineteenth century there were perhaps as many as twenty million bison on the Great Plains. These grazing animals were divided by the Platte River into two herds, with that south of the river somewhat larger than the northern herd. For most of the year the animals lived in groups of 50 to 200, but in the late-summer mating season they would congregate into herds that amazed white observers would sometimes estimate to include half a million bison.

The gregarious instincts of the bison, their slowness, and their relative inattention to danger made them highly vulnerable to hunters. Indians on horseback, using lances and bows and arrows, killed many; by 1800, the bison was virtually the sole support of many Plains Indian groups. But the killing became even more efficient when it was transformed into a systematic commercial enterprise. Entrepreneurs prized bison hides, which they processed into leather and sometimes into winter coats and robes for coach and buggy passengers. Pickled buffalo tongue was also a delicacy enjoyed by some easterners. Before the Civil War, Native American groups such as the Comanche on the southern Plains and Métis (mixed bloods, usually the children of Ojibwa Indians and French or Scots fur traders) on the northern Plains engaged most enthusiastically in the commercial exploitation of the bison. By 1840, 100 thousand bison hides were being shipped out of St. Louis every year, and by 1850 bison numbers had been reduced to less than 12 million. After the Civil War Indian hunters were joined by whites, who discovered they could earn up to $15,000 in a good year, a princely sum in postbellum America. Soon the Plains was filled with rotting carcasses—hunters took only the hide and the tongue—especially of young cows, the suppleness of whose hides made them particulary desirable.

Harried by the petty capitalists—white and red—who scurried after them, the bison herds declined steadily and dramatically. The southern herd went first and was effectively gone before 1875. The northern herd held on longer, and as late as 1882 there were still enough around that nineteen tons of hides could be sent off from one minor shipping point in western North Dakota. But the northern herd went quickly, too, and by 1890 it was estimated that only about a thousand bison survived on the Plains. Long before that date the Native Americans were ground down between military pressure on one side and diminishing resources on the other. By the end of the nation's centennial year most of the Plains Indians were confined to reservations.

SETTLING THE PLAINS

The post–Native American future of the Plains began to be revealed long before the last Indians were confined to reservations. The harbinger of that future was open-range cattle ranching. Though it is popularly associated with the Plains and probably always will be, open-range cattle ranching was a fixture of the American frontier as early as the sixteenth century. Spanish explorers commonly seeded lands they touched with cattle, and vibrant ranching cultures eventually developed in some of these places. In California, for example, cattle ranching was the primary economic occupation until the discovery of gold and American annexation in 1848. English colonists in the Chesapeake and elsewhere ranged cattle in the forests, and ranching contin-

140 ued to be a thriving enterprise in the piney woods of Mississippi, central Florida, and other sparsely settled areas east of the Mississippi, long after the Civil War. But it was on the Great Plains after the Civil War that ranching became a big business.

Open-range cattle ranching matured in Texas in the early postbellum years. Cattle had been introduced in Texas by eighteenth-century Spaniards, who organized the ranching enterprise in conformity to practices that had been successful on other Hispanic frontiers. Americans entering Texas in the 1820s and 1830s brought their cattle—and their cattle-herding ways —with them. The result was that by the end of the Civil War there were between three million and five million cattle in Texas, many of them wild for all intents and purposes, as well as hundreds of thousands of feral hogs and many wild horses.

Cattle were a resource on which Texans depended, both for subsistence and for commercial exploitation. Before the Civil War they drove animals hundreds of miles to market, and in the difficult economic climate of the postbellum years they eagerly anticipated resuming the beef trade. Initially, Texans drove cattle to market at St. Louis, but there were problems with that destination. For one thing, the distances were very great. Moreover, western Arkansas and Missouri were in a chaotic, almost anarchic, condition at the end of the Civil War, and cattle drovers were subject to rustling and even murder by the Pukes, as they styled inhabitants of the region. Pukes were not the only challenge facing the Texans. Many Texas cattle carried a tick-borne disease called Texas fever. While the Texas longhorns had developed an immunity to this malady, the cattle with which they came in contact were vulnerable, a situation about which non-Texans complained bitterly even before the Civil War. In 1866 Kansas and Missouri passed laws prohibiting Texas cattle in areas where local stock were raised, and vigilantes were more than willing to put teeth in these laws.

In 1867 Texans Charles F. Gross and W. W. Sugg and transplanted Illinoisan J. G. McCoy pioneered a drive that avoided Arkansas, Missouri, and the settled areas of Kansas by going north to Abilene, Kansas. There the cattle were loaded on rail cars for shipment east. Safer and shorter, the drive to Kansas quickly came to be preferred by Texans. From 35 thousand in 1867, the number of cattle driven to Abilene reached 700 thousand in 1871.

The style of open-range cattle ranching that developed in Texas synthesized American and Hispanic traditions. Prospective ranchers had first to choose ranchsteads. They looked for arable land on a year-round stream, where they could raise oats or some other feed for horses, but they did not usually own much land, preferring to exploit the public domain. It was in their interest to be far enough from neighbors to have plenty of range for the use of their cattle but not so far as to make cooperative activities impossible.

Spring and fall were the busiest times in ranching. In spring ranchers and hands rounded up all the cattle they could find on the range and separated them by their brands, with unbranded calves going to the owners of their mothers. Most of the young males were castrated; as steers they would gain weight more rapidly than as bulls and were easier to handle. Calves and other unbranded cattle were branded, and the herds were turned back to pasture to regain the weight they commonly lost in the winter. In the late summer or early fall the cattle were rounded up again, sometimes by ranchers and sometimes by independent entrepreneurs who contracted to drive them to market. Most cattle were usually returned to the range, but mature steers and older heifers (females) were separated from the herds to be marketed.

Cattle drives, like the roundups, were usually cooperative neighborhood ventures. Drives could take from a few days to several weeks, depending on the distance from ranches to railheads. The drive was a dull, dirty, and sometimes dangerous enterprise. At best it was boring. Excitement, such as that represented by a stampede or an Indian raid, endangered ranchers' pocketbooks and sometimes their lives. Arrival at a cowtown was cause for relief— and release—for all concerned. Employer and employee alike enjoyed a payday and an opportunity for recreation in places whose saloons and brothels gave them a well-deserved reputation for moral laxity. Then it was back to the ranch, to start the process all over again.

The people who pursued the ranching enterprise were romantic figures in the popular imagination a century ago, and Hollywood did little afterward to dull their appeal. Ranchers and cowboys attracted Americans because they appeared to be free beings in the wide-open spaces. They appealed to that impatience with restraint that has always been an important subcurrent in the American character.

Like most stereotypes, this one was connected to reality without being perfectly descriptive of reality. Ranchers were substantial businesspeople, and such staples of the Hollywood western as the shoot-out at the O.K. Corral never entered their consciousness. That they were tough, determined, confident, and sometimes ruthless is certainly true, but they were not free, being burdened with debts and responsibilities and concerns about weather, prices, meeting loan payments, negotiating with labor, and whatever else affected their businesses. Nor were they as individualistic as we might like to believe. Like other businesspeople, they banded together to advance their purposes. Cattlemen's associations registered brands, marked trails, settled disputes, conducted cooperative roundups and drives, disciplined miscreants, and lobbied the government for favorable treatment, often successfully. Ranching was a business, not an opportunity for living out a romantic fantasy. Those—such as Theodore Roosevelt—who failed to recognize it for what it was were not destined to stay in it very long.

As with ranchers, so with cowboys. They did enjoy solitude, and if they were misanthropes, that quality passed for freedom. But they are perhaps best understood in the context of their contemporaries in the urban working class. Their work was arduous and dull, and they were poorly paid. They spent much of their time wet and cold and seldom enjoyed the comforts of family life; their diet and living conditions were bland and unvaried, and they lived mainly for moments of intense self-indulgence that allowed them briefly to forget the tedium and pointlessness of their existence. White, black, or Hispanic, they were probably illiterate men with undistinguished pasts and unpromising futures. They put meat on American tables, and their romantic image was much admired, but the reality of their lives holds little appeal for us.

In the two decades after the end of the Civil War, open-range ranching rapidly overspread the Plains, stimulated by the supply of range and the demand for beef grazed thereon. The reduction of the Indian threat and the rapid decline of the buffalo herds opened massive portions of the range. Simultaneously, the eastern market for beef expanded rapidly, and the extension of rail lines into the Plains made it easier for western ranchers to tap that market. The increasing use of refrigeration for maintaining the freshness of beef, and especially the growing availability of refrigerated railcars, made beef more accessible to more consumers in more places more often, and aggressive marketing by Chicago packers overcame the aversion of eastern consumers to beef slaughtered elsewhere.

For a time rising demand and rising supply interacted in a dynamic fashion, creating a boom psychology. Demand seemed insatiable, and increases in supply did not seem to depress prices. Ranchers responded by expanding and upgrading operations. Large Texas ranchers established spreads in the central and northern Plains. Eastern and European capitalists joined in. By the late 1870s the ranching frontier had reached Montana and the northern Dakota territory. Such cowtowns as Dickinson and Glendive relived the rowdy early experience of the Abilene and Dodge City, further south. As the business became larger, it became more sophisticated. Purebred bulls were introduced to upgrade herds composed of hardy, but tough and thin-bodied, Texas longhorns. Ranchers managed far-flung operations with hundreds of employees. Some even moved cattle from summer pastures on the Plains to winter quarters in the Midwest and back again.

In the agricultural economy, as in life, all good things must come to an end, and the end began for open-range cattle ranching in the mid-1880s. Supply finally met and even began to exceed demand, with a resultant decline in cattle prices. On the eastern edge of the Plains, prospective farmers pressured the government to force cattle ranchers to remove their stock from the public lands they were accustomed to exploiting unchallenged. Environmental factors also played a role. In a sense, ranchers were not much different from the Native Americans who had dominated the Plains before them. They lived off grazing animals, which in turn lived off the abundant grass of the Plains. The problem came when ranchers, deluded by wet years and bewitched by high profits, put too many animals on the range. Between 1885 and 1887 disaster struck. Two dry summers followed by bitterly cold and stormy winters decimated many herds on the open range. While losses varied and probably averaged 15 percent throughout the region, some operations on the northern Plains lost over half their cattle in the first winter alone, with losses of longhorns especially heavy. It was becoming clear that those who wanted to stay in ranching would have to change.

Ranchers began claiming land, often using their hands as dummy entrants under the Homestead Act, and throwing up fences around it. They discovered that closer attention to their cattle and their range enhanced their ability to survive an enterprise with high risks and low margins. Ranchers began managing their range more carefully and rotating cattle on it systematically. They planted hay in place of some native grasses and began cutting fodder for use as winter feed. Attention to the winter comfort of cattle cut winterkill and resulted in a higher survival rate for calves in the spring. When cattle were supervised closely, diseased animals could be removed before entire herds were infected. And herds could be more easily upgraded when they were more closely controlled. Blooded bulls had been sprinkled among open-range cattle, but they bred promiscuously and unsystematically, as cattle are inclined to do, so that as late as 1890 over 80 percent of cattle were still classified as scrubs (mongrels). That situation was changing, however, as open-range cattle ranching passed away in all but a few places on the Plains.

Plains boosters never believed that cattle ranching represented the future of the region. They always thought that the Plains would become comparable to the contemporary Midwest, a land of prosperous small farms and numerous towns with diversified economies. They worked hard to make reality fit their dreams, and for a time they seemed to succeed.

Government at all levels endeavored to induce farmers onto the Plains. The federal government bent its efforts toward familiarizing potential settlers with the Plains environment and helping them meet its challenges. Government scientists surveyed surface and groundwater resources. John Wesley Powell, who eventually concluded that the Plains could not duplicate the midwestern agricultural regime, experimented with dry-farming techniques that enthusiasts hoped would make the West bloom. The United States Department of Agriculture scoured the world for cultivars appropriate for the Plains. And in 1887 Congress passed the Hatch Act, providing federal funds for the creation and maintenance of agricultural experiment stations in the states. In the West these institutions concentrated on developing appropriate crops and methods for the region.

As it came to appreciate more fully the special challenges of the Plains, Congress passed legislation designed in part to allow farm operations to conform more closely to environmental realities and in part to encourage changes in those realities. Recognizing that the 160 acres available under the Homestead Act might not be enough to support a family in much of the region, Congress sought to make more land available for settlers. The Timber Culture Act, passed in 1873, allowed farmers to claim 160 acres in addition to what they held if they planted 40 acres with a specified number of trees (realizing how onerous planting 40 acres of trees actually was, Congress in 1878 amended the Timber Culture Act to require only 10 acres of trees). This legislation was designed to allow larger, more economically viable operations and to help overcome the problem of lack of timber in the West. Some believed that trees actually interacted with the atmosphere in such a way as to enhance rainfall.

Other legislation attacked the water problem more directly while allowing further expansions of acreage. The Desert Land Act of 1877 allowed individuals to claim up to 640 acres at twenty-five cents an acre if they were able to bring water to the land. Later measures further encouraged irrigation. In 1894, the Carey Act distributed the proceeds of federal land sales to the states for the construction of irrigation works, and the Newlands Act of 1902 put the federal government itself into the irrigation business.

States, territories, and localities were also eager participants in the promotion of the West. States maintained immigration departments that flooded the United States and Europe with favorable propaganda, and towns and counties added their voices to the chorus of praise for the region. Integrity was an early casualty in the war for settlers. Editors wrote of soil so rich that a nail dropped in the morning would grow into a crowbar by sundown. Northern Plains boosters shamelessly promoted "Jay Cooke's banana belt" along the Northern Pacific line in Minnesota and North Dakota, an area supposedly sheltered from harsh winters by unexplained climatic peculiarities.[2] Most prospective settlers no doubt recognized the humbuggery of all of this. Many came anyway, usually to acquire land on the farmer's last frontier.

Boosters fervently grasped any theory that promised relief from the problems of the region, regardless of how dubious it might be. Rainmaking, styled "pluviculture" by its pseudoscientific practitioners, always enjoyed a respectable hearing among optimists in an age when meteorological principles were just beginning to be understood. University of Nebraska scientist Samuel Aughey's theory that cultivation would in itself cause an increase in precipitation, that "rain follows the plow," was understandably popular in a land where dreams were much more pleasant than realities.[3]

The railroads were not as silly as many western boosters but no less committed to the future of the Plains. Unbroken horizons and sweeping landscapes might have appealed to romantics, but railroaders knew that their future prosperity depended on numerous settlers and a vital economy. The railroads encouraged agricultural experimentation and improvement, running seed trains, promoting improved livestock, and granting passes to agricultural scientists and farmers' institute workers. The railroads were eager sponsors of the Dry Farming Congress and supported such panaceas as that of Hardy Webster Campbell, whose dry-farming system promised bounteous yields on arid lands. In North Dakota, the Northern Pacific encouraged the creation of huge demonstration grain farms, called bonanzas. On one such operation, the Cass-Cheney Bonanza west of Fargo, manager

Taking a break in the field during grain planting, North Dakota, circa 1910.

Courtesy of the Fred Hultstrand History in Pictures Collection, North Dakota Institue for Regional Studies and North Dakota University Libraries, Fargo.

Oliver Dalrymple produced 600 thousand bushels of wheat on 30 thousand acres in one year, a stunning achievement in a nation of small-scale family farms.

As the bonanzas showed, farmers could overcome the problems of the West. Technology helped. Improved steel plows facilitated the breaking of prairie sod. Windmills helped farmers raise groundwater, and barbed wire, sod housing, and buffalo chips helped them compensate for the shortage of wood, at least temporarily. Some were better able to cope than others. Germans from Russia, immigrating from the treeless Russian steppes to the Dakotas and Colorado, were ready to move into sod houses and heat them with *mistholz*, a mixture of straw and manure dried and cut into blocks.[4]

The Plains was a postindustrial commercial frontier. Its settlement depended on the perception of settlers that they could produce salable commodities at a profit, not that they could simply survive. And they could profit, at least sometimes. European and American urbanization and industrialization produced a dependable, if fluctuating, market for wheat. The Plains was prime wheat country, when enough rain could be had, and wheat was the premier lazy man's crop, taking relatively little labor to produce. Further encouraging wheat production was development of the Minnesota Patent process, whereby hard spring wheat, the only type feasible on the cold and dry northern Plains, could be milled economically. By the mid-1870s farmers were flowing onto the Plains, building farms and towns as their parents and grandparents had on earlier frontiers.

But the Great Plains was different from those earlier frontiers. Cattle and wheat could support relatively fewer and larger farms than in the Midwest. Fewer farms and smaller population meant fewer and weaker towns, less vital and prosperous local industry, and less local demand for farm products. The economy was hostage to commodities processed elsewhere whose prices fluctuated unpredictably, and to an environment that remained precarious. Population rushed in when prices were high and rain was abundant and fled away when prices were low and drought was on the land. In the six years between 1888 and 1894, for example, the population of Haskell County, Kansas, dropped from 2,666 to 831, while that of neighboring Stevens County plummeted from 3,000 to 797. Usually in less dramatic fashion, this pattern was repeated several times in the century and a quarter after the end of the Civil War.

The demographic and spatial realities of the Plains had emotional effects.

The relatively large farms and the requirement that homesteaders live on their claims, along with a difficult climate that made it hard for people to visit neighbors or go to town, made farmers more isolated than they had been in the East or in Europe. Physical surroundings sometimes contributed to a sense of desolation. A journalist captured the despair most visitors and many settlers felt in 1893 when he wrote that "on every hand the treeless plain stretches away to the horizon line. . . . One mile of it is almost exactly like another. . . . When the snow covers the ground the prospect is bleak and dispiriting. . . . The silence of death rests on the vast landscape, save when it is swept by cruel winds."[5] Such sentiments came less frequently from Plains residents, perhaps in part because their expression would be an implicit admission that settlers had made a mistake in choosing to live there. Those settlers who did express unhappiness with the Plains were more commonly women than men. This is not surprising, in light of the cultural expectation that men be stoical and the reality that women were separated from family and friends and transplanted to an isolated and forbidding place by husbands who often failed to consult them or solicit their opinions. "Frequently I questioned in my own mind how a sane man could be dragging his family into such a desolate country," one South Dakota plainswoman remembered.[6] "The sod shacks and log houses along the trail looked dismal, and I wondered if the women who lived in them had any happiness." Of course, many were happy, and many enjoyed the challenge of building a home and farm in a new country, but others, isolated from neighbors and lacking the public outlets their husbands enjoyed, undoubtedly shared this South Dakotan's mood.

Eventually people came to accept and even appreciate life on the Plains, seeing virtue in the very characteristics that had repelled them initially. Today hundreds of thousands of plainspeople would not trade what they see as a superior existence for life anywhere else, and they bristle when outsiders dismiss their home as flyover country or suggest that it should be turned back to the buffalo.

However satisfactorily society there developed, economically the Great Plains proved to be America's most disappointing frontier. In a nation in which successive frontiers proceeded smoothly from wilderness to greatness, the Plains always fell short. Even today, most of the region remains economically marginal. Distance from markets and an adverse climate dictate that products from the Plains suffer a competitive disadvantage. As a region, the Plains remains overwhelmingly dependent on commodities, such as beef, wheat, coal, and oil, that are subject to dramatic price fluctuations. The region remains a colonial one, exporting raw commodities and importing capital and manufactured products. For most of this century the Great Plains, like most of the rest of the West, has been a ward of the United States, maintaining its standard of living only because more money flows in through federal transfer payments than flows out in the form of taxes. It is an ironic position for self-consciously independent people to find themselves in.

THE PLEASURES AND PAINS OF COMMERCIALIZATION

The market behavior of ranchers and wheat producers underscored the reality that the settlement of America's last great agricultural frontier took place in the context of increasing commercialization of the farm enterprise. American farmers had always been in the market to a large extent, but a century ago they were becoming relatively more commercial, partly because they chose to and partly because they had to. Helping fuel commercialization was a surge in industrialization and urbanization in the United States and Europe. Economic development increased the numbers of farmers' customers and made them more affluent. Manufacturers turned out more, better, and cheaper consumer goods for farmers and others to buy. And advertisers and merchants made these goods ever more alluring and seductive. Sophisticated merchants specifically targeted the rural market. In 1872 salesman Aaron Montgomery Ward launched a modest mail-order house, and within a dozen years his catalog offered rural shoppers over ten thousand items. By 1890 his firm was facing stiff competition from an aggressive Sears, Roebuck, which also shaped its offerings to farmers' tastes.

Montgomery Ward, Sears, Roebuck, and the advertisers in newspapers, magazines, and farm periodicals revealed an expanding world of consumption to rural people. Drowning in goods and taking consumption for granted, it is easy for us to overlook the fascination of people a century ago for a Baldwin piano, a manufactured carpet, or even a Stetson hat or the way in which such items brought joy into people's lives. Rural people wanted these things and believed they deserved them, but wants have an insidious way of becoming needs that have to be filled, and that demands steady and dependable income.

In addition to increasing farmers' needs for income, the new consumer-goods industries and mass retailers weakened local communities. Local manufacturers found it increasingly difficult to compete with distant firms able to produce better, cheaper, and more heavily advertised goods. And local merchants suffered when farmers purchased expensive items from Sears, Roebuck or Montgomery Ward in Chicago rather than from the stores in town. Farmers still purchased convenience goods, such as food items, hardware, or everyday clothes, locally, but they bought more of their big-ticket items and fancy goods through the mail.

A major part of the reason was price, of course, but there was more to it than that. The national publications, advertisers, and mail-order houses helped define taste. They suggested what rural people should have and how they should arrange, display, or wear it. It was not enough that one had parlor furniture, it had to be fashionable and it had to be arranged just so. This is not to suggest that farm people followed along blindly, manipulated in any direction urban media or catalog houses desired. The process was a subtle one, marked by unconscious mutual accommodation and compromise. Montgomery Ward and Sears, Roebuck succeeded in part because they stocked goods they knew would appeal to rural consumers. And rural people bought pianos or davenports not simply because such items were advertised in urban publications but because they believed these goods would enhance the family and neighborhood sociability that was such an important part of their lives. But their consumption of goods designed, manufactured, advertised, and sold by urban businesspeople involved a degree of rural deference to urban standards.

The subtle shaping of the tastes of rural consumers was one of the more benign indications of growing urban cultural hegemony in the late nineteenth century. The urban definition of standards of value had a harder edge. Jeffersonian agrarianism suggested farmers were important mainly because of who they were—independent, hardworking people meeting elemental human needs in natural surroundings. But the more complex and sophisticated society of the late nineteenth century valued what people knew and what they did over who they were. It was no longer sufficient just to be a particular type of person or display admirable character traits. Increasingly, society's ideal was the educated professional possessing a specialized and esoteric body of knowledge.

To those whose paragon was the professional, the farmer was a drudge, pursuing an occupation demanding no special skill or training, only hard and thoughtless labor. Some within the agricultural community decried this negative image and sought to overcome it by making farming a profession that demanded education and rewarded intelligence. Supporters of the Morrill Land-Grant College Act and the Hatch Act were motivated in part by the desire to make agriculture a scientific endeavor practiced by educated professionals. But while they sought to redraw its unfavorable image, those who sought to professionalize farming unconsciously conceded the correctness of an urban standard of value.

Even the agrarian notion that farmers were more moral than others because of their independence and their contact with nature came under urban attack in the late nineteenth century. Novelists, such as Edgar Howe in his bitter *Story of a Country Town,* began to define rural morality as narrow and puritanical self-righteousness, and early social scientists questioned whether it existed at all.[7] In 1877, sociologist Richard Dugdale published *The Jukes,* a study of a rural New York family with a history of degeneracy reflected in illegitimacy, criminality, insanity, and retardation.[8] Others jumped on Dugdale's bandwagon, creating the inescapable impression that the countryside was filled with idiots, perverts, and throwbacks.

Of course, negative urban attitudes regarding rural people were as old as cities themselves, and the hegemonic role of cities in defining American culture could be seen well before the Civil War. But while urban attitudes toward country cousins had been patronizing or gently mocking before, they now seemed almost savage. Increasingly, such derogatory labels as hick, rube, and yokel became regular parts of public discourse about people who were defined as distinctly—and perhaps dangerously—inferior. We cannot know how all of this affected rural people. But we do know that they were surrounded by messages of urban superiority, some subtle and others blatant. It is reasonable to hypothesize that sensitive rural people picked up on these urban cultural cues, imbibing a sense of their own inferiority and perhaps developing self-contempt in the process.

Economic changes in agriculture in a more commercial and industrial milieu are easier to delineate than subtle alterations in the rural self-image. As farmers became more oriented to the market and as the market became more accessible, regional production patterns changed. During the 1880s, when the flood of wheat from the Great Plains made their profits precarious, Dave Wood and his Trempealeau County neighbors switched to dairy farming, which was harder work but provided more dependable returns.[9] In the lower Midwest, farmers switched out of wheat and into corn-and-hog production.

Farmers in the South devoted more acres to the cotton that fed the looms—and satisfied lien holders—and fewer to the corn and pork that fed their families. In New England and the Middle Atlantic states producers continued to deemphasize small grains and livestock in favor of dairy products, fruits, and vegetables for the local urban markets.

Even as they became more commercial, farmers struggled to fulfill as many of their needs on the farm as they could with the finite resources at their disposal. On their farm near Bellefontaine, Ohio, to cite a typical instance, the Gebbys grew a stunning variety of berries, fruits, and vegetables, preserving what they did not eat fresh.[10] For example, they ate apples fresh and in pies and turned the surplus into sweet cider, vinegar, and apple butter for the winter table. They kept their own cattle, swine, and poultry and butchered and preserved their own hogs, sometimes in cooperation with neighbors. In common with most farm women, Margaret Gebby was mainly responsible for these endeavors, as well as for home manufacturing and for the preparation and sale of butter and eggs. In 1888, her butter and egg receipts composed more than 20 percent of the Gebby family income. Clearly, urban cultural hegemony was not so powerful as to turn the Margaret Gebbys of the world into rural imitations of contemporary middle-class city women living in conformity to the ideal of domesticity.

Farmers like the Gebbys were wise to stress the safety-first principles that had guided their ancestors, because in their commercial lives agriculturalists were increasingly vulnerable to economic problems. Some of these were new. Glucose and oleomargarine produced by modern chemistry threatened the livelihoods of sugar and dairy producers, for example, and the rise of the monopolistic American Tobacco Company confronted small growers with an unjust exchange relationship. But most farmers' problems were traditional ones that became more onerous with increasing commercialization. Virtually all late-nineteenth-century farmers suffered to a greater or lesser degree from the three Ms—markets, middlemen, and money.

The market was at once benefit and bane to commercial producers. Without it families' standards of living would not have advanced in the way they wanted. But as they became more dependent on the market, they became more vulnerable to its fluctuations. One hundred years ago American farmers operated on a world market, in which prices fluctuated, sometimes wildly, with alterations in supply. The demand for most basic agricultural commodities remains relatively steady, regardless of changes in supply.

Bread is an important part of most people's diets, and they will consume about the same amount when it is two dollars a loaf as when it costs one dollar. This reality means that a shortfall in the supply of wheat or some other basic commodity will result in a disproportionate price increase, while an oversupply will result in a disproportionate decrease in prices. As a general rule, the trend in agricultural supplies in the late nineteenth century was up, and the trend in prices was down. American cotton producers, as we have seen, faced growing competition from Asians, Africans, and Latin Americans, and cattle ranchers and wheat farmers in Canada, Australia, Argentina, and Russia dumped growing quantities on the same markets their contemporaries from the Great Plains were serving.

To control world production and thus world market prices was impossible. To control domestic production and the domestic market was impractical. As a debtor nation, the United States needed to sell commodities on the world market at whatever price they would bring in order to maintain a favorable balance of trade. To attempt to limit production or to inflate domestic prices through crop loan rates or tariffs would have been economic suicide. In theory, farmers might have been able to control production, but they were too numerous and individualistic to organize, and few would risk cutting output for fear that their fellows here or abroad would increase theirs to gain a temporary advantage.

The nature of farming itself aggravated the marketing problem. The economic integration of the nation and the world meant that commodity producers lost once stable local markets. The absence of substantial on-farm storage facilities meant that farmers had no practical alternative to marketing at harvest, when prices were lowest. And the relative ease with which farmers could shift from crop to crop in response to market forces meant that diversification was no more than a temporary solution.

Then there was the problem of middlemen. As small and unorganized producers, farmers found themselves in an unfavorable position relative to many of those with whom they did business. Others had the ability to set both the prices farmers paid and the prices they received. Farmers took what the cotton factor or elevator manager or commission merchant offered, and they paid what the railroad and the merchant and the manufacturer charged. For farmers, the stick had two short ends.

The money problem was the third of this terrible triumvirate. Commercial farmers borrowed money long term to buy land and make capital improvements, and they borrowed it short term to get from planting to harvest. There was a worldwide shortage of capital in the late nineteenth century. The money supply did not keep pace with economic activity, resulting in rising value of money or falling price of goods, however one wants to look at it. Adding to the cost of money in this country was the lack of a national banking system with the flexibility to move money from where it was to where it was needed quickly and cheaply. As a general rule, the farther one was from New York, the country's major capital market, the more one paid for money. What all of this added up to was high real interest rates. Ten percent was common on the Great Plains. Those borrowing from southern merchants sometimes paid 40 percent or more. Forty percent is a high rate under almost any circumstances. Ten percent could be reasonable if prices were inflating at 5 percent per year, but with prices deflating by that much or more, it was a great burden to bear. The late nineteenth century was a bad time to be in debt.

COMMERCIAL FARMERS' PROTEST

Farmers responded to the problems that accompanied commercialization as individuals, but they also banded together to cope with the challenges of markets, middlemen, and money. The first of the important protest groups of the late nineteenth century was the Patrons of Husbandry, more commonly referred to as the Grange.

The Patrons of Husbandry was founded in 1867 by Oliver Hudson Kelley, a Minnesotan who was convinced that the major problems of farm life were boredom and the absence of social and intellectual stimulation. As Kelley conceived it, the Grange was to serve as a social center for the rural community, providing educational and recreational programs. Reflecting this purpose, Kelley's Grange was a family organization, in which women played a prominent, if not exactly equal, role. The Grange grew slowly until the Depression of 1873, when hard-pressed farmers and rural merchants poured into the organization. As its membership swelled to perhaps as many as 750 thousand by 1874, its original mission of enhancing rural family and social life was supplemented by the goal of devising solutions for the problems of commercial agriculture. Grangers understandably believed that the maintenance of a strong rural family and society was intimately related to the economic health of agriculture.

The depression-era Grange focused on problems with middlemen and money. In the Ohio and Upper Mississippi Valleys, where the organization was strongest, Grangers pressed state legislatures to aid small shippers by regulating railroad rates and ending such discriminatory practices as rebates to major customers and higher rates in areas where there was no competition. Railroad regulation on the state level was achieved in many places, but it was not as satisfactory as the Grangers had hoped. State regulators were few, and enforcement was often lax. Moreover, many doubted that it was constitutional for states to regulate commerce that was interstate in nature. In the 1876 case of *Munn v. Illinois,* the Supreme Court suggested that they could, but in the *Wabash* case ten years later it reversed itself, concluding that the regulation of interstate commerce was exclusively the prerogative of Congress. In 1887 Congress partially filled the void by passing the Interstate Commerce Act, which provided some minimal regulation of railroads.

The Grangers could not do without the railroads, but they believed they could do without other middlemen. Grangers formed cooperatives to buy and even produce the products they bought and process the products they sold. They also created cooperative banks and insurance companies to meet their financial needs. While there were individual success stories, as a general rule Grange cooperatives failed. They tended to be insufficiently capitalized and poorly managed. Lending institutions distrusted them, experienced managers shunned them, and established businesses competed with them vigorously and, many Grangers believed, unfairly. The major problem was often insufficient loyalty on the part of cooperative members. Willing to patronize private businesses that lowered prices temporarily, Grangers undercut the entities that promised to release them from thralldom to middlemen.

Grangers attacked the farmers' money problems mainly by promoting inflation, the debtors' friend. During the 1870s inflationists favored maintaining and even expanding the supply of greenbacks, paper money printed by the government during the Civil War as an expedient to help pay for the conflict. Greenbacks carried the implicit promise of redemption in gold or silver, and when redemption began during Ulysses Grant's administration the inflationary feature of the paper money was sharply minimized. Frightened by the dramatic deflation that accompanied the depression of 1873, Congress suspended redemption and increased the supply of greenbacks by a little less than 5 percent, to $400 million. Redemption was resumed in 1875, however, and the inflationary value of the greenbacks was again largely lost. Struggling for greenbacks led Grangers into political action, in the established parties and in a Greenback party established specifically to promote inflation through paper money.

The Grange was in decline by the late 1870s, undone by the failure of its economic and political program and the return of better conditions to the rural economy. Farmers tend to be individualistic people, and many could see no compelling need to remain in an organization of economic and political reform when the conditions that had promoted their original membership changed. As those who defined the Patrons of Husbandry mainly in economic and political terms drifted away, the organization reemphasized its original social and educational purposes. Today it remains an important social organization in rural communities throughout the United States and a part of the conservative farm lobby in Washington.

Commodity agricultural production was a boom and bust enterprise a century ago, and by the mid-1880s hard times again beset many farmers. This time the Alliance movement became their favored vehicle for protest and redress of grievances. The Farmers' Alliance was less a well-organized and unitary movement than three separate ones. The Northern Alliance, founded by Chicago farm editor Milton George, bore many similarities to the Grange. It accepted most of the principles of the older organization, with the major exception that it embraced public ownership of railroads rather than regulation. Like the Grange, the Northern Alliance was a nonsecret, inclusive organization which nonfarmers were free to join. In local areas the Alliance often allied with nonfarm groups such as the Knights of Labor in political activities. When hard times hit the wheat growers of the Great Plains in the late 1880s, they flocked into the Northern Alliance.

More interesting and innovative in some ways was the Southern Farmers' Alliance, centered in Texas and the Southwest. Farm journalist C. W. McCune, who founded the Southern Alliance, recognized that people wanted more from an organization than mere formulation and advocacy of agricultural policy. Consequently, he devised a farm organization that had many of the characteristics of a fraternity or a lodge, including initiation ceremonies, secret rituals, and so forth. The Southern Alliance thus fulfilled an important social function, and the picnics and public meetings it held often had the revivalist ambience with which its largely evangelical Protestant membership was familiar and comfortable. Also befitting a fraternal organization, the Southern Alliance was exclusive. Only farmers could be members, and only white farmers at that. The Colored Farmers' Alliance soon developed in the Southwest to serve blacks excluded from the Southern Alliance.

The founders of the Southern Alliance expected its fraternalism to be functional in its economic program. McCune and his colleagues envisioned a cooperative structure of sufficient wealth and strength to allow small farmers to escape the clutches of furnishing merchants who paid minimum prices for their cotton and charged usurious rates for the goods farmers had to borrow. The problem with the cooperative structure the Southern Alliance created was not that it lacked elan or the support of farmers. It lacked capital. The sad reality was that people who spent their lives in debt to crossroads merchants could not generate the capital necessary to escape those local capitalists.

The failure of self-help led the Southern Alliance to search for political solutions to the problems of small farmers. The main product of that effort was the Sub-Treasury Plan, which addressed the farmers' marketing, middleman, and money problems. This proposal envisioned a system of government warehouses in counties where more than $200 thousand worth of agricultural produce was marketed annually. At harvest, the farmer would have the option of depositing his crop at the Sub-Treasury in return for a loan, in federal notes, worth 80 percent of its current market value. At any time during the ensuing year, the farmer could redeem his crop by repaying the loan and paying a small fee for storage, handling, and interest. If he failed to redeem the crop and retire the loan, the government would take the stored produce to satisfy his obligation.

To McCune and other Southern Alliance members, the Sub-Treasury Plan was a panacea that promised to solve all the farmers' problems. It would let farmers market their crops when prices were favorable rather than when low. It would allow them to get credit while avoiding the high interest charges of bankers and furnishing merchants. And, by pumping paper money into the economy, it would inflate prices. To most contemporary policy makers, however, the Sub-Treasury Plan seemed paternalistic, bureaucratic, and expensive and represented an unprecedented and disturbing kind of federal involvement in local affairs. Still, it was an imaginative and prescient idea. The Commodity Credit Corporation, a New Deal agency that supported farm prices through loan rates, was based largely on the Sub-Treasury idea (see chapter 10).

Like the Grange before it, the alliance soon found it necessary to partici-

158

pate in partisan politics. In 1890 the Southern Alliance, which was spreading rapidly eastward from its Texas base, endorsed Democratic congressional candidates willing to support its program. Alliance members on the Plains formed independent parties, usually called the Peoples party or the Populists. Both strategies resulted in impressive electoral victories, but by 1892 disappointment with unresponsive Democratic endorsees led most Southern Alliance leaders to embrace the idea of a farmers' political organization divorced from the old parties.

The national Populist party held its first convention in Omaha, Nebraska, in 1892. The Populists wrote a broadly reformist platform that included a number of planks of general reform as well as others directed at solving farmers' problems. The Populists saw themselves speaking for all those oppressed by industrial capitalism, not just farmers, and the Omaha platform reflected that expansive self-image. Iowan James B. Weaver, once a presidential candidate of the Grange-supported Greenback party, was picked as the Populist standard-bearer.

The Populist campaign of 1892 was enthusiastic and exciting. Rallies, which often had a strongly evangelistic style, attracted people from miles around. While the old parties were exclusively male in most areas, the Populists had a family flavor, befitting their role as saviors of the embattled family farm. Women and children were prominently represented at Populist gatherings, and such female orators as Mary Elizabeth Lease and Annie Diggs were featured speakers, shocking conservatives who believed women should play no public role.

The message of the Populists blended economic discontent with social resentments of people who felt the sting of urban contempt. The Populists were agrarian fundamentalists who argued that, as producers of elemental goods and fillers of basic needs, they were superior to those who manipulated money and produced nothing. But instead of dominating the nation and enjoying living standards justified by their hard and important labor, the farmers were themselves dominated by crafty monopolists and ignored by corrupt politicians. The Populists promised a return to the nation's Jeffersonian foundations, when people were supposedly valued for who they were and what they contributed to society, not for how much money they had.

The Populists' showing was impressive, especially in light of the fact that they were poorly financed and faced a vigorous and often unprincipled opposition. They overcame Republican ridicule in the West and Democratic fraud and violence in the South to pile up over one million popular votes, out of about nine million cast, and twenty-two electoral votes. Populist momentum carried over to the congressional elections of 1894, when candidates of the farmers' party garnered nearly 1.5 million votes and were particularly strong in the South.

These successes partially obscured serious Populist weaknesses. One of these was disunity. In such northern states as Kansas and North Dakota former Republicans in the party complained that it had been taken over by former Democrats, and in the South the alliance between black and white Populists, tenuous at best, was fraying. A more serious problem was that of limited appeal. The Populists ran well in areas where commodity producers were suffering, but they had virtually no appeal in cities, among industrial workers, or even among prosperous farmers. There were enough suffering farmers around that the Populists could represent a substantial minority position, but in a system in which congressional representation is not divided in proportion to votes and in which electoral votes are cast on a winner-take-all basis, minority parties have no power, only frustration.

Part of the reason for the Populists' limited appeal was that, regardless of the breadth of the Omaha platform, they quickly became a one-issue party, embracing inflation through monetization and coinage of silver. The growing preoccupation with silver was understandable. First, it was easy for debtors to see how inflation would help them, and silver seemed a reasonable way of inflating prices and a more legitimate way than greenbacks had been, given the fact that silver had been monetized through most of the nation's history. Second, a large portion of the Populist electorate was more interested in silver than in any other portion of the platform. Indeed, in 1892 most of Weaver's electoral votes had come from Colorado, Idaho, and Nevada, silver states all. Third, Populist campaigns were bankrolled largely by the silver-mining industry. In America, those who pay the piper call the political tune, even when the tune has a reformist beat.

There was nothing irrational, and certainly nothing immoral, about the Populist embrace of silver. Parties are supposed to respond to the wants and needs of those who support them. However, the Populist obsession with silver did indicate that this party lacked a complete or sophisticated understanding of the situation confronting commercial agriculturalists. Their radical rhetoric, combining republican and Christian values in a potentially volatile mixture, promised something more exciting than silver could deliver. Moreover, as the Populists became a more narrowly focused, one-issue party, the likelihood that they would be taken over by one of the major parties increased.

That is precisely what happened. In 1896, the Democrats wrote a platform endorsing the free and unlimited coinage of silver at the ratio of sixteen ounces to one ounce of gold. The Populists confronted an unhappy dilemma. They could continue to exist as an independent political party, but they faced the certainty of a crushing defeat and the probability that they would be blamed if the Democratic standard-bearer, William Jennings Bryan, was beaten. On the other hand, if they fused with the Democrats, whose platform was unattractive aside from the silver plank, they would almost certainly cease to exist as an independent political entity. Southern Populists, who had suffered fraud, intimidation, and violence from the unscrupulous Democrats, were especially loath to rejoin their literally mortal foes. But in the end there was not much of a choice. The Populists endorsed Bryan and nominated Georgian Tom Watson for the vice presidency as a token of their independence. Bryan lost anyway, and the Populists ceased to exist as a significant political organization.

The Populists were the first and last major farmers' political party. Their failure to capture the presidency showed that farmers—or at least unhappy ones—had neither the numbers nor the cohesiveness required to control the government. But the demise of Populism did not mark the end of politically active farm organizations, nor did it end the debate over the nature and source of farmers' problems. The heirs of the Grange and the Alliance movement and the Populists continued to believe that the source of the farmers' economic difficulties lay outside agriculture and that government action was required to rectify the situation. In the years after Populism's demise such organizations as the American Society of Equity and especially the Farmers Union, founded in 1902 in Texas and strong thereafter in the Southwest and on the Plains, continued to keep the Populist faith. And conservatives continued to believe that the farmers were the authors of their own problems and that they could advance by becoming better businesspeople and more skilled producers. The lines drawn in the late nineteenth century remain clear in the rural community today, as clear as the section lines drawn by surveyors a century ago.

EIGHT

Prosperity
and Its Discontents

The first two decades of the twentieth century represented a time of such rare prosperity for American farmers that the period is referred to as the golden age of agriculture. During this twenty-year period, gross farm income more than doubled, and the value of the average farm more than tripled. The contrast between the golden age and the periods preceding and succeeding it, when economic hardship and political discontent were all too frequently the farmer's lot, could not have been more stark.

Rural people responded to prosperity in predictable ways. They participated more enthusiastically in the market, emphasizing commercial products to the neglect of those providing family self-sufficiency. The United States Department of Agriculture estimated in 1920 that the average farm family produced only 40 percent of what it consumed, down from 60 percent twenty years earlier.

Farmers put some of their profits into improving their operations. They purchased machinery, land, fertilizer, and purebred livestock and built improved barns and silos. They made their homes more liveable for their families. They purchased more carpets, drapes, wallpaper, and furniture. They installed pumps in their houses and sometimes plumbing and electricity as well. They enriched their lives by putting in telephones and purchasing automobiles. And they improved their neighborhoods. They upgraded roads, improved schools and churches, hired better-trained ministers and teachers, and sometimes sent their children to high school and even to college.

The signs of rural prosperity were impressive but misleading. Urban material standards remained much higher, urban institutions were judged far superior, and urban life was reckoned far richer. Rural young people continued to vote with their feet, moving to town regardless of prosperity in the countryside. Those who did not leave lusted after automobiles that allowed them to escape the farm even for brief periods.

The early twentieth century was remarkable not just for agricultural prosperity but also for the high level of urban interest in agriculture and rural life during the period. The first two decades of the century witnessed a flourishing Country Life Movement, composed of urban-based educators, ministers, social and agricultural scientists, bureaucrats, and policy makers who aimed at renovating rural society in such a way as to make it more satisfying to rural people and more beneficial to the nation and at reforming agriculture in order to make it more efficient and productive.

The golden age of agriculture and the struggle of the Country Life Movement to redefine, redirect, and reform agriculture and rural life both reached a climax during World War I. Farmers emerged from that experience in a vulnerable economic position but more fully integrated into American society and its interest-group-oriented political system than they had ever been before.

THE GOLDEN AGE OF AGRICULTURE

Agricultural prosperity characterized the golden age. Farmers generally did well, both in absolute terms and relative to urban wage earners. Gross farm income doubled between 1900 and 1920, while real farm income (gross income adjusted for inflation) increased by 40 percent. Farmers expected prosperity to continue. The value of the average farm—which remained smaller than 150 acres throughout the period—tripled over the first twenty years of the century. This was an index of expectations for the future as well as a matter of substantial tangible importance to farmers, who anticipated that their relatively low incomes would be supplemented by the increase in the value of their property. The farmer, it is often said, has only one real payday—when he sells his farm.

The prosperity of agriculture played a role in attracting urban people to it.

A substantial number of organized colonization ventures were launched. The Salvation Army created several farm colonies for unemployed urbanites in the West, basing its agrarianism on the premise that life in the countryside would allow its clients both to feed themselves and to reconstruct their characters. Jewish philanthropic agencies, especially the Baron de Hirsch Fund, settled Eastern European Jews in agricultural colonies throughout the United States, reasoning in part that dispersion of Jews in nonurban areas would slow the rise of anti-Semitism in America. Others urged a return of urbanites to the land, mainly on economic grounds. In 1907 Bolton Hall, a Malthusian (a follower of Thomas Malthus, the early-nineteenth-century British economist who believed that population growth would inevitably outstrip increases in food supplies), wrote a book entitled *Three Acres and Liberty,* in which he argued that urban refugees could live comfortably on small agricultural plots.[1] His ideas spurred a number of individual and communal experiments, most notably at San Ysidro, California, where urban colonists mixed small-unit agriculture with employment in light manufacturing. Henry Ford, the eccentric automaker, was another enthusiast who saw promise in a future of decentralized communities feeding themselves through farming and generating income through local industry.

The belief of Hall and other back-to-the-landers that population was outrunning increases in food production appeared to be correct. Agricultural prosperity in the early years of the twentieth century was due mainly to an imbalance between supply and demand. Through most of American history agricultural output had increased mainly because more fertile land was brought into production. As we saw in chapter 7, the amount of land in farms more than doubled between 1870 and 1900, and the production of the major American agricultural staples advanced apace. By 1900, though, most of the best agricultural land in the United States was already producing, and over the next twenty years the acreage in farms increased by only 12 percent. Moreover, much of this land was in the arid High Plains, the Great Basin of Nevada and Idaho, the Oregon desert, cutover timber lands in the Great Lakes region, and other marginal areas.

Compounding the difficulty caused by fewer acres being added to the national agricultural domain was sluggish farmer productivity. Between 1900 and 1910, agricultural productivity barely budged, and for the entire twenty-year period it advanced at less than 1 percent per year. The result was an increase in agricultural production of only 30 percent between 1900 and

1920, while the population of the country rose by 40 percent. Inevitably, farm prices rose faster than the general price level, and farmers claimed a bigger piece of the economic pie.

American farmers were able to prosper in part because what was happening here was being duplicated in much of the rest of the world. In South America, Canada, Russia, Australia, and Africa the dramatic agricultural expansion of the last third of the nineteenth century slowed perceptibly. The result was that the world market became the friend of American farmers, for a change. The volume of American exports remained basically flat between 1900 and 1920, yet their value nearly quadrupled.

From the standpoint of profit maximization, farmers should have plowed money back into their operations, but until the frothy days of World War I reinvestment levels were not impressive. Few farmers expanded, meaning that average farm size barely changed, and they were reluctant to mechanize, buy purebred stock, or otherwise upgrade their businesses. Risk-averse farmers remembered the periodic hard times of the late nineteenth century and avoided behaviors that might harm them when periods of economic difficulty returned. Those who forgot hard times often paid a high price for their amnesia.

Farmers in the golden age did spend money, especially on improvements in their communities and their homes. Rural people taxed themselves to upgrade their schools. One-room schools proliferated as more people in the countryside concluded they could afford a school close by. By 1910 there were over 210 thousand one-room schools in the United States. Farmers hired more fully trained teachers, and they painted their schools, installed new privies, and purchased blackboards, maps, and desks. Those committed to providing further education for their children could now afford to do so more readily. Attending high school was a hardship, because children usually had to board in town, creating a financial burden on the family and depriving it of valuable labor. But more began attending high school, and some even enrolled in college.

Other important indications of the relative prosperity of the golden age included improvements in the farm home. Rural people purchased more furnishings, kitchen devices, specialty food items, and other goods they believed would make their lives richer, easier, and more modern. They made their homes more convenient. A common improvement involved putting a hand pump in the kitchen, usually connected to a cistern, ending the onerous and seemingly endless woman's task of carrying buckets of water from a pump or well in the yard into the house. They built privies if they did not have them, or improved them if they did, and began screening doors and windows to limit the number of flies and other insects in the house.

One popular improvement adopted by many farmers was telephone service, provided by hundreds of tiny companies, frequently locally owned cooperatives. The telephone was attractive because it diminished isolation, facilitating rural visiting and allowing help to be summoned in the event of an emergency. But it also proved to be an entertainment medium for the people along the line who listened in whenever one neighbor called another.

Far and away the most popular acquisition for rural people in the golden age was the automobile. In 1900 there were only a few thousand automobiles in the entire nation, most of them the playthings of wealthy hobbyists. By 1920 there were nearly two and a half million cars in the countryside alone, and over 30 percent of farmers owned at least one.

The Model T Ford was the farmer's car until the 1920s. Henry Ford, a farm boy himself, shrewdly designed and marketed the Model T with rural pocketbooks and problems in mind. It was inexpensive enough—about $240 in the early twenties—that farm people could afford it, and simple enough that rural tinkerers could repair it themselves cheaply. Moreover, its tight turning radius, high center of gravity, and light weight made it attractive to people on unimproved rural roads that were often narrow, rutted, and muddy. Farmers' fealty to the Model T waned in the 1920s, when General Motors offered annual model changes, color choices, and pay-as-you-drive financing. The progressive abandonment of the farmer's car by the farmers was a significant indication of their decreased willingness to be set apart culturally and materially from urban people.

Automobiles were attractive to farmers in part because they made work easier. If a plowshare or reaper cog broke, the car allowed the farmer to get to town quickly for a replacement. Trucks, which became an increasingly prominent feature of life in the country during and after World War I, facilitated marketing of produce. Moreover, ingenious farmers and automobile manufacturers devised a variety of ways in which internal combustion engines could be used for farm tasks, such as sawing wood, washing clothes, and even pulling plows.

But the automobile was mainly attractive as a device for leisure and play. It became an entertainment medium for families, and the Sunday drive quickly developed as a rural institution. The automobile allowed people to visit friends and participate in community social life more easily and made it possible for them to go beyond local villages and towns for recreation, cultural enrichment, and shopping. Young people discovered that the automobile revolutionized courtship by allowing them to escape the prying eyes and wagging tongues of neighbors, by affording them a degree of privacy the horse and buggy did not provide, and by widening the range of their acquaintances.

Automobiles widened the rural world in other ways as well. Advocacy of road improvements involved farmers in competition with other interest groups, especially on the state level, broadening their horizons and increasing their political sophistication in the process. And automobiles made it easier for schools and churches to be consolidated and for farm children to attend high schools while living at home.

But rural communities often paid a price for increased automobility. Village merchants complained that their customers stopped patronizing them, preferring to shop in larger and more distant towns, and ministers argued that the Sunday drive was too often taken in lieu of attendance at services. The automobile accelerated the process whereby leisure became increasingly a private individual or family matter, thereby potentially diminishing community cohesion. Perhaps most significant, automobiles represented a major drain on rural finances, especially in marginal areas. In Lee County, South Carolina, in 1920, for example, the investment in automobiles was four times the capital stock of the banks, and it took one-third of the value of the cotton crop just to service and fuel the cars. Obviously, expenditures of this magnitude limited the ability of farmers to enhance their local institutions, upgrade their farm operations, or improve their homes.

Regardless of whether expenditures on automobiles were the wisest investments rural people could make, their ability to assume such substantial financial burdens clearly demonstrated the relative prosperity of agriculture during the golden age. But prosperity was always limited by the realities of country living. Rural people might aspire to live like middle-class urbanites, but that goal remained beyond their grasp. The farm family might put a pump in the house, but it was unlikely to have indoor plumbing or a water heater. Because central-station power was unavailable, electricity was a rarity in the countryside, effectively denying farm families a whole range of devices that made urban living easier and more convenient. Even the material possessions rural people acquired reminded them of how far behind they were, planting the seeds of discontent in their souls.

The sober fact was that even in the golden age the economic, technological, and public-policy realities under which the nation and its farmers lived decreed that there would be a gap between rural and urban standards of living. But there was no gap in expectations, and rising rural expectations that could not be met was a sure prescription for frustration, discontent, and an active desire to leave the countryside for the cities.

THE COUNTRY LIFE MOVEMENT

The golden age of agriculture was remarkable for more than the level of agricultural prosperity it witnessed. This was also a period in which urbanites devoted unprecedented attention to rural developments and problems. Concern both with rural life and institutions and with the economic behavior and performance of farmers was reflected in what was called the Country Life Movement.

The origins of the Country Life Movement lay in the growing apprehension of urban-based educators, religious leaders, social scientists, philanthropists, and other public figures regarding the rapid ascendancy of urban America and the apparent tendency of the smartest and most promising young people in the countryside to move to cities. Country Life reformers recognized that the United States was becoming an urban nation, and they believed that urban-to-rural migration refreshed and improved cities and the nation as a whole. But they were concerned that so many bright people were leaving the countryside that it would become blighted, with severe consequences for the nation.

These socially oriented Country Lifers believed that intelligent and ambitious people left the countryside because of urban cultural hegemony and unsatisfactory rural living standards and social institutions. Cities represented a style of living, a level of cultural advancement and intellectual stimulation, and a concentration of recreational and social resources—such as the theater, libraries, schools, churches, and so forth—that sowed rural discontent and seduced rural migrants. Exacerbating this problem was the dullness and stultification of rural life and the reluctance of rural people to develop social institutions and resources that would satisfy bright young men and women. If rural society and living were not enlivened and reformed, these people believed, then the countryside would eventually be populated mainly by ignorant and inefficient people, and the nation would no longer have that vital rural pool of potential leaders in business and public life on which it had always drawn.

Also uneasy about an ignorant and inefficient rural population and the implications of that situation for the nation was a more economically oriented group of Country Life reformers. Bureaucrats, businesspeople, and agricultural scientists were among those who worried that low agricultural productivity, while not necessarily harmful to farmers, was ominous for the country. The golden age was positive for farmers, but consumers complained that food prices rose faster than wages and had become a main component of the high cost of living.

The high cost of living was a problem because the United States was historically a cheap-food country. Cheap food meant that working people lived relatively well, that their wages could be kept in check, and that, consequently, the price of American exports could be kept competitive. Should population growth continue to outstrip increases in agricultural production, people would live less abundantly, labor unrest would become a more serious threat, and American industrial exports might be priced out of the market.

An inefficient and unproductive agriculture threatened more than just industrial exports. Eventually, American farmers would be squeezed out of world markets by more efficient competitors. That would be a serious blow to the country. The United States was a debtor nation before World War I. We needed to export more than we imported in order to generate the gold and foreign exchange we required to meet our obligations to foreign lenders, and we traditionally enjoyed a healthy trade surplus in agricultural products. Should that situation come to an end, we would have difficulty meeting our obligations, making capital flight and economic collapse distinct possibilities. Economically oriented Country Lifers did not begrudge farmers their prosperity. But they believed that the nation would be imperiled if that prosperity continued to be rooted in low productive efficiency.

Country Life reformers received a major boost in 1907, when President Theodore Roosevelt created a Country Life Commission to study rural problems and recommend solutions. The chair of the Country Life Commission was Liberty Hyde Bailey, a Cornell University horticulturist who had long been concerned with revitalizing rural institutions as a means of slowing the cityward population drift. Other important commission members included

Kenyon L. Butterfield, generally acknowledged to be the father of the academic discipline of rural sociology, Gifford Pinchot, chief forester of the United States and a well-known expert on economic efficiency, and Henry Wallace, the editor of *Wallace's Farmer* and the father and grandfather of future secretaries of agriculture.

The Country Life Commission traveled extensively, taking testimony from hundreds of witnesses and collecting surveys from thousands more. In its 1909 report, the commission cataloged an array of social and economic problems and concluded that "better farming, better living, and better business" were needed if rural Americans were to keep pace with their increasingly sophisticated urban cousins and to continue to make important contributions to the United States.[2] Specifically, the commission called on rural people to beautify their homes and make them more convenient. It argued that the rural church should be reenergized and redirected and that rural schools should be reformed. And it warned that farmers had to become more efficient producers and marketers of food and fiber if they and the nation were to prosper in the long run.

The very existence of the Country Life Commission lent legitimacy to the Country Life reformers, and its report structured and focused their many concerns. While the movement had many suggestions for rural social revival and economic reform, it tended to concentrate on education. Of the existing social institutions in the countryside, none drew as much attention from reformers as the school. The school was a crucial agency in the effort to reform rural life for several reasons. First, most rural people had children in schools, and schools were important social institutions in most rural communities. Second, the schools dealt with children, who were more pliable than adults. To truly endure, changes in rural society had to begin with children. Finally, because they appropriated money and set curricular and instructional standards, state governments could influence schools in ways they could not influence other institutions. Churches, by contrast, were also important to rural people, but they were self-directive and could not be influenced easily by outsiders.

Reformers suggested that rural schools be substantially redirected. They believed that a curriculum stressing the basics of literacy, numeracy, history, and civics was simply too narrow. Music, art, physical education, and other subjects that had enriched—or diluted—the urban curriculum were sug-

170 gested to make rural schools livelier and more interesting places. Schools with richer curricula would presumably stimulate intelligent young people, holding them in the countryside.

Country Lifers also thought the curriculum should be made more relevant to agriculture and rural life. Liberty Hyde Bailey favored nature study as a means of helping children understand and appreciate country living, but most reformers championed more practical courses in vocational agriculture and home economics, or domestic science, as it was often called. Such courses would not only enhance students' appreciation for farming and homemaking as honorable and even sophisticated professions but might lead them to carry better practices home, thereby influencing their parents. The practicality of vocational agriculture and domestic science led Congress to pass the Smith-Hughes Act in 1917, offering federal aid to schools initiating such courses of study.

Such substantial curricular revisions as Country Lifers envisioned would necessarily involve considerable reorganization. Schools would have to hire more professional supervisors and teachers trained in the new subjects. Most reformers favored the consolidated school, created by uniting several one-room school districts. Consolidated districts would have wider tax bases, facilitating the hiring of better qualified teachers who were specialists in their subject areas. Consolidated schools could be graded on the basis of age and skill levels, which reformers considered to be a more efficient educational organization than that of the ungraded one-room school. And consolidated schools could be better insulated than one-room schools from local patrons intent on directing the educational process.

School reformers were well-intentioned people who had the best interests of rural people at heart, or at least what they perceived those best interests to be. They believed that rural education had to be reformed if country people were to keep pace in an increasingly sophisticated nation and that farm people deserved better and more satisfying institutions. It was ironic that these reformers, who were concerned about the social effects of increasing urban cultural hegemony, usually took urban educational innovations as their models, but as a practical matter other workable modern guides were not available.

Rural people disappointed Country Lifers by demonstrating little enthusiasm for reshaping their schools in accordance with reformers' specifications. Part of the problem was that rural people became defensive when they

Morning roll call at a typical one-room schoolhouse, this one in Tyrol Township, Griggs County, North Dakota. Courtesy of the Myrtle Porterville Collection, North Dakota Institute for Regional Studies, Fargo, North Dakota.

or their institutions were criticized by outsiders, especially urban outsiders. Rural people did not agree that there was a crisis in their schools or even that there was anything very wrong with them. The schools did what they had always done, and that was what the patrons wanted. The curriculum was fine. Art and music were frills, and children could learn agriculture and homemaking on the farm. Rural people were especially wary of school consolidation. The one-room school was close physically and emotionally to the people of the neighborhood, who could control it and make it be what they wanted it to be. The consolidated school was a distant and somewhat forbidding institution. There, children would come in daily contact with people from other neighborhoods, with different religious beliefs, ethnic backgrounds, and values. And it would be so large and so distant that neighborhood patrons would have little influence over its operation. The one-room school was an educational agency, of course, but to rural people it was also a social institution that helped unite neighborhoods, uphold their values, and express their identities. They were reluctant to sacrifice an institution that provided such fundamental social benefits for one promising educational advances that were only potential.

Rural resistance did not stop reform; it only meant that reforms would come more slowly and be undertaken less voluntarily. Gradually, states set curricular requirements and minimum teacher qualifications that moved rural schools in the direction desired by Country Life reformers. By providing special financial inducements or by denying aid to schools under a certain size, states advanced the goal of consolidation. After 1920, declines in rural population and economic hardship made it difficult to maintain one-room schools in many areas. Still, consolidation proceeded at a glacial pace. Most rural people cherished their little local schools and were loath to give them up.

Those concerned about slow agricultural-productivity growth also focused on education, but not primarily in the schools. Reformers came to believe that productivity was stagnant not because the means of enhancing it did not exist but because the methods of disseminating new agricultural knowledge were deficient. The scientific bureaus of the United States Department of Agriculture, the land-grant colleges, and the state experiment stations had all been conducting research for some time. The big breakthroughs in agricultural science—hybrid corn, chemical pesticides, and advanced machinery, for example—all still lay in the future in the early years of the twentieth century. But publicly sponsored agricultural science had identified area-specific crop varieties, developed methods of increasing animal production, and formulated sound principles of crop rotation, fertilization, and cultivation that enhanced the productivity of the land and conserved topsoil. Had farmers used the scientific arsenal available to them, they would have been much more productive, but according to Secretary of Agriculture David Houston's estimate in 1913, only one-eighth of the land in the country was being farmed with reasonable efficiency.

The problem was conveying the knowledge effectively from where it was generated to where it was to be consumed. It appeared that abundant means of dissemination were available. Local agricultural societies and Granges existed in many places; most farmers took agricultural newspapers; and the county fair was an institution nearly everywhere. Moreover, the USDA and the state agricultural experiment stations printed and distributed bulletins, railroads sponsored seed, crop, and milk trains to encourage better methods, and virtually every state had a farmers' institute program through which experts carried the latest agricultural information to local gatherings of farmers. But the return on this substantial investment was disappointing. Farmers continued to scoff at book farming, embracing instead moon farming or some other traditional method.

The most promising new means of disseminating knowledge was agricultural extension, pioneered in Texas by Iowa scientist and entrepreneur Seaman Knapp beginning in 1902. The principle of Knapp's program was that extension personnel, or county agents, as they quickly came to be called, would work directly in the local community to upgrade agriculture. The agent would identify farmers who were willing to cooperate and would help them plant new crops and improve methods on their own lands. These innovations would then be demonstrated to neighbors. While other types of agricultural education involved telling and sometimes showing farmers what to do, Knapp's emphasized learning by doing on the farm. He assumed, correctly, that practical experience would be a more effective teacher than precept and that farmers' characteristic reluctance to innovate could be best overcome if they saw their neighbors innovating successfully.

Knapp's methods caught the attention of those hoping to reform agriculture. Extension was especially attractive to southerners, who saw it as a means of moving their region away from its overwhelming dependence on cotton. The desire to escape the tyranny of cotton became especially intense in the early years of the twentieth century, as the boll weevil—a beetle that lays its eggs in the bolls of cotton plants where its larvae can consume the fibers—spread slowly eastward through the cotton belt from Texas. The General Education Board, a Rockefeller-family philanthropy devoted to improving southern health and education, and the Rosenwald Fund, a rurally oriented philanthropy created by the head of Sears, Roebuck, provided financial support for extension. By 1910 white and black county agents were operating in every southern state (a separate Jim Crow extension structure was created to avoid offending racist sensibilities), and the program had been introduced in a few places in the North.

The popularity of extension in the South excited those who saw it as a potential means for reforming agriculture everywhere in the country. Bills were introduced in Congress calling for federal support, and in 1914 the Smith-Lever Act was passed into law. This legislation provided federal funds to hire county farm agents and home agents (female agents who worked with rural women) when those funds were matched by states and counties, each of which was to contribute one-third of the cost of maintaining agents. The program was to be headquartered at each state's land-grant college.

The Smith-Lever Act demonstrated the degree to which extension had captured the imagination of agricultural policy makers and reformers, but it was not welcomed by all farmers. One major problem was that few farmers had demanded the program. They resented the implication that they did not know how to farm, and they suspected that agents wanted them to produce more to drive down prices. In most areas, town chambers of commerce and commercial clubs were the main supporters of agents, increasing the distrust many farmers had for them.

When extension began to operate in rural areas it was not always relevant to farmers' problems and concerns. Many farm women were frustrated by the gender division of the program and the urban bias it reflected. Home agents focused on advancing such domestic skills as cooking, canning, clothing construction, and child rearing, while farm agents with information on crops and animals worked exclusively with men. This division reflected the belief of County Lifers and of some progressive farm women, such as those with leadership positions in the Grange, that rural women's lives should revolve around the home, but it was irritating to female farmers who played significant roles in the productive side of the farm business.

Even when agents had relevant information their success was not assured. Farmers had to be receptive to their advice and their suggestions, and such receptivity was not automatically or universally forthcoming. Moreover, it was easy for agents to fail among suspicious farmers. Bad advice or suggestions that did not work could devastate a county program. Agents also had to be sensitive to farmers' beliefs and feelings. The Minnesota agent delivering advice "while he sits in a livery rig" and the Ohio agent whose suggestions were "said in a patronizing way" were doomed to failure, and their failure might poison the program for years to come.[3] It was not easy being someone few people wanted, thrust into tight local communities that were often proud, insular, and distrustful of outsiders. Extension endured, because even with its problems it was the most effective means available for disseminating agricultural information, but it was far from the cure-all reformers sought for the agricultural productivity problem.

Country Life organizations remained active until the early 1940s, but as a broad-based movement Country Life reform faded after World War I. Because it was not rooted in the rural community it could not revolutionize rural life, but it did enjoy some successes, such as inducing incremental changes in rural education and helping agricultural extension become an important component in the agricultural policy apparatus.

The Country Life Movement was most significant for what its existence indicated about the evolving position of rural America in the nation. For most of the history of the country rural had been normal, and urban had been peculiar. The typical person was a farmer, the atypical person was not. According to American mythology, the farmer was the paragon of virtue and the backbone of the republic; those who did not farm were, in some way, deficient.

Now farmers had become peculiar. They were objects of concern. They drew the attention of altruistic reformers who suggested urban innovations for their institutions and solutions for their problems. The farmer had been transformed from paragon to problem, and rural America from backbone to backwater. Whatever its intentions and accomplishments, the Country Life Movement represented the diminished status and growing peripheralization of rural America.

The remarkable interest of policy makers and reformers in rural America during the golden age intensified when the United States entered World War I, in 1917. The government was especially anxious about the ability of agriculture to meet the heightened food and fiber needs that would accompany the war. Not only would Americans need at least as much to eat as they had before the war, given the reality that many in the service and working overtime in civilian pursuits would be burning more calories, but to the United States would also fall a large part of the burden of feeding British and French allies. Given the sluggish growth in agricultural productivity before the war, the government was not optimistic about the ability of farmers to meet these demands.

Congress addressed the problem of agricultural production in the early weeks of the war by passing the Food Production Act. This legislation provided a special appropriation to allow the placement of farm and home extension agents in every agricultural county, without regard to whether local communities wanted the program. It also granted the United States Department of Agriculture emergency authority to allocate seed, fertilizer, and other production goods that might be in short supply. The USDA used this authority in only a few instances.

A companion measure to the Food Production Act was the Food Control Act, which gave President Woodrow Wilson virtual dictatorial control over food. Wilson turned administration of this legislation over to a special emergency agency called the United States Food Administration. The Food Administration was headed by Herbert Hoover, a mining engineer who had made a name for himself by his efficient organization of food relief for Belgium after the Germans invaded that country in 1914. The Food Administration motto, Food Will Win the War, reflected the seriousness with which Hoover and his associates approached their task.

The Food Administration attempted to encourage food production and saving, allocate scarce supplies, and keep consumer prices within reason. Encouragement of food production and saving involved an impressive modern propaganda campaign. City people were urged to plant gardens and can fruits and vegetables, and farmers were asked to produce as much of everything as they could. Consumers were requested voluntarily to limit their consumption of certain foods by observing meatless Mondays and wheatless

Wednesdays and were urged to use substitutes for scarce items, such as honey or sorghum syrup for refined sugar. In some cases, Food Administration propaganda altered fashions and styles. Shorter skirts were justified as a means of saving cotton, for example, and Food Administration championship of slimness helped the trim female figure replace a more ample and matronly one as the American ideal.

Food saving was further advanced by the Food Administration's power over processing, retailing, and exporting. Processors and retailers of critical food items received licenses that limited what and how much they could handle and sell and the prices they could charge for it. Failure to comply with the provisions of the license could result in revocation of the right to do business. Exporters, too, received a license that strictly stipulated the buyer, price, and quantity involved for each international sale.

The Food Administration tried to ensure that consumers were not priced out of the market by setting the prices of a few basic commodities such as wheat, pork, and sugar. The affected farmers grumbled that their prices were capped while those of other producers were allowed to rise, but the prices—$2.20 for a bushel of wheat, for example—proved to be high enough to encourage production without working a severe hardship on consumers. The Food Administration also sought to ensure availability by punishing food hoarding.

In rural areas federal food legislation was largely enforced by county agents. Agents found seed, fertilizer, machinery, and scarce capital for farmers who could use such items to best advantage. In a situation of tight supplies of labor and high demands for labor, agents devoted much of their attention to finding workers. They advertised in distant towns for farm labor, issued "work or fight" orders threatening transients with the draft if they did not secure jobs on farms, and organized townspeople to help with harvests. In the South, Negro agents tried to dissuade black laborers and sharecroppers from moving to cities in search of wartime employment. Everywhere agents were called upon to sit on draft boards or to advise them regarding who should be deferred from the draft as essential farm labor. Their activities on draft boards indicated how difficult it was for agents to confine their activities to the agricultural economy. Actions dealing with labor, capital, and even the allocation of productive materials inevitably had social ramifications.

Agents' involvement in rural society was encouraged and intensified by the government. During the long debate that had preceded American entry into the war, midwestern and southern farmers had been unenthusiastic at best regarding the prospect of participation by the United States. Without the wholehearted support and cooperation of rural America, government officials believed, the war effort might be weak and unsuccessful. As they considered the need for social mobilization in rural America, officials naturally looked to county agents, the only federal employees in many areas, aside from postal workers. County agents were called on to aid the Committee on Public Information, a government propaganda agency, in its efforts to build enthusiasm for the war, and to help the Justice Department find seditionists and draft dodgers. Likewise, agents were required to play a leading role in the efforts of the Treasury Department to sell Liberty Bonds to finance the war, and they also commonly participated in the fund-raising endeavors of the American Red Cross, the YMCA, and other quasi-public agencies. Some agents were swept up in the excitement of emergency war work. It is hard to imagine, for example, that the South Dakota agents who organized vigilante "home guard" units to ferret out German sympathizers or the McPherson County, Kansas, agent who took it on himself to conduct classes for draftees on the meaning of the war had much time for agricultural work.[4]

The multiplication of their duties troubled some agents, and veterans of the Extension Service complained that many of their long-term programs had to be neglected during the emergency. Many called on supportive local groups for help. When the extension program was introduced in the North around 1910, agents often found that organizing local farmers and businesspeople who favored their work gave them a valuable base of support. When the Smith-Lever Act went into effect, some states required that such organizations, usually called farm bureaus, be organized in counties even before agents were assigned. With the onset of American participation in the war, farm bureau organization accelerated dramatically, especially outside the South.

Farm bureaus provided agents with significant help and support during the war. Bureau members enjoyed the opportunity to support what they saw as a valuable agricultural program and to contribute to their country's war effort. Farm bureau membership carried more tangible benefits as well. Bureau members believed, rightly or wrongly, that their support of extension made it more likely that their sons would be deferred as essential agricultural labor, that they would secure a bank loan they needed, or that they would get a necessary piece of farm equipment. Those outside of the bureaus believed the same thing, and they resented what they saw as government favoritism for some farmers to the detriment of others.

The divisions engendered by the agents and the farm bureaus were not the only ones facing rural America during World War I. Opposition to the war did not cease simply because the United States decided to participate, and many communities were split between proponents and opponents. German-Americans were especially likely to be against American participation, and divisions between them and their neighbors often became bitter and enduring.

Community problems frequently went beyond social divisions. Churches lost ministers to the military chaplaincy or to larger and more lucrative urban posts. Schools were disrupted. Teachers took better opportunities and sometimes could not be replaced. And school terms were made irregular by pressing labor demands. Shortened terms, sanctioned by states in the interest of winning the war, reversed a generation of progress in lengthening the school year.

The high level of physical mobility brought by the war was also disruptive. Hundreds of thousands of rural men entered an army that eventually numbered four million. Adding to the poignancy of their departure was the almost universal perception that they would not return to rural America even if they survived the war in the trenches. The popular song, "How Ya Gonna Keep 'Em Down on the Farm (After They've Seen Paree)"[5] expressed the belief that once the boys left they would never come back and reflected the self-contempt that was becoming a significant subtheme in rural life.

Part of the reason rural people lacked confidence in their ability to get their sons back was that their undrafted neighbors were leaving the countryside in droves. The urban economy boomed during the war, especially in those areas where defense industries were concentrated, and labor agents recruited aggressively in rural districts. For the first time, large numbers of southern black sharecroppers and laborers—as many as 500 thousand between 1916 and 1921—fled the region, especially for such midwestern and eastern cities as Chicago, Detroit, Cleveland, Pittsburgh, Philadelphia, and New York. Their move was difficult. Not only did they find that racial discrimination was more of a factor of northern life than they had hoped, but they also faced the challenge of developing habits and behaviors appropriate for urban living. But they persevered, becoming the first link in a chain of southern black migration that would continue for more than a generation. The migration of some blacks from southern agriculture changed the lives of those who remained. The relative shortage of labor resulted in improved terms for those who chose to stay, and the fact that they now had neighbors and kin in northern cities made their own future relocation more feasible.

The paradox that struck observers of the rural scene during World War I was that rural-to-urban migration was taking place at a time of unprecedented agricultural prosperity. The period from 1916 to 1920 represented a dramatic spike in agricultural prices at the end of an era when farmers had generally done well. Farm incomes rose in step with crop prices, exceeding average urban incomes for one of the few times in the history of the country. It was difficult to avoid the conclusion that material and social shortcomings endemic to rural life—not incomes—were the main factors driving migrants away.

Those farmers who remained took advantage of high incomes to rectify some of the shortcomings that drove their neighbors to town. They spent money to provide richer material lives for their families, and they committed themselves to higher property taxes to improve their schools and roads. Farmers poured some of their wartime profits into upgrading their operations. Gasoline-powered tractors became important items of capital investment, especially in the Midwest, on the Great Plains, and on the Pacific Coast. Tractors helped those who could afford them do without scarce labor and freed land that had been used to feed draft animals for production of income-producing crops. The fact that tractors were expensive, hard to acquire in wartime, and primitive meant that fewer than 4 percent of farmers owned them at the end of the war, but virtually all observers agreed that they were the wave of the future. In addition to mechanizing, farmers bought expensive blooded livestock and purchased land at inflated prices. Many convinced themselves that this boom was different from earlier booms and would not be followed by a downturn. Previous boom periods had stimulated expansion and overproduction, but now the best land in the country was already being farmed. Meanwhile, populations here and abroad continued to grow. As farmers liked to say, "they keep making babies, but they aren't making any more land." Farmers who thought in terms of permanent prosperity turned out to be wrong, but their optimism seemed justified during the war.

Continuing rural-to-urban migration and high farm prices kept the attention of urban reformers focused on the countryside. During the war and the years immediately following it, reclamation through irrigation caught the imagination of those who hoped to revolutionize agriculture and rural life. Reclamation especially attracted those concerned about finite land supplies and high food prices because it allowed unproductive land to bloom. Those concerned about rural depopulation and urban overpopulation were drawn to reclamation because irrigated farms were small, densely populated, and highly productive on a per-acre basis. Some, including Interior Secretary Franklin K. Lane, whose department included the Bureau of Reclamation, saw in irrigated farms the answer to the troubling national question of what would be done with the soldiers and sailors once the war ended.

Country Life reformers worried about the condition of rural society were also entranced by reclamation. Irrigation demanded close cooperation among farmers, diminishing what some saw as a destructive and unhealthy rural individualism. Country Lifers also liked the fact that irrigation communities could be created from scratch, in accordance with organizers' specifications. Hence, schools, churches, community organizations, and cooperatives could all be created *for* farmers, in conformity to correct principles, rather than *by* them, in accordance with traditions reformers perceived to be flawed.

Several planned irrigation communities, designed especially for veterans, were developed at the conclusion of the war. The most important of these were Durham and Delhi, created by the California State Land Settlement Board at the behest of irrigation enthusiast Elwood Mead. Mead and his colleagues left little to chance at Durham and Delhi. The irrigation works were carefully planned, of course, but so, too, were schools, cooperatives, and other community organizations. Community managers even decreed breeds of livestock to be raised, types of fencing to be erected, styles of houses that could be built, and colors of paint residents could use on their buildings! Within a few years of what seemed like a promising start by social engineers, both communities collapsed, in large part due to the settlers' resentment of micromanaging by Mead and his subordinates.

The failure of the World War I–era irrigation communities did not deter reclamation enthusiasts who hoped to revitalize rural society and revolutionize the agricultural economy. During the Great Depression of the 1930s, dams and ambitious irrigation works were among the most favored relief projects, and small-scale, irrigated farms were touted as the solution for a

182 country that seemed overurbanized and overindustrialized. But the results of reclamation were already proving by the 1930s to be dramatically different from what supporters of irrigation had promised. Instead of being the province of the small family farmer, irrigation in California and other areas of the West became the foundation for corporation agriculture. In violation of the spirit, and often the letter, of reclamation laws, large-scale growers put together massive irrigated farms, worked by impoverished laborers—Filipinos, Asian Indians, Chinese, Japanese, Okies, Hispanics, or some combination thereof—and managed in accordance with cold business calculation. The results of government agricultural programs frequently diverge from the intentions, and nowhere is that divergence clearer than in the case of irrigation.

Country Life reformers were not the only people who had a vision for agriculture and rural life during World War I. Farmers had several themselves. In North Dakota a new farmer-oriented political movement called the Nonpartisan League developed rapidly between 1915 and 1918. League founder A. C. Townley and his followers believed, as many Populists had, that farmers could get fair treatment from government only if they controlled it. Running its candidates in the primary of the dominant Republican party, the Nonpartisan League swept to victory in North Dakota in 1916 and again two years later. Leaguers proceeded to enact an ambitious program that struck especially at middlemen by creating a state-owned bank and a state-owned grain elevator and flour-milling complex, institutions that still exist in North Dakota.

Flushed with its success in North Dakota, the Nonpartisan League spread into Minnesota, South Dakota, Montana, Nebraska, and Colorado. The league's membership grew, but it was defeated outside of its home state by determined opponents who unfairly but successfully portrayed the organization as pro-German and as an instrument of revolutionary socialism. Even if the Nonpartisan League had not been victimized by wartime hysteria, its potential was quite limited. While it could take power in North Dakota, where three-fourths of the people lived on farms, and while it had the potential to seize the statehouses in a number of other heavily rural states, its national prospects were nonexistent. If a farmers' party was unable to gain control of the government in 1892, when two in three people were rural, one had no chance in 1920, when the census showed that for the first time in the nation's history the majority of Americans were urban.

Some farmers grasped that the relative shrinkage of the farm population and the changed conditions of agriculture demanded a new style of political behavior. Farmers could no longer credibly claim to be "the people" fighting to uphold liberty and equality. Increasingly, they were an interest group jostling with other interest groups in competition for economic benefits. Unlike the Nonpartisan League, the new American Farm Bureau Federation was a narrow economic-interest group from the beginning. The Farm Bureau, as it was commonly called, had its origins in the county farm bureaus formed to support extension agents. The businesspeople and farmers in these bureaus were usually friendly to productive innovations in agriculture, believed farmers' business practices should be better, and thought farmers and government could more effectively solve agricultural problems as partners than as adversaries. As early as 1918 state and local leaders had discussed creating a national organization out of the county bureaus, and in 1920 that goal was reached with the formation of the American Farm Bureau Federation.

The creation of the Farm Bureau placed the Extension Service in a delicate position. County agents had frequently created bureaus and had benefited from their existence. And the Extension Service as a whole gained important support from an organization of people who shared its vision for agriculture and were willing to lobby for it aggressively at every level of government. At the same time, the Extension Service was a public agency, supported overwhelmingly by tax dollars, and many people thought it inappropriate that such an entity would have a close relationship with a private economic group that made it clear that it would be pressuring the political system in the interest of its members. The solution to this problem came in 1921, when the Farm Bureau and the Extension Service negotiated a Memorandum of Understanding declaring that extension agents were public employees, not employees of farm bureaus, and that they worked with and for all farmers, though farm bureaus were allowed to contribute funds to maintain agents and further their work. The memorandum also strictly forbade extension agents from engaging in such political and economic activities as lobbying, forming cooperatives, and organizing local bureaus. The Memorandum of Understanding was necessary, but a piece of paper could not end a relationship, especially one based on mutual support and a shared agenda. In practice, the Extension Service and the Farm Bureau remained closely linked. Both benefited from this relationship, but it was also the source of much suspicion and resentment within the rural community.

184   Many of those who remained in rural America emerged from World War I better prepared in some ways for the future. They lived less isolated existences and enjoyed more of the material advantages that characterized urban life. Their horizons had expanded beyond those of their parents, and their expectations for the future were great. Farmers were becoming more commercial, and their growing market involvement was frequently accompanied by a greater appreciation for science, an increasing technological sophistication, and a determination to behave in accordance with sound business principles. They were thinking of themselves less as downtrodden yeomen, or representatives of the common man, and more as members of an economic interest group. Rural people were becoming more modern, and their modernity prepared them for the century that lay ahead. Unfortunately, their modernity did not prepare them for the period of economic and social difficulty that began in 1920, a period in which their expectations would be frustrated and their economic assumptions would be refuted.

NINE

From the Best of Times

to the Worst

The prosperity agriculture enjoyed during World War I continued after the Armistice, carrying through 1919 and into 1920. Some had anticipated a downturn after the fighting stopped. When it did not come, the arguments of those who repeated that dangerous but seductive phrase, "this time it's different," gained credence. Worried that the gravy train would leave the station without them, some who had been reluctant to invest before the war rushed to pay high prices for land, stock, and machinery afterwards.

The correction came late, but it came. Commodity prices broke sharply in 1920 and remained flat throughout the decade. All farmers complained, but some were hit harder than others. Those who had borrowed heavily in the late teens had difficulty surviving. Those who were not able to mechanize and thereby achieve economies of scale suffered more than those who were. And those who produced basic commodities that competed with products on a world market were hurt more than those who grew specialty crops for niche markets.

Producers of basic commodities demanded government aid, but it was not forthcoming. They were effectively thrown on their own resources. Farmers tried to economize, diminish their expenditures, and lower their taxes, but it was difficult. They had developed material standards and made commitments during the golden age that made it harder for them to tighten their belts.

Under the pressure of financial stringency the structure of agriculture began to assume a more modern shape. The number of farms and farmers declined, with the middle-sized producers most likely to be squeezed out, and population flowed away from the countryside. The future seemed to belong to the large, highly mechanized, and abundantly capitalized producers. The farmer was no longer the average American, and it was becoming clear that the average American could no longer hope to be a farmer.

A bad situation became much worse in the early thirties. The stock market crashed in 1929, and agriculture was a full participant in the economic depression that followed. For farmers, the issue was no longer prosperity, it was survival. Rural people and their communities cut expenses to the bone, "lived at home," and in general reduced their living standards to the lowest level in any person's memory. But still it was not enough. Hundreds of thousands lost farms, and many were thrown on the labor market of a country in which one of every four workers was unemployed.

Farmers became desperate in this situation. They demanded federal aid, but the government seemed paralyzed. They talked of farm strikes and foreclosure moratoriums, they blocked farm-to-market roads to inflate prices, and they intimidated bidders at farm foreclosure auctions. Some observers thought, as they had in the 1890s, that farmers had become a dangerous and potentially revolutionary force, but they were wrong. Farmers were just small, commercial property owners attempting to influence a situation beyond their control.

THE TWENTIES

To the great surprise of many observers, farm prices plunged in the early summer of 1920. Prices stabilized in 1921, then remained relatively flat until after the stock market crash in 1929. When compared with prices during the frothy days of the wartime and postwar eras, prices in the twenties appeared especially low. In 1919, wheat sold for $2.19 per bushel, potatoes went for $2.20 per hundredweight, and cotton fetched $.35 per pound; in 1929 the prices for these products were $1.05, $1.29, and $.17, respectively.

A number of factors contributed to the decline in prices. To a large extent the decline represented a return to a normal supply-and-demand situation following the extraordinary years of the middle and late teens. The artificially high demand on the part of warring and recovering Europeans and Americans had distorted prices. European recovery naturally diminished our exports, but its effects on our international trade were compounded by a major shift in the world financial position of the United States. Before World War I, the United States was a debtor nation. The countries to which it owed money, especially Great Britain, had an incentive to buy American products, because doing so made it possible for the United States to acquire the gold and currency (pounds, in the case of the British) needed to service its debts to them. During the nearly three years of war in which it did not participate, the United States served as supplier and banker to the Allies. In that position, it not only escaped its status as debtor but also became the world's leading creditor. Now the trade shoe was on the other foot. The British needed to sell to the United States to acquire the dollars to service their debts, and they hoped to use as few of those dollars as possible to buy the products the United States had to sell. Consequently, when alternative suppliers were available, the British and others of the United States' debtors preferred to buy from them, and there were alternative suppliers for many agricultural commodities. Europeans began eating more Argentine, Canadian, or Australian wheat, beef, and pork and less of these products from the United States.

Trade figures illustrate that, while not all American agricultural exports were devastated, there was an overall decline, with some commodities particularly hard hit. Exports of wheat, for example, plummeted from 366 million bushels in 1919–20 to 186 million bushels in 1928–29, and meat exports fell by 85 percent in those years. United States farm income from exports dropped from 27.7 percent in 1919–20 to 16 percent in 1928–29. Of course, 1919 and 1920 were extraordinary years, but in the last two prewar years, 1913 and 1914, 17.4 percent of United States farm income came from exports.

The disheartening export situation was compounded by unfortunate trends in domestic consumption. The population grew at a slightly lower rate than in the 1900–20 period, mainly because of restrictions on immigration. Alterations in the national diet and in styles affected many commodity producers. People ate more fruits, vegetables, and dairy products but fewer starches, fats, and carbohydrates. In a society in which machines did more of the work that once depended on human muscle and in which slimness had become the ideal, fewer potatoes and loaves of bread were consumed. When the Prohibition Amendment banned the manufacture and sale of alcoholic beverages, beginning in 1919, the market for barley and other grains was constricted. Shorter skirts and synthetic fabrics, especially rayon, became popular, diminishing the demand for cotton and wool. And the growing substitution of cars and trucks for horses in cities shrank markets for hay and oats. Farmers were also harmed by the growing preference of more-affluent consumers for highly processed foods. Between 1913–14 and 1928–29, the farmer's share of the food dollar fell by 10 percent.

While each of these factors was of marginal importance when viewed alone, in combination they put severe downward pressure on farm prices. Magnifying their effect was the inelastic nature of most farm prices. While falling prices for such durable goods as radios or automobiles induce consumers to buy more, thus helping to stabilize prices, the same cannot be said for most agricultural products. Few people eat more sandwiches when the price of bread falls, and it is only the rare woman who will buy a longer skirt in defiance of current fashions because the cotton in it is cheaper.

The spike in agricultural prices between 1916 and 1920 makes the subsequent decline look more dramatic than it really was, and some agricultural economists and historians have argued that the farm depression of the twenties was less an economic fact than a statistical artifact.[1] Such scholars correctly point out that prices receded only to prewar levels, which were relatively high, and that intense suffering was confined mainly to those who had taken on heavy debt burdens under the erroneous assumption that extraordinary prices would become ordinary. Indeed, most of the half million who lost their farms to bankruptcy during the twenties were people who had expanded unwisely during and after the war.

Those who question whether the agricultural depression was real help us put it in perspective, as does the unquestioned depression that began in 1929, but there is more to the story than price comparisons. One factor that contributed to rural hardship during the twenties was the reality that the prices farmers paid for the goods they purchased did not decline to the same degree as the prices they received. Hence, their real incomes were not as robust as they had been before the war. It is also true that farm families were less well prepared to weather economic stringency than they had been in the past. They were less self-sufficient, their standards of living were higher, items that had once been luxuries for them—such as automobiles—had become necessities, and they had committed themselves to higher taxes to pay for roads and schools. One might argue that rural people were imprudent to try to live as middle-class urbanites lived, but it is understandable that they should aspire to that standard, especially when all the urban media as well as the USDA, the land-grant colleges, and the Extension Service told them they should. Finally, it should be kept in mind that farmers judged their positions not only in light of their own experience but also in relation to urban contemporaries. During the war average rural incomes had exceeded those of urban wage earners, but that was not the case during the twenties. The cities enjoyed remarkable prosperity while the countryside languished, and by 1925 the average rural income was only 70 percent of that in the city.

Whether or not it is accurate to label the price slump of the twenties a depression, it was felt intensely by farmers, many of whom called for government action. There was some sentiment for another agrarian party and, indeed, a Farmer-Labor party was created in 1920 that survived for a time in a few places, most notably Minnesota. But most farmers, including those in the three big farm organizations, the Farm Bureau, the Farmers Union, and the Grange, inclined toward interest-group politics through the existing parties. Responding to farmers' concerns, a group of senators and representatives from the Great Plains, the Midwest, and the South created an informal organization called the Farm Bloc in 1921.

By working together, the congressional representatives in the Farm Bloc were able to pass some legislation favorable to farmers. In 1921 they helped push through the Packers and Stockyards Act, designed to curb the manipulation of meat prices by buyers, and the next year the Capper-Volstead Act, cosponsored by Kansas Senator and Farm Bloc leader Arthur Capper, exempted agricultural cooperatives from prosecution under the antitrust laws.

Unfortunately, these and other pieces of legislation had no detectable effect on farm prices and incomes. Republican leaders believed that high tariffs on imported agricultural products would inflate prices, so they raised rates dramatically in the Fordney-McCumber Tariff in 1921. The problem was that tariffs were ineffective in raising the prices of products whose domestic supply exceeded domestic demand, as was the case with the basic agricultural commodities. Such products would continue to trade at the world price, regardless of tariff rates. Indeed, by making it harder for foreign countries to export to the United States and thereby acquire dollars, tariffs actually discouraged our trading partners from buying our agricultural products.

Illinois implement manufacturer George Peek devised a plan for providing producers of basic agricultural commodities with the same level of protection the tariff afforded manufacturers. Peek believed the government should purchase commodities from farmers at what he called the parity price. *Parity* was defined as fair equivalent value between what farmers received for what they produced and what they paid for what they consumed. Peek established the 1909–14 period—before the wartime price surge—as his base period for identifying fair equivalent value between agricultural and industrial prices. The parity price for any given commodity would fluctuate from year to year as a reflection of changes in an index composed of the prices of a number of goods farmers bought. Under the Peek plan the parity price paid by government would become the domestic price for a commodity, because the government would purchase the supply in excess of domestic demand and would maintain tariff rates high enough to keep competitive commodities produced elsewhere out of the country. So far so good, but what would the government do with the commodities it held, and how would the program be paid for? Under Peek's plan, the government would dump its commodities on the world market (sell them at whatever price it could get, even if that price was below what it had paid for them) and would make up its losses by charging farmers an equalization fee on every unit of the covered commodities produced.

Commodity producers favored the Peek plan because, while it would not allow the achievement of full parity (the equalization fee would be deducted from the parity price), it would raise prices. With strong support from the Farm Bureau and other organizations, the Farm Bloc introduced a series of McNary-Haugen bills—named for Oregon Senator Charles McNary and Iowa Representative Gilbert Haugen—between 1924 and 1928 to put the Peek plan into law for corn, cotton, pork, rice, tobacco, and wheat. Conservatives attacked the McNary-Haugen proposal on the grounds that it would create a monstrous bureaucracy and would involve the government in agriculture in a paternalistic and un-American way. They argued effectively that it would encourage even more production of commodities that were already in oversupply and would shield weak producers from the consequences of their inefficiency. They doubted that the equalization fee would cover government losses, and they feared that international dumping would invite retaliation by our trading partners. These concerns resulted in congressional defeats for the McNary-Haugen bills in 1924 and 1926 and in vetoes by President Calvin Coolidge in 1927 and 1928 that Congress sustained.

Farmers did not put all of their eggs in the McNary-Haugen basket. Economic cooperation also entranced them. The Farm Bureau was enthusiastic about the possibilities of cooperation, just as had been the Grange, the Alliance movement, the Society of Equity, and the Farmers Union before it. If farmers would buy, sell, and process in concert, advocates of cooperation argued, they could capture many of the profits that had traditionally gone to middlemen.

Enjoying the support of a friendly Congress and USDA and buoyed by the enthusiasm of the Farm Bureau, cooperation became something of a mania during the early and mid twenties. Helping the process along was a magnetic, evangelistic California attorney named Aaron Sapiro. Sapiro had put together successful cooperatives in his home state, and he and his associates formed others throughout the country during the twenties.

Well-managed and broadly supported cooperatives could provide some advantages for all farmers. Farmer loyalty was a key. In Trempealeau County, Norwegian-American farmers' traditions of community activism and ethnic loyalty made cooperative creameries a success,[2] while Grange co-ops had been largely undermined by fickle members. The crop being handled by the cooperatives was another important determinant of success. The farmers who benefited most from cooperatives were those who produced perishable products, items that sold on a national rather than a world market, crops whose production was restricted by climate or growing peculiarities (one barrier to entry in the fruit-growing business, for example, is that one must wait several years for trees to mature), crops grown by only a handful of farmers, and crops aimed at a market niche rather than at the mass consumer. Cooperatives in such endeavors as dairy and fruit production fit some or all of these conditions, so it is not surprising that such cooperative products as Sunkist oranges, Land O'Lakes milk, Diamond walnuts, and Ocean Spray cranberries have become nationally renowned.

Cooperation resulted in fewer benefits for producers of such basic commodities as cotton, tobacco, pork, or wheat. For one thing, it was difficult for cooperatives to pull enough of the numerous and scattered producers together to exert market power, and the nature of the commodities foreclosed the possibility of the sort of quality differentiation Sunkist was able to provide in oranges. Because these commodities tended to be less perishable than, say, milk or fruit, nonmembers could hold inventories and benefit from any price rises cooperative action might induce. Likewise, because these commodities flowed freely through the channels of world trade, foreign producers could also take advantage of favorable local market situations created by cooperatives. Cooperation could benefit producers of basic commodities when its aim was the achievement of economies of scale and greater efficiencies in handling or processing, but cooperatives that aim at market control of basic commodities—as the Sapiro cooperatives did—are almost certain to fail. The inability of the Sapiro-inspired cooperatives to live up to their promises resulted in a decline in the number of farmers marketing cooperatively from 13.9 percent in 1924 to just 11 percent in 1929.

Cooperation continued to have its champions, however, including Herbert Hoover, the wartime food administrator who became president of the United States in 1929. Hoover's experience in government, especially as secretary of commerce between 1921 and 1928, made him a strong believer in economic corporatism or associationalism. This was the belief that voluntary producer groups could solve problems of production and marketing by working together. Government could encourage and help them, as it had with the Federal Farm Loan Act of 1916, which provided government start-up capital for cooperative agricultural lending agencies. But if government imposed a bureaucratic solution—such as the McNary-Haugen bills contemplated—paternalism, economic inefficiency, and a loss of personal liberties would likely result.

Hoover believed that the only problem with cooperation—associationalism in agriculture—was that it had been ill conceived and unsystematically executed. He was willing to put the federal government behind a realistic program encouraging cooperation. In 1929 Congress passed the Agricultural Marketing Act at Hoover's behest. This legislation created the Federal Farm Board, an agency that was provided with a $500 million fund to advance agricultural cooperation. Most of this money was to be used for loans to allow cooperatives to acquire facilities, but the board was also authorized to purchase commodities on the open market in order to underpin cooperatives' efforts to stabilize prices. Whether the Federal Farm Board would have solved the economic problems of agriculture is one of the great unanswered questions of American farm policy. The thinking behind it was sound and it was well funded, but the depression that began shortly after its creation prevented it from getting a fair test.

For all practical purposes, rural people had to cope with the economic downturn of the twenties on their own. It became more difficult for them to support small local schools and churches, making consolidation an increasingly attractive option. Their material wants became more difficult to fulfill, and they were forced to make some painful choices. Some things they were loath to give up—their automobiles, for example—but many reluctantly surrendered their telephones. Making material privation all the more acute was the fact that there were more things to buy all of the time. The most exciting new product of the twenties was the radio. Like the automobile, the radio had its practical utility. It carried farm and household hints, quoted commodity prices, and advised of impending weather developments. But, also like the automobile, it was mainly a medium of escape, allowing families to feel less isolated from world and national events, to lose themselves in soap operas, adventures, and comedies, and to forget the tedium of the day with an evening of dance music. It advanced the privatization of leisure and helped rural people compensate for deficiencies in neighborhood and community life. It is hardly accidental that the radio was most popular on the Great Plains, where neighbors were often distant and visiting was difficult.

Rural people accepted radio on their own terms, approaching it as they did other consumer products. They were not empty vessels into which just anything could be poured. Some programs appealed to them more than others, a fact that networks and advertisers were quick to grasp. Country music, for example, had a strong appeal in many rural areas, and such programs as the "National Barn Dance" and later the "Grand Ole Opry" facilitated a degree of rural cultural penetration of urban America. On balance, though, cultural penetration mainly went the other way. The process was subtle and was characterized by mutual accommodation, but radio proved marvelously effective in advancing urban cultural standards in the countryside.

While the networks made radio a national medium, much of the programming was local and conformed closely to local tastes and standards. Such was not the case with movies or music. Farmers complained bitterly of the movies that fascinated their children, films that were violent and sexually suggestive, glorified urban living, and upheld unrealistic material standards. Also disturbing was jazz music, quickly introduced in the countryside over the airwaves, and what many rural people considered to be the improper dances boys and girls did to it. Culturally assaulted as they were, it is small wonder that some rural people felt besieged during the twenties. While it is misleading and unfair to label such conservative cultural reactions of the age as Protestant Fundamentalism and the Ku Klux Klan as rural, as many historians have, people on farms frequently shared the anxieties of those who belonged to such movements.

However ambivalent they were about urban life, rural people tried to keep pace materially, and the most effective way to do so seemed to be by making farms more productive. The surest way to greater productivity in the twenties was through mechanization, especially the replacement of horses and mules with tractors. Doing away with draft animals had long been a dream of many farmers. Horses and mules required a good deal of care and feeding (a workhorse was estimated to consume six acres of hay and oats per year), could not be worked continuously, and were sometimes stubborn or dangerous. Moreover, operators of horse-drawn machinery "were in the direct line of fire of all discharged solids, liquids, and gasses, usually disposed of in enormous quantities," as one Iowa farm boy remembered.[3] Steam- and later gasoline-powered tractors offered potential escape from draft animals, but their shortcomings were numerous before 1920. Early tractors were large but underpowered and usually had to be used with implements designed for horses. Their utility was limited because they lacked lifts that let farmers raise implements out of the soil at the ends of fields and because their wheels were configured in such a way as to make them useless for cultivating row crops. The absence of power take-offs that allowed machinery to operate at the speed of the engine rather than the speed of the tractor—almost a necessity for farmers harvesting heavy stands of hay or grain—also made the machines unattractive. All of these problems and more were addressed during the early and mid twenties, with the result that the number of tractors on American farms surged from 246 thousand in 1920 to 920 thousand in 1930.

Because tractors allowed the more rapid and timely completion of field operations, they were the main reason agricultural productivity surged by 18 percent during the twenties, the second highest advance in any decade up to that time. Farm men liked the idea of freeing acres previously devoted to keeping draft animals for market production, and farm women liked the idea of replacing hired men—often one of the banes of their existence—with machinery. Tractors also made it easier for women to do field labor when it

Adams County, North Dakota, farmer killing a starving cow, July 1934.
Courtesy of the North Dakota Institute for Regional Studies and North Dakota University Libraries, Fargo.

was necessary. On the other hand, tractors were expensive, and the petroleum they consumed could not be produced on the farm, as hay and oats had been. Moreover, only a minority of farmers could use tractors cost effectively. In 1920 three-fifths of American farms were under one hundred acres, but the USDA estimated that a minimum of 130 acres was necessary to make a tractor pay.

The minority of farmers whose ownership of tractors increased productivity unconsciously intensified economic pressures on others. Those especially pressured were middle-sized farmers, whose farms were large enough to demand their full attention but not large enough to allow them to capture the economies mechanization offered. Some of these people strove to increase the size of their farms during the decade, and the fact that the percent of mortgaged farms increased from 37.2 in 1920 to 42.0 in 1930 suggests that many were borrowing to do so. Others withdrew from agriculture, usually by selling to expanding neighbors. Overall, average farm size rose from 145 acres to 157 acres during the twenties, and there were 160 thousand fewer farms in 1930 than there had been in 1920. It is noteworthy that the number of farms under 50 acres, which could often be handled by a farmer holding a nonfarm job, rose, as did the number of farms 175 acres or larger. Meanwhile, the number of farms between 50 and 175 acres decreased by 206 thousand. In what would become a pattern in twentieth-century American agriculture, the middle was getting squeezed out.

Fewer farms and a declining labor demand on those that remained combined with the economic and social attractions of cities during the roaring twenties to increase the pace of rural-to-urban migration dramatically. The countryside suffered a net outmigration of 6.25 million people in the decade. Even though the rural birthrate exceeded the rural deathrate, there was still an absolute rural population decline of 1.2 million people between 1920 and 1930. Those most likely to leave were the young, whose family and property responsibilities were usually minimal. The flight of young people from agriculture was reflected in the fact that 52.6 percent of farm operators were over age forty-five in 1930, as opposed to 48.1 percent ten years earlier. Outmigration had important social effects. It meant fewer parishioners for churches and fewer pupils for schools. It put added pressures on small towns that were already reeling from the effects of the mail-order catalog, rural free delivery, parcel post, and the automobile. And it damaged rural morale, imparting a sense of abandonment in the people who remained.

Country Life reformers a few years earlier had worried about out-migration, but the attitude of urban observers in the twenties was much different. As farm journalist Wheeler McMillan succinctly put it in 1929, there were "too many farmers," far more than a mechanized agriculture demanded.[4] Country Lifers believed a vital rural life was necessary to refresh and revitalize the nation socially and morally. By the twenties, farmers were not commonly seen as anything special. Indeed, they were more likely to be seen as backward and retrograde elements in an increasingly sophisticated society. One observer captured the new mood when he expressed his pleasure that modernization was "driving the old-time, bucolic, turkey-in-the-straw style of farmer from the . . . countryside."[5]

The twenties foretold the course of agriculture over the rest of the century. Farming would become more highly mechanized and scientifically and technologically sophisticated. Farmers would become better educated, and farms larger, more heavily capitalized, and more commercial. And their numbers would shrink, far more than even farsighted observers like Wheeler McMillan imagined. These trends were probably positive for the national economy. Whether they were positive for the agricultural economy was less clear. That they were negative for a vibrant and flourishing rural society is beyond question.

THE GREAT DEPRESSION

The collapse of the stock market in the fall of 1929 initiated the most severe and prolonged depression in the nation's history. The downturn could be seen first in the commercial and industrial sectors of the economy. The crash shook consumer and investor confidence. Demand dropped as consumers curtailed discretionary spending, especially for such flashy durable consumer goods as automobiles and radios. Retailers, burdened with high inventories, slashed prices and cut factory orders. Factories consequently cut production, diminishing payrolls and purchases of raw materials and capital goods. Soon a deflationary spiral was evident as wages and prices fell, feeding on one another.

Deflation was a serious matter for debtors. Money borrowed for homes or businesses when prices and wages were high could not be easily repaid when prices and wages fell. The problems of debtors became problems for bankers. Borrowers could not make payments, and foreclosure was not an attractive option at a time when collateral values were plummeting. Banks were further pressured when depositors withdrew funds and when returns from their portfolios—often heavy with stocks and bonds—eroded. Driven to illiquidity, large numbers of banks collapsed, dragging even solvent borrowers down with them.

The United States was the world's leading economic power in 1929, and its problems inevitably affected every other nation. American investment abroad declined dramatically, harming Germany and, indirectly, Britain and France, to whom the Germans owed money. As nations decreased consumption and raised tariff barriers to protect domestic enterprises, exporting nations such as Japan suffered. And diminished manufacturing activity inevitably harmed developing regions that exported raw materials.

When the United States had been mainly a nation of farmers, downturns in agriculture triggered depressions in commerce and manufacturing. Now the opposite was true. What started as an industrial depression soon reverberated in rural America. Demand for agricultural products fell away. Export markets virtually disappeared as former customers hastened to protect their own producers and find alternative suppliers to whom they did not owe money. Between 1927–29 and 1931–33 wheat exports fell from 354 million bushels to 143 million, the value of meat exports dropped from $246 million to $81 million, and the value of cotton exports went from $2.497 billion to $1.069 billion.

Domestic demand also declined. People living through a depression have to eat, even if they are unemployed or underemployed, but they do not have to eat as much or to eat the same things. Specifically, they substitute cheap starches and carbohydrates for meat, dairy products, fruits, vegetables, and other relatively expensive fresh foods. In 1929 Americans spent $19.544 billion on food and beverages. Three years later, they spent only $11.365 billion. As with food, so too with clothing. People must be clothed, but they can make last year's dress serve again or can get along with one shirt rather than two. Producers of cotton and wool suffered when expenditures on clothing fell from $7.682 billion in 1929 to $4.022 billion in 1932.

It was not just farmers who faced declining demand, but in relatively oligopolistic industries, such as steel and automobiles, producers were better able to manage supply, thereby preventing prices from declining as dramatically as they might have. Producers of major agricultural commodities were too numerous to restrict output, and they also faced the problem that their production was influenced by forces beyond their control. The flick of a switch shuts down an assembly line, but rainfall and sunshine are not subject to human influence. Optimal growing conditions in 1931, for example, resulted in the second-largest cotton crop and the third-largest wheat crop ever, exacerbating the difficulties of producers awash in commodities.

Farmers' inability to control production, declining domestic and foreign demand, and the inelasticity of agricultural prices resulted in a price decline in farm products that made the collapse in industrial prices appear comparatively tame. Between 1929 and 1932 the average price of corn dropped from $.77 to $.32 per bushel, wheat from $1.05 to $.38 per bushel, cotton from $.168 to $.05 per pound, and hogs from $12.93 to $6.13 per hundredweight. Overall, gross farm income in 1932 was but 40 percent of what it had been in 1929. Because the prices farmers received fell further than the prices they paid, their situation became especially critical in the early years of the depression. In 1929, farm prices had stood at 92 percent of parity. Three years later they were at 58 percent of parity. Rural incomes were already relatively low in 1929—about 70 percent of average earnings in manufacturing—but by 1932 they had declined to barely 50 percent.

Rural people struggled to hang on in this desperate situation. Families retrenched heroically, cutting all but the most essential expenses. Farmers shared machinery. Some returned to horses and mules to avoid the expense of running and maintaining tractors. Tenants in the South depended on landlords to provide furnish, which became more a form of welfare and less a means of tiding people over until harvest. The fact that farmers lacked money translated directly into pain for local communities. Merchants extended credit, but they eventually reached the point where their own creditors would carry them no longer. Local professionals such as lawyers and physicians accepted chickens or cream for their services, returning to the barter system of previous generations. Farmers had difficulties paying property taxes, and counties were understandably reluctant to press them in this time of hardship. But counties without revenue could not continue to provide services, so roads and bridges fell into disrepair. School districts could not pay teachers, so they offered warrants that functioned as IOUs. Sometimes banks and merchants would accept them—at substantially less than face value—and sometimes they would not. Many districts could not hire teachers by any means and were forced to depend on volunteers or even close schools altogether.

State agricultural officials, farm and home extension agents, and agricultural experiment stations encouraged greater rural self-sufficiency by launching "live at home" campaigns. Farmers were urged to can vegetables, butcher and preserve meat, raise poultry, keep dairy cattle, and engage in home manufacturing. The emphasis on self-sufficiency relative to commercial production placed a heavy burden on women, who had traditionally been responsible for such enterprises. Extension belatedly recognized the economic significance of women on farms. Home agents in New York State helped farm women produce salable crafts, and elsewhere extension conducted poultry and dairy demonstrations for women. The contributions of farm women frequently transcended their customary economic roles, significant as those were. In many cases husbands seemed paralyzed by the challenges they faced, forcing women to play family leadership roles to which they were unaccustomed and adding stress to their lives. Farmers let their hired help go during the depression, increasing the emphasis on family labor. One Iowa farm woman remembered that "all farm women . . . were expected to do what was euphemistically known as 'help out.' Translated, this meant that you were supposed to do all the work that your husband didn't have time for, didn't like to do, or considered beneath the dignity of a man."[6] It was not an attractive situation, but the alternatives were worse.

The live-at-home movement highlighted one major advantage that rural people had over their urban cousins—they could feed themselves. That reality attracted many unemployed urbanites in the desperate years of the early thirties. The flow of rural-to-urban migration slowed and then reversed; in 1932–33, there was a net in-migration of 750 thousand people to the countryside. Most of the migrants to rural America were young men and women who had moved to cities during the twenties and returned to live with their families when they lost jobs. A minority of the migrants were urban people who tried to scrape out livings on unowned or abandoned lands, sometimes under communal arrangements. This last enterprise was romanticized by King Vidor's 1932 film, *Our Daily Bread,* and was institutionalized in some experimental government programs during Franklin D. Roosevelt's New Deal administration.

The Great Depression reinvigorated the back-to-the-land movement. American disciples of English Distributism such as Alfred Bingham and Lewis Mumford argued that the crisis proved that the country had become overindustrialized and overurbanized, and that people should be scattered about in decentralized communities where they could combine subsistence agriculture with light manufacturing. Ralph Borsodi, a New York advertising man who had moved his family to a Long Island farm during the twenties, advanced a plan for communal farming by the unemployed and developed a model community near Dayton, Ohio. And the Nashville Agrarians, eight faculty members in the liberal arts at Vanderbilt University, published "I'll Take My Stand," a plea for rural living based on the notion that such rural institutions as the church and the family were stronger than their urban counterparts and that rural people had superior moral characters.[7]

Most of this involved urban people talking to one another, sharing romantic and sometimes fanciful visions of rural life and harsh and even apocalyptic visions of urban life. Such discussion had no noticeable impact on farmers. What urban commentators saw as an admirable self-sufficiency, commercial farmers saw as a bitter necessity. They did not "live at home" because they wanted to, however charming that might have seemed to observers, but because they had to.

Families could struggle along on their own resources, canning and milking and butchering, parking their tractors and putting horses back in harness. They could let their property taxes slide for a couple of years. If they couldn't make the payments they could let the banks and finance companies repossess their cars and radios and appliances. They could forego coal by burning wood or even corn, as many did. But they could not do without the land. "Living at home" depended on holding on to the farm, and that was not an easy proposition for farmers carrying mortgages, as over 40 percent did when the depression began.

The problem was that people purchased income-producing assets—such as land—when prices were adequate to service the debt they assumed, but when prices fell they found themselves in difficulty. An interest payment that is easy to make when wheat is a dollar a bushel becomes impossible when wheat falls to thirty cents. The land can only produce a finite amount, and when prices fall it might be too little to cover costs.

Contrary to popular American mythology, bankers, insurance companies, and other lenders do not enjoy seeing borrowers fail, not least because the creditor can seldom recover the full value of the loan he has made. The market value of the average acre in 1932 was just half what it had been in 1929, making it highly unlikely that many lenders could recapture their investments. Consequently, lenders usually tried to be liberal, extending loans and delaying payments when they could. The problem was that they, too,

202 had obligations to meet. When they could not do so, they had to foreclose in order to recover at least part of their investment. Banks that could not remain liquid otherwise demanded payments of loans that were being serviced adequately; they simply could not leave the funds out any longer. Sometimes even that was not enough, or it could not be done in time. Banks closed, and their assets—good loans as well as bad—were sold to satisfy their creditors. In these ways hundreds of rural banks failed and hundreds of thousands of farmers lost their farms between 1929 and 1933.

This was a painful and poignant process, in which both lenders and debtors were victimized. It was not always devastating. The land had to be farmed, and new owners frequently engaged old ones as tenants. When Kenneth Hassebrock's parents lost their Iowa farm in 1931, the Travelers Insurance Company rented it back to them.[8] This kept them off the glutted urban labor market but failed to soften the blow to their pride and status that reduction to tenancy symbolized in their community.

FARMERS RESPOND

President Hoover's farm program was already in place when the depression began, and he counted on it to cushion the economic blows to agriculture. The Federal Farm Board was authorized to engage in crop-holding operations as a means of helping cooperatives capture more of the benefits of their actions. Buying crops on the open market and holding them could also have the effect of combatting price deflation, and the board found itself heavily committed to this purpose as the depression deepened. Eventually, the agency spent $180 million on crop-holding operations. While it is impossible to tell where prices might have been had the board not engaged in this enterprise, it did not appear to contemporaries that crop holding had done any good.

Farm organizations had their own solutions to the problem of the depression. The Farm Bureau, led by Alabama cotton planter Ed O'Neal, favored the McNary-Haugen approach and compulsory reductions in planted acreage. The Farmers Union, under John Simpson, preferred monetary inflation and government payments to guarantee farmers their cost of production. While there were differences among these plans, it is important to note that each of them was targeted at land-owning commercial farmers. Tenants, farm laborers, and others at the bottom of the rural social scale were generally ignored by the farm organizations. That was a pattern that would continue.

The divisions among farm groups made it unlikely that the federal government would enact any substantial new program of agricultural relief, as did the serious flaws many could see in these plans. The McNary-Haugen proposal seemed foolhardy at a time when prices were far below parity, production was high, and export markets were evaporating. A Congress struggling with declining revenues and growing demands for aid was understandably reluctant to create such a potentially expensive and open-ended program. Guaranteeing farmers the cost of production would also be expensive, would subsidize inefficiency, and would encourage farmers who already produced too much to produce more. Determining a fair cost of production, given the tremendous variations among farmers, also promised to be controversial and a potential bureaucratic nightmare. Acreage reduction seemed immoral at a time when many people were ill clothed and ill fed, and inflation, by cheapening the value of the dollar, would further destabilize trade and would invite commercial retaliation from others.

Congressional concerns about flaws in suggested farm programs were more or less academic, because Hoover opposed going beyond the Federal Farm Board. His concerns were partially budgetary and trade related but mainly ideological. Hoover was willing to help farmers develop associational arrangements to help themselves, but he opposed government paternalism or bureaucratic regimentation that would diminish freedom or sap individual initiative. Hoover's attitude effectively doomed any new federal programs for farm relief.

The states could do some things for farmers, if they were willing. One popular idea was the enactment of property-tax and foreclosure moratoriums. The former probably saved a few farms, even while it exacerbated the struggles of local government. The latter was an unconstitutional abrogation of contractual rights and obligations and was often ignored by judges, sheriffs, and other officers of the court. Desperate times call for desperate measures, and the willingness of some states to take action they knew violated the United States Constitution is a sign of how serious things really were.

States also toyed with the idea of limiting production. The near-record cotton crop of 1931 prompted Louisiana Governor Huey Long to spearhead a movement for a regionwide, one-year holiday on cotton production. This idea was doomed by farmer disunity and lack of sufficient support from other governors. In North Dakota, Governor William Langer declared a brief embargo on the shipment of wheat from the state as a means of raising prices. Because only Congress has power over interstate commerce, this action was blatantly illegal, but one does not gain the sobriquet "Wild Bill" by being overly fastidious about the Constitution.

Even when the states were willing to take action, they were distinctly limited in what they could do for farmers. They could undertake little that required money. They suffered from shrinking revenues, in part because of the direct effects of the depression and in part because they often cut taxes to relieve burdens on citizens. At the same time, most were required to have balanced budgets, and many were prohibited from borrowing funds. The hands of the states were tied.

Farmers themselves could take action, however. In 1931, when Iowa health officials attempted to identify and destroy tubercular cattle, angry farmers resisted, sometimes violently, in what came to be called the Cow War. The next year Iowa—never a particular hotbed of agrarian discontent—became the center of the Farmers Holiday movement. The Farmers Holiday Association was the brainchild of Iowa Farmers Union official Milo Reno, and its membership was drawn largely from that organization. As the name implied, the organization advanced the idea of farmers taking a holiday from production to drive prices higher. The association called a national farm strike for August 15, 1932, urging producers to hold products off the market. Farmers responded with crop-holding operations in several midwestern and Great Plains states, but the Farmers Holiday caused its greatest stir in its homebase of Iowa. Holiday members there set up roadblocks around major towns to prevent hogs and such perishable products as milk from coming to market. Other farmers saw these actions as an intrusion on their freedom, and violent incidents occurred at several roadblocks. Eventually, the governor called out the National Guard to clear the roads.

Less spectacular but more effective were the efforts of the Farmers Holiday Association to prevent farm foreclosures. Local members of the association attempted to mediate between creditors and debtors in an effort to refinance mortgages or restructure payments. If they were unsuccessful, the association sometimes tried to intimidate lenders or judges (foreclosure is a civil proceeding demanding a court order). When such efforts were unavailing, farmers would occasionally attempt to thwart the purposes of foreclosure by staging penny auctions. These were farm sales in which farmers bid trivial amounts of money for property, which was then turned back to the original owner. For penny auctions to be successful two separate conditions had to be met. First, it was necessary to dissuade legitimate bidders from participating, which often required intimidation. Second, it hinged on the tacit cooperation of the county sheriff, the local official charged with carrying out the order of the court. Should the sheriff declare a sale to be fraudulent—as the auctioneer and the lender's representative at his elbow invariably urged him to do—it would be canceled and rescheduled for a later date. Penny auctions were obviously not the solution to the farm-debt crisis, just desperate acts by desperate people.

The activities of the Farmers Holiday Association and other groups led some observers to believe that normally conservative farmers were becoming a revolutionary force. Some were excited by this prospect. The Communist party, for example, launched a major effort to organize farmers into its United Farmers League. Others were disturbed that people who had once been considered the backbone of the republic might now prove its undoing. The reality was that farmers remained commercial property owners who had been driven to uncharacteristically extreme actions by a deteriorating situation. When they were given reason to hope for something better, their radicalism evaporated like the dew on a sunny midwestern morning.

TEN

The New Deal
and Rural America

The inauguration of President Franklin D. Roosevelt and the beginning of his New Deal program in March of 1933 signaled a dramatic shift in the relationship between the federal government and rural America. In contrast to Hoover, who offered little to farmers but support for cooperation, Roosevelt launched a program for agricultural recovery based mainly on acreage reductions and price supports. His administration also developed programs to enhance security for farm property, supplement credit resources, encourage cooperation, and insure crops against weather-related losses. Within a few months of the change of administrations, there were precious few areas of the agricultural economy in which the federal government was not at least indirectly involved.

New Deal programs inevitably had effects that went beyond the farm economy, though the recovery of the agricultural sector was the administration's primary aim. Some agencies attempted to reorient the rural social structure, making it possible for laborers and tenants to live lives of dignity and even become landowners. Relief agencies operating in rural America improved buildings and transportation facilities, hired unemployed people, maintained institutions, and enriched lives. And the New Deal undertook a revolutionary—and successful—effort to electrify the countryside. More federal activities were undertaken in response to the Dust Bowl, an ecological crisis that beset the Great Plains with especial severity between 1934 and 1938. Government agencies promoted conservation, retired highly erodable lands from farming, resettled some victims on more viable lands, and provided sustenance for others.

This explosion of government activity confused many rural people, and for good reason. Programs were based on diametrically opposed philosophies and on contradictory visions of the nature and the future of rural America. Some agencies advanced initiatives that were canceled by others. This bureaucrat battled openly with that one. This bureau established a relationship with these farmers and organizations, while that bureau appealed to their adversaries.

Part of the confusion was attributable to the depth of the crisis and to its varied facets, but part of it was due to the Roosevelt style. The president had sympathies and inclinations but, unlike Hoover, he was not wedded to one particular understanding of a problem or approach to it. If one thing did not work, he tried another thing, seldom bothering to abolish the agency established to do the first thing. Roosevelt also tried to maintain a broad political coalition by giving everybody something he or she wanted. One result was programs that lacked coherence and a clear sense of direction.

As a result, while it was clear that the New Deal was changing rural America, for a while it was not clear how. By the beginning of World War II, however, it was becoming obvious which programs were significant and which were not and what changes were really taking place. It was apparent first that programs maintaining and supplementing the incomes of commercial producers of basic commodities were destined to be permanent legacies of the New Deal. And it was also certain that the main effect of most New Deal programs would be to strengthen the existing socioeconomic structure of rural America and accelerate the economic and technological trends that had helped bring that structure into being, regardless of the goals of some bureaucrats and social scientists.

AGRICULTURAL PROGRAMS OF THE NEW DEAL

The agricultural programs of the New Deal were responses to a severe crisis and were thus largely children of necessity. But they were also shaped by the economic and fiscal constraints under which government operated, both domestically and internationally, and they were influenced by the beliefs and personal inclinations of the people responsible for proposing and executing them. Franklin Roosevelt himself had a strong emotional commitment to farming. Born and raised at Hyde Park, his family's country estate in the Hudson River Valley north of New York City, he fancied himself a farmer and identified himself as such on census returns. Throughout his presidency, his shrewd grasp of political realities was tempered by a sentimental attachment to the family farm.

His secretary of agriculture was Iowan Henry A. Wallace, the grandson of a member of Theodore Roosevelt's Country Life Commission and the son of Warren Harding's secretary of agriculture. Wallace edited an important farm paper, *Wallace's Farmer*, and was an agrarian fundamentalist who believed that a strong and vital agriculture and rural life was essential to the nation's economic and social health. He was also a believer in scientific and technological progress in agriculture, who had himself played a role in the development of hybrid corn. Other early agricultural advisors included George Peek, the father of McNary-Haugenism, and Rexford Guy Tugwell, a Columbia University economist who believed in national economic planning and who sympathized with agriculture's underdogs. Most of the people in his administration shared Roosevelt's enthusiasm for experimentation.

Most policy makers agreed that it was necessary immediately to provide greater security for the property of farm debtors caught in the deflationary spiral. This problem was addressed by the Farm Credit Administration (FCA), created by executive order in May of 1933. The FCA purchased farm mortgages from lenders or from the receivers of insolvent banks at discounted prices, pursuant to an application by the lender and the borrower, scaled them down, and refinanced them over longer terms and with lower interest rates. This was good for lenders, because it allowed them to liquidate mortgages that were often in default for more than they would have received in bankruptcy auctions, and it was good for borrowers, because it allowed them to retain their property and made their debts more manageable.

The Farm Credit Administration quickly became the dominant lender in agriculture, holding 40 percent of the nation's farm-mortgage indebtedness by 1937, but that situation was meant to be temporary. The long-term solution to agricultural credit problems was cooperation, New Dealers believed, and the FCA provided start-up and expansion money to the Land Bank, the Production Credit Association, and the Bank of Cooperatives, rural lending agencies that were farmer owned and operated.

As the creation of these agencies shows, the New Deal repudiated Hoover, but it did not completely abandon his emphasis on cooperation. In addition to encouraging the creation of new cooperative facilities, the New Deal recycled old ones, turning back to farmers properties that were purchased with Federal Farm Board funds and then repossessed by that agency. The Farm Security Administration, created in 1937, was an especially enthusiastic participant in this process. Its close relationship with the Farmers Union helped make it possible for that organization to acquire the facilities that allowed the creation of one of the most impressive cooperative structures in American agriculture.

Significant as it was, cooperation was a long-term solution for agricultural problems, and the mortgage refinancing the FCA undertook would be effective only if agricultural prices and farmers' incomes were raised quickly. That was the New Deal's second big agricultural goal in 1933, and there was no shortage of suggestions for accomplishing it. Most of the usual suspects, such as McNary-Haugenism and guaranteed cost of production, were still around, but open-ended programs that might encourage greater production or that depended on virtually nonexistent foreign markets had glaring flaws. Roosevelt's early advisors, especially economist Raymond Moley, believed that the depression had been caused by overproduction. Because too much of everything had been produced, they argued, prices had fallen, triggering a deflationary spiral that fed on itself. The answer to this problem was to limit supplies in order to bring them into better balance with demand. When that was accomplished, prices would stabilize and then rise, reversing the deflationary spiral, relieving debtors, increasing consumer and investor confidence, and stimulating employment and production.

Production control was not a new idea for either industry or agriculture, having been discussed at length before Roosevelt became president. Hoover had not opposed it in theory, but he had wanted it to be voluntary and had refused to provide government encouragement by suspending antitrust laws. Agriculture was so fragmented, with hundreds of thousands of producers of each basic commodity, that voluntary restriction of production was impossible.

The effective production control agriculture required came with the passage of the Agricultural Adjustment Act in May of 1933. A product of political consensus-building, this legislation threw bones to a number of howling farm dogs, including McNary-Haugenites and inflationists, but the meat of

210 the Agricultural Adjustment Act was the acreage-limitation program. Under the act, producers of seven basic commodities—corn, cotton, hogs, milk, rice, tobacco, and wheat—were encouraged to participate in voluntary programs to reduce production, in most cases through limitation of planted acreage. Quickly perceiving the benefits of the program, producers of other commodities demanded seats on the federal gravy train, and over the next two years barley, beet and cane sugar, cattle, flax, peanuts, potatoes, rye, and sorghum were added.

Acreage limitation was fairly simple. For purposes of illustration, a cotton farmer might offer to remove half of his forty acres from production. Upon approval by a county committee, which received allocations from the national Agricultural Adjustment Administration (AAA), he would be allowed to do so. The farmer would sign a rental agreement with the secretary of agriculture, with the per-acre rent set at the parity price minus the market price, multiplied by the average production. So, if the parity price was fifteen cents a pound, the market price was a nickel a pound, and average per-acre production was 250 pounds, the farmer would receive $25 per acre [($.15 - $.05 = $.10) × 250 = $25], or $500 for twenty acres. The money for the rental would come from a tax on the processors of agricultural products, which was really a tax on consumers, because the middlemen simply passed it through.

Acreage limitation was designed to raise farm incomes in two ways. First, it provided direct cash payments to participating farmers for what was not produced. And second, because production was restricted, the prices of what was produced would rise. This program was not supposed to be permanent. As market prices rose and the gap between them and parity prices narrowed, fewer farmers would find it in their interest to participate in the program. Everyone hoped, and many expected, that market prices would eventually approach and even surpass parity prices, at which point the program would presumably atrophy or be abolished.

In order to further buttress farm incomes, President Roosevelt created the Commodity Credit Corporation (CCC) by executive order in October of 1933. In its operations the agency bore a strong resemblance to the Sub-Treasury suggested by the Southern Alliance in the late nineteenth century (see chapter 7). The CCC provided loans to farmers who participated in acreage limitation on the crops they produced. Originally, the loan rates were set at 60 to 70 percent of parity. To illustrate how this worked, let us go back to our cotton farmer. If he enjoyed an average year, he produced 5,000 pounds on the twenty acres he still had in production. He could receive a loan on that cotton from the CCC of, say, a dime a pound—or 67 percent of parity—for a total of $500. If, in the course of the next year, the market price of cotton rose enough above a dime a pound to compensate him for his effort, he could sell the cotton and repay the loan to the government. If he did not repay the loan—as he probably did not if the market price approximated the loan level or was below it—then the CCC seized his collateral (the cotton) to fulfill his obligation. The loans were nonrecourse loans, meaning that the CCC could take no property but the crop on which the loan was made. Like the AAA, the CCC was conceived as a temporary measure to inflate prices and incomes until agriculture recovered from the depression. But in fact, acreage limitations—sometimes tied to marketing agreements—and commodity loans—sometimes supplemented by target prices or other subsidies—became permanent fixtures of American agriculture.

The New Deal agricultural program quickly became unpopular with consumers. It raised food and fiber prices for people who already had trouble feeding and clothing themselves; in a sense, it involved a tax that fell most heavily on the disadvantaged to benefit commercial farmers. It seemed particularly immoral to many that crops should not be grown—indeed, should even be destroyed, as they were in the spring of 1933—at a time when many Americans were ill fed and ill clothed.

Agricultural prices would have risen more had the New Deal program actually worked as planned. Prices went up but not as dramatically as farmers and policy makers had hoped. Commodity prices averaged about 80 percent of parity between 1934 and 1940. This meant that, in several years for several commodities, prices were not enough above loan rates for many farmers to justify market sales. As a result, the CCC found itself awash in surplus commodities that could not be sold. To dispose of these domestically would defeat the purpose of the program by deflating prices. To dispose of them internationally at prevailing prices would invite charges of dumping, because the loan level almost always exceeded the world price. As a consequence, the United States voluntarily curtailed its participation in world markets for a number of agricultural commodities. This seemed a small sacrifice in light of the trade situation in 1933, and, as a creditor nation that did not need to sell commodities, the United States could afford to do it. But in the future, when world markets again beckoned and the United States needed them, production-control and price-support programs were impediments.

Prices did not rise enough because production did not fall enough. Production declined, certainly, but not in proportion to the amount of land retired. Moreover, at least some of the decline was due to the Great Plains drought and other natural factors. There were several reasons for this unanticipated result. First, some farmers did not participate, and some of them actually increased commodity production in the expectation that prices would rise. Some of those who participated cheated, and virtually all who took part in the programs understandably removed their least productive acres from production. Moreover, the crop loan program ironically encouraged production of the very commodities New Dealers wanted to limit. Loan rates constituted a floor under prices, removing much of the risk from commodity production. In order to take advantage of this new situation, farmers worked their unretired acres more intensively, increasing their yields. Science and technology also drove yields up. The introduction of hybrid corn, which provided a yield advantage of about 20 percent over open-pollinated varieties, was especially significant in increasing production. This last point illustrates the contradictory effects of government agricultural policies. While one portion of the USDA was trying to curtail production the scientific establishment in the department and in the land-grant research complex was trying to increase it.

The programs, then, did not work exactly as planned, and farmers did not benefit as much as hoped. But they did benefit, and by 1938 over a third of farm income came in the form of government payments of various sorts. The benefits were spread very unevenly, though. In order to participate, one had to be a producer of a covered commodity. Farmers who grew tobacco or corn were included, while those who produced oats or oranges were not. Moreover, only commercial producers benefited; those who made corn or tobacco for their own use derived nothing from the programs. And the more commercial farmers were, the better off they were, at least in most of the programs. The tobacco program involved an acreage-allotment system that benefited small producers, but that was the exception that proved the rule. In cotton, which was much more typical, farmers large enough to take 100 acres out of production and get a CCC loan on 25 thousand pounds were obviously better off than neighbors who retired 20 acres and got a loan on 5 thousand pounds.

The problem was that commodity-based programs were not very effective means of addressing such human problems as low income, rural poverty, and the demise of the family farm. Had farmers all been commercial commodity producers of roughly equal size the programs would have been socially just. In the Midwest and on the Great Plains, where most farmers produced corn, hogs, wheat, beef, or milk for market, benefits were spread broadly and relatively evenly. But such was not the case in most other sections of the country. Farmers in the Northeast and in the Appalachian region, who were often weekend subsistence producers or truck gardeners, received nothing, despite the fact that many were quite poor. Farmers in other regions were actually harmed by the operation of the programs, and none suffered more than sharecroppers in the cotton South.

New Deal agricultural programs came to a suffering, backward South. Not only were prices low, but infertility was a problem in many areas, as was the boll weevil. The region had not changed appreciably in the seventy-five years since the Civil War. Cotton agriculture remained an undermechanized, undiversified, labor-intensive enterprise. Most cotton was grown by sharecroppers and laborers on land owned by others. Prices and production were too low to provide decent standards of living in the overpopulated rural areas, even before the depression pushed marginal people into despair. Only a crisis as severe as the Great Depression could have induced many conservative landowners to welcome federal programs. But they quickly grasped that the cotton program of the AAA held out the prospect of higher prices for the crop, and some realized that it extended the possibility of removing sharecroppers.

The AAA realized that cotton agriculture was a human endeavor of great complexity, and the agency attempted to assure that the interests of croppers were protected. AAA cotton contracts stipulated that landlords share acreage-reduction payments with tenants in the same proportion as they had shared the crop. But the first question landlords asked was, which tenants? Landlords removing land from production had to decide whether to apportion acreage reductions among all of their tenants or simply to put some off the land. In other words, should a landowner with ten croppers on 400 acres who had a contract to retire 160 acres have each cropper plant sixteen fewer

214 acres or simply dismiss four croppers? Recognizing that there was a labor surplus for most of the year anyway, more often than not the landowner chose the latter option. Such an action violated the spirit of a AAA stipulation that planters maintain cropper numbers insofar as possible, but that phrase was flexible and had no apparent effect on the actions of many landlords.

It got worse. Landlords, cash poor for most of their lives, suddenly found themselves with capital in the form of government checks. Some of them used the money to buy tractors, which allowed them to put all of their croppers off the land. This was risky, because hand labor would still be required to chop and pick the crop, but New Deal unemployment relief programs provided a means for laborers to live when they were not needed in the fields. In this way, the New Deal played the planter's historic role of providing furnish for croppers.

Even those who kept their croppers did not usually share with them as AAA contracts stipulated. Sometimes they reasoned that sharecroppers were laborers rather than tenants and were thus unprotected. In other cases they kept tenants' shares as compensation for excess furnish they had provided over the years. Whatever explanation landlords might have given for their behavior, they were used to making the rules by which their croppers lived, and they had no intention of living by rules imposed from Washington. The people in the Cotton Section of the AAA generally accepted that reality. They also accepted planters' domination of the county committees that interpreted and enforced Washington's rules. And they recognized that a strong effort to assert and protect croppers' rights would probably doom the cotton program altogether.

Not everyone in the AAA proved as willing as the administrators of the Cotton Section to accept a situation that empowered those who were already powerful at the expense of the powerless. In 1935 the efforts of several young attorneys in the AAA to secure justice for croppers culminated in a public fight that resulted in their being purged—removed—from the agency. That same year the actions of the Southern Tenant Farmers' Union (STFU), founded by socialist Harry Mitchell to publicize the plight of displaced and abused croppers, brought the issue to public attention.

The New Deal, which championed society's downtrodden at its best moments, was understandably embarrassed by the publicity generated by the

AAA purge and the STFU. Henceforth, more resources were directed to agencies that addressed the problems of those on the bottom of rural society, and the AAA exerted a bit more energy in upholding croppers' rights. These efforts were more cosmetic than substantive, however, and did little good in the long run. In retrospect it is clear that a revolution was beginning in the cotton South that would alter it economically, socially, technologically, and structurally and that New Deal programs had unintentionally launched it.

Everything was in surplus in 1936, including critics of government agricultural programs. Liberals and radicals inside and outside of agriculture, including leaders of the Farmers Union, argued that the AAA was unfair to the rural poor. Conservatives, such as those in the Farmers' Independence Council of America, complained that the programs stripped farmers of their independence and removed them from the free market. And farmers themselves, self-consciously independent, were embarrassed to receive government checks and complained of bureaucratic regimentation and red tape. Farmers in 1936 willing to say they really liked the agricultural programs of the New Deal were few and far between.

But liking and needing are two different things. In the case of the *United States v. Butler* (1936), the Supreme Court ruled the Agricultural Adjustment Act unconstitutional on the grounds that regulation of agricultural production was beyond the power of Congress and that the processing tax was not a direct tax as defined by the Constitution. Farmers faced with the prospect of going cold turkey clamored for a replacement, and Congress responded with the Soil Conservation and Domestic Allotment Act. This legislation removed land from production on the basis of its erodability and paid farmers in the program out of general funds. Not surprisingly, highly erodable lands were defined as those used to produce basic commodities. With thousands of tons of midwestern soil flowing down the Mississippi every year (and thousands more suspended in the air as dust over Washington and other eastern cities), the Supreme Court was convinced that soil conservation was an interstate problem and thus an appropriate area for congressional action.

In 1938, Congress followed with a second Agricultural Adjustment Act. This legislation emphasized acreage allotments and flexible crop loans through the CCC. It also provided for binding marketing agreements among farmers as a means of underpinning prices. Secretary Wallace hoped that this legislation would allow the maintenance of what he called an ever-

216 normal granary, a situation in which supplies and prices were stable in good years and bad. The second AAA also elaborated the government safety net under agriculture by providing for federal crop insurance.

Names and details of programs changed, but underlying apparent flux were several stable concepts. First, programs were targeted at commercial producers of basic commodities. Second, acreage limitation was the most popular means of curbing production. And third, loans provided floors under farm prices. Finally, and most basically, while nobody realized it yet, the government was in the agricultural market to stay.

THE NEW DEAL AND RURAL LIFE

The benefits of government-sponsored mortgage refinancing, acreage limitations, and crop loans came disproportionately to landowning commercial producers of basic commodities, with the largest among them enjoying the greatest advantages. New Dealers believed such programs would benefit the whole rural community, mainly because a rising tide supposedly lifts all boats, but such an outcome was more often the exception than the rule.

The New Deal, however, was a complex and frequently contradictory enterprise, and while its main thrust benefited the top half of the rural community, some of its programs helped those on the bottom. New Deal relief agencies were created for the urban unemployed, but administrators quickly recognized that farm people—laborers, tenants, and even landowners—could also be in desperate need. Consequently, such early agencies as the Federal Emergency Relief Administration, the Civilian Conservation Corps, and the Civil Works Administration extended relief to rural as well as urban people. Virtually all relief was work relief, in which recipients performed public-service labor in return for their payments. In most rural areas early relief programs were oriented toward such infrastructure projects as repairing roads or clearing ditches.

Relief was supposed to be a stopgap measure to tide people over until economic recovery took place. In 1935 the anticipated recovery had still not occurred, so Congress created the Works Progress Administration (WPA) as a permanent relief agency. Because the WPA was to be permanent, its administrators had the luxury of designing more ambitious and imaginative projects than predecessor agencies had undertaken. The WPA still emphasized infrastructure development, but it was able to embark on more enduring projects, building roads, bridges, parks, swimming pools, schools, and courthouses rather than simply repairing or painting existing facilities. Hundreds of WPA facilities and structures continue to serve rural America today. In the West and on the Plains, WPA workers fought drought by building check dams and stock ponds and by undertaking land-conservation activities such as terracing, reseeding, and tree planting. The WPA also recognized that some of the unemployed could better serve the community with their brains than with their brawn. Thousands of WPA workers taught in rural schools or staffed rural libraries. WPA artists painted murals on rural public buildings, WPA historians interviewed local pioneers, and WPA actors and musicians performed for rural audiences, free of charge.

New Deal relief programs helped rural communities maintain essential services and even provided them with some enrichment, but their main purpose was to help relieve personal distress. Tens of thousands of farmers took relief work—in North Dakota alone over ten thousand farmers were employed by the WPA in 1936—and it helped their families survive. Relief was controversial in rural America, however, even more than in cities. Employers, especially in the South, complained that laborers would rather go on relief than work for wages. But relief was controversial even among those who received it. Self-consciously independent, farmers were reluctant to take government handouts unless they were in dire need, even when they worked for payments. Adding to their reluctance was the reality that some of their neighbors viewed them as shiftless or lazy. When the crisis had passed, former relief recipients looked back on their experience with embarrassment and began a process of suppressing their memories of it. They were so successful that it is difficult today to find anyone in rural communities who will admit that people in his or her family received unemployment relief during the thirties.

Relief activities helped rural casualties of the depression, but the New Deal's agricultural recovery program had ironically created many victims of its own. To its credit, the New Deal was willing to take at least some responsibility for these people. In 1935 Roosevelt created the Resettlement Administration (RA) by executive order. The purpose of the agency was to oversee some ongoing rural projects—including the Subsistence Homestead program, a back-to-the-land enterprise launched by the Interior Department in 1933—and to develop some new ones. Among the RA's new programs were the resettlement of tenants and owners displaced by government programs or environmental disaster on new farms, the provision of rehabilitation loans

Georgia sharecropper and his mule cultivating cotton in 1937. Photograph by Dorothea Lange. Courtesy of the Library of Congress.

for small farmers with degraded properties, and the creation and maintenance of camps for migratory farm laborers. In 1937 its activities were transferred to a new agency, the Farm Security Administration (FSA).

The brave effort of the RA and the FSA to uplift some of the people on the bottom of rural society turned out largely to be a fool's errand. The agencies were funded with conscience money that reflected the determination of an embarrassed administration to relieve its guilt. New Dealers had no intention of revolutionizing the countryside. Neither agency ever began to have enough money to address the needs it confronted. There were simply too many displaced croppers, too many tenants who wanted to be owners, and too many farmers whose operations were not commercially viable. The agencies learned that it was expensive to provide people with the land and machinery they needed to succeed. All too often, the answer was to provide marginal farmers with new farms that were only slightly less marginal. To do more was too expensive and invited criticism of the government for favoritism to a few. The agencies also discovered that poor farmers frequently lacked agricultural and business skills. Providing skills demanded intensive casework, and that was also expensive. The RA and the FSA found themselves involved in a sort of agricultural triage, saving a handful of relatively promising farmers and letting the rest go. Southern blacks were disproportionately represented among those let go. The most severely displaced, they enjoyed the fewest opportunities for resettlement.

The fiscal constraints on the RA and the FSA compounded their confusion of purpose. The main functions of the agencies involved enhancing commercial agriculture by making marginal producers viable, providing support services for agricultural laborers, and encouraging cooperatives, an important FSA enterprise. Others in the agencies believed in social experimentation with subsistence homesteads and cooperative farms uncomfortably similar to Soviet collectives. Subsistence homesteads and collective farms were attractive to some romantics during the depression, but few knowledgeable observers saw any future for them in an agricultural system that had always been commercial and capitalistic.

These agencies could never afford to fulfill any of their tasks very well, but what they did—and especially what they represented—aroused savage opposition to them from powerful groups in agriculture. By the early 1940s the FSA had come under intense political pressure. Critics claimed that it aided shiftless ne'er-do-wells undeserving of help. Employers complained that it

220 spread discontent among tenants and gave laborers unrealistic expectations. To some it seemed un-American. Soviet-style collectives raised suspicions totally disproportionate to their numbers. Conservatives argued that the whole idea of resettlement violated individual freedom and represented a paternalism alien to the American experience. Rexford Guy Tugwell, much maligned during his tenure as head of the Resettlement Administration, wryly noted in later years that the clients' "freedom . . . was limited to the right to be dispossessed and to migrate, or perhaps to sink deeper into misery" but that these unfortunates suddenly found themselves objects of solicitude by conservatives who had never appeared to care for them before.[1]

Underlying the broad and multifaceted assault on the FSA was the issue of political power. The FSA had allied itself with the Farmers Union, but beyond that it had little political support in agriculture. Tenant farmers and migrant laborers do not generally belong to powerful lobbying organizations or contribute to political campaigns, and congressional representatives are not much interested in their opinions. On the other side were the Farm Bureau, which opposed the FSA both for what it stood for and for who it stood with, the Grange, which usually followed the Farm Bureau's lead, and the USDA, which had never shown much sympathy for anyone in agriculture who was not a substantial commercial producer. It was an unequal contest. Congress slashed FSA appropriations, most dramatically in 1943, and abolished the FSA altogether in 1946, folding its remaining functions into a new agency, the Farmers Home Administration, which also took over the functions of the Farm Credit Administration. The existence of the RA and the FSA had proved that the New Deal had a heart, but neither had a noticeable effect on the structure of rural society.

The New Deal enterprise that had the most enduring impact on daily life in rural America was electrification. In 1933 the near-universal absence of electricity on farms represented one of the sharpest qualitative differences between rural and urban living. Urban electrification proceeded dramatically in the early twentieth century, and by 1920 most middle-class city people enjoyed the convenience of central station power. Electrification underwent an especially impressive surge in the twenties, as the number of kilowatt-hours produced nearly doubled. By the end of the decade, relatively few urbanites of any social class lived without the benefits of electricity. But as urban America electrified, rural people were left behind. Farmers could generate their own power, and some did, but home electrical plants were expensive and demanded technological sophistication. Central-station power was sometimes available to a handful of farmers living near towns, but it was out of the question for most. Power companies contended that it was not cost effective to string miles of wire just to serve a handful of scattered farmsteads. In an electrifying country, the absence of electrical power did not mean only that people had to depend on gas or kerosene for illumination. It also meant that they beat rugs, heated flatirons on wood or coal stoves, and cooled food in dripping iceboxes while their more fortunate urban cousins had access to a range of electrical conveniences. And it meant that a device like a radio could not simply be plugged in but had to be hooked up to cumbersome batteries that needed frequent recharging.

The New Deal got into the rural electrification business in 1933 with the creation of the Tennessee Valley Authority (TVA). The TVA was a sweeping project for comprehensive development in a region comprising parts of seven southern states. At the heart of the project was a series of dams to control floods and generate hydroelectric power, but it also included an ambitious program of rural revitalization consisting of land reclamation, erosion control, manufacture of cheap nitrogen fertilizer, and electrification. The TVA was a boon to the farmers of the Tennessee Valley—or at least to those whose homes were not inundated by the lakes that filled the valleys behind the dams—but most of the rest of rural America could not be electrified in the same way. Moreover, the TVA raised shrill opposition from conservatives to whom it represented a Soviet-style government intrusion into what had traditionally been a private enterprise.

Committed to enriching the lives of all rural Americans, Roosevelt decided to use local cooperation as the predominant means to electrification. In May of 1935 he issued an executive order creating the Rural Electrification Administration (REA), an agency given permanence by congressional legislation the following year. The REA was authorized to make low-interest, long-term loans to entities that would generate or distribute electricity to rural areas. While private utilities could apply, consumer-owned cooperatives and nonprofit organizations received priority.

Managers of private utilities believed that conservative farmers would neither assume the debts electrical distribution required nor put power in their homes, but rural people moved quickly to take advantage of the opportunity the REA presented. In addition to funding generation and distribution, the REA provided long-term, low-interest loans to farmers who wanted to wire their homes and farm buildings and to buy appliances. The farm family could pay the estimated average cost of $600 for line construction, wiring, and appliances over twenty years for about $3 a month under the liberal terms offered by the REA. Farmers were not inclined to look this gift horse in the mouth.

Because original REA regulations required a minimum of three customers per mile, most early co-ops were formed in the relatively densely populated East and Midwest. Rules were liberalized in 1944, however, facilitating electrification in the West and on the Great Plains. Electrification was interrupted when World War II brought a shortage of labor and materials, but by 1950 over half the farms in the country had central station power. A decade later only a handful of farms lacked electricity.

The electrification of rural America provided a short-term economic stimulus there and beyond. People were employed putting up lines and wiring homes. Appliance and equipment manufacturers and dealers enjoyed a vast new market for their wares. And farm-implement manufacturers moved an array of devices from the drawing boards to the assembly lines. But the effects of electrification on rural America were much more enduring. Electrification made all kinds of farm work easier and dramatically altered such enterprises as dairy and poultry production, facilitating mechanization and a stunning increase in efficiency. It also altered the rural home, allowing the introduction of a vast range of devices and conveniences urban people enjoyed. Because many of these devices were related to homemaking, electrification allowed manufacturers, advertisers, and home extension agents to underpin the ideal of domesticity that had been deemphasized by the demands the live-at-home thirties had placed on women. Rural women continued to have their own agendas, however, sometimes welcoming electricity precisely because it allowed them to escape the house and do more farm work.

For its part, the REA became a powerful government bureaucracy, gaining authority in 1949 to lend money to telephone cooperatives on terms similar to those it offered electric co-ops. It also benefited from the 1942 creation of the National Rural Electric Cooperatives Association, a lobbying group that established a relationship with the REA similar to that existing between the Farm Bureau and the Extension Service. By the 1980s the REA had become an object of criticism and controversy. To many, it symbolized government favoritism to one social group at the expense of the general public. At times it seemed that an agency created to electrify farms had been abused by wealthy suburbanites and penny-pinching manufacturers who enjoyed cheap power subsidized by taxpayers. But it is difficult for anyone who remembers the literally dark days before the REA to discount the good that the agency has done for rural America.

THE DUST BOWL

The challenge of the Dust Bowl further increased government involvement with agriculture during the thirties. The term Dust Bowl referred both to the phenomena of drought and wind erosion that plagued the entire Plains region and to the area of western Kansas, eastern Colorado, the Oklahoma panhandle, the northern panhandle of Texas, and eastern New Mexico where the impact of these phenomena seemed especially severe. The climatological causes of the Great Plains drought were easy to understand. Most of the region received fewer than twenty inches of rain in normal years, and much of it received under fifteen. But the thirties was not a normal period. In eight of the ten years rainfall was below normal at most reporting stations. In 1934 and 1936, probably the two driest years overall, rainfall in many places was less than half of normal. This problem was aggravated by extraordinarily high temperatures that accelerated evaporation of whatever moisture fell. Low moisture and high evaporation meant that natural vegetation receded and crops did not thrive. When the ubiquitous wind moved across the uncovered land it lifted the soil, and dust storms resulted.

None of this was totally new. Drought and dust had been a major feature of the 1850s and 1860s in the Plains and had returned to plague the region in the 1890s. Even in normal years dust storms were common phenomena, especially in the spring. What was different in the thirties was the scale, scope, and frequency of the storms. The dust boiled up into massive clouds that filled the space above the ground all along the horizon. Stunned observers' powers of description were challenged by the storms; most often they called the dusters black blizzards or black tidal waves. "Blizzard" was a fairly accurate description. People caught in their midst became disoriented, drivers could not see roads, and towns turned streetlights on in the middle of the day. The scale of the storms made them frightening. One duster in May of 1935 lifted an estimated 350 million tons of soil into the air and moved it to the East. Meteorologists figured that 12 million tons sifted down on Chicago, and as far east as Buffalo, New York, motorists switched on headlights during the day to cut the gloom. Western dust reddened the afternoon sun in Washington, D.C., and hundreds of miles into the Atlantic grit was deposited on the decks of ships. Nobody could remember anything quite like this before.

If the storms of the dirty thirties were different it was at least partially because the Plains were different. In the 1890s virtually all of the western Plains remained unbroken. But with high crop prices in the early-twentieth-century grain farmers pushed farther west. The huge demand for wheat during World War I rapidly accelerated the farm-making process in the semiarid grasslands. More land was broken during the twenties, much of it by mechanized, "suitcase" farmers (farmers who were not residents of the region but exploited economic opportunities there) who achieved economies of scale by bringing huge tracts into production. When the land was broken it was more vulnerable to wind erosion, and agricultural methods intensified the problem. One-way disc plows, which pulverized the soil more completely than the moldboard type traditionally preferred on the Plains, became popular, and farmers often burned off trash (crop residue, such as stalks) rather than leaving it on the ground where it could help hold the soil.

While it seems reasonable today to attribute the Dust Bowl to a combination of natural and human causes, observers at the time tended to take sharply divergent positions on the question. Most residents of the Plains blamed the weather and argued, on the basis of their experience, that adequate rain would again make small grain production feasible in the region. On the other hand, a number of federal officials, buttressed by range scientists and plant ecologists, argued that people had caused the Dust Bowl by upsetting a fragile ecosystem. That view was dramatically captured by Pare Lorentz's documentary film *The Plow That Broke the Plains*, which laid the disaster on the doorstep of Plains farmers.

The effects of the Dust Bowl were much clearer than its causes. It put farm families under tremendous strain. Farmers who would have had difficulty surviving even with crops in those depression years failed without them. In 1935, Hamilton County, Kansas, farmer George Friesen realized only $134 from his wheat crop.[2] The only thing that kept the Friesens going was the $182 Martha earned selling chickens and eggs. Especially hard hit were those, like George Friesen, who raised wheat or cattle exclusively; farmers who mixed the two in a common regional diversification were better able to weather the crisis. Adding to farmers' woes were the plagues of grasshoppers and jackrabbits that accompanied the drought; what did not dry up and blow away was likely to be eaten by these ravenous vermin.

Communities suffered along with the farmers on whom they depended. Economic hardship made it difficult for town merchants and professionals to survive, and maintaining schools, churches, and other local institutions was a tough proposition. Special health problems appeared. People with respiratory conditions found the dust debilitating, and some—the very young and the very old, especially—suffered from "dust pneumonia," which was often fatal. The morale of what had been optimistic, booster communities eroded with the fields.

The suffering of the Dust Bowl region was genuine, but it must be kept in perspective. After Roosevelt's inauguration in 1933, aid poured in. People in the region enjoyed disproportionate benefits from federal relief agencies, they participated fully in agricultural-recovery programs, and they were favored with special initiatives created for them. On a per-capita basis, the people in the Dust Bowl received more federal largesse than people in any other agricultural area. They would have preferred to be in a position where they did not need the help, of course, but they were certainly not abandoned by the country in their time of trial.

As far as the nation was concerned, the major effect of the drought was the so-called Dust Bowl migration of hundreds of thousands of people—usually called Okies because so many seemed to come from Oklahoma—mainly to California. The Okies became the focus of special attention between 1937 and 1940 for several reasons. First, they endured tremendous hardship and dislocation, especially after they arrived in California, where many of them joined an already swollen migrant-labor stream in agriculture. Innumerable Mexicans, Filipinos, Chinese, and others had long lived marginal lives as transient workers in the fields and orchards of the Golden State, but the fact that the Dust Bowl migrants were old-stock Americans made their plight especially poignant. This touched on a second reason for the remarkable attention given to the Okies—they were white. The Dust Bowl migrants did not suffer any more than black croppers put off cotton farms by the tens of thousands in the same years, but the sufferings of blacks were accepted by a racist nation while those of whites were not. A final reason for the extraordinary attention paid to the Okies was that they went to California. In a state with a remarkable history of xenophobia and class frictions, their presence quickly became a public issue. Moreover, because California was already a major me-

226 dia center, the Okies were sure to be thrust into the national spotlight. In 1939, John Steinbeck immortalized the Dust Bowl migrants in *The Grapes of Wrath*, and the next year John Ford put Steinbeck's Joad family on film. By that time, the Okies and the Dust Bowl were inextricably linked in the public mind.

People on the Plains howled that it was all very misleading. Oklahomans especially complained that they had been unfairly portrayed as backward and ignorant. They argued that the people who had left were mostly at the bottom of society—and thus, presumably, were not typical. They ordered their libraries not to buy *The Grapes of Wrath*, and they boycotted theaters showing the movie. Everywhere on the Plains, people had the feeling they were being stereotyped and pitied, and they did not like it.

The complaints were defensive and myopic, but they were not without substance. In the first place, migration from the Dust Bowl region itself was not extraordinary, though it appeared to be because in-migration virtually ceased. Indeed, in many areas out-migration declined, simply because there were no jobs elsewhere and one needed to establish residence to get on relief. Migration was much more pronounced from areas like eastern Oklahoma, where the AAA's cotton program worked its wicked ways on tenants. In the second place, most migrants went to a town in their state or to an adjacent state, not to California. And they were not extraordinary migrants. They were most likely to be young people with minimal family and property responsibilities, and they commonly undertook chain migration, going where friends or kin had gone before. Many of them got caught temporarily in a difficult situation, to be sure, but by the early forties most had improved their situations dramatically.

The myths of the Dust Bowl migration stuck because so many people needed them. Social reformers needed the Dust Bowl–migration myths if they were to induce structural changes in California agriculture. The Farm Security Administration needed them to justify its programs for the rural underclass. The New Deal needed them to deflect attention from the embarrassing reality that most migrants had been displaced by its own programs. The Dust Bowl region itself needed the myths to justify continuing government aid. And, perhaps most important, the public needed the Dust Bowl myths. People beset by depression needed someone white with whom they could identify and who was worse off than they were, someone they could feel sorry for and who could make them count their blessings, and the

Okies filled the bill. For the first time in the history of the country, a substantial body of rural Americans were the subject of urban pity. It was an important milestone on the road rural America was traveling from majority to marginality.

Most of the victims of the Dust Bowl stayed in the region, and the federal government developed programs to help them survive and eventually thrive. As was so often the case during the New Deal, the solutions suggested for the drought problem were premised on divergent analyses and contradicted one another. Land-use planners, led by Lewis Gray of the USDA's Bureau of Agricultural Economics, took what might be called a "plow that broke the plains" position on the Dust Bowl. They believed that the more arid portions of the region were naturally short-grass country, that they should never have been broken, and that they should be returned to something resembling their natural condition. This was the point of view that dominated the government-appointed Great Plains Committee and was reflected in its 1936 report to the president, *The Future of the Great Plains*.[3] Specifically, Gray and the Great Plains Committee proposed a three-part program for the Plains. First, the committee wanted to retain all remaining unbroken lands in their natural condition. Second, they wanted the government to purchase submarginal lands in the region, return them to grass for grazing purposes, and resettle the farmers whose land had been purchased on more viable properties. Gray thought 75 million acres—an area equal in size to all of South Dakota and more than half of North Dakota—should be handled in this manner. The third part of Gray's program involved the creation of county committees to enforce sound conservation practices on lands still being cropped.

The other New Deal position on the Dust Bowl was represented by the Soil Conservation Service (SCS), led by the charismatic Hugh Hammond Bennett. The SCS took the position that, while unwise agricultural methods had exacerbated the crisis of the drought, lack of rain was the major problem, and farmers had to learn to cope with that reality. The SCS did not agree with Gray that most of the land was marginal and should be retired from crop agriculture. Bennett believed that better methods and crops, not the return of the Plains to its short-grass past, was the answer to the Dust Bowl problem. The SCS program for the Dust Bowl, like that of the Great Plains Committee, consisted of three parts. First, the SCS advocated new crop mixes, emphasizing grass, soil restorative crops, and such new dryland

228 crops as sorghum. Second, the SCS advocated the restoration of seriously depleted soils and the preservation of endangered ones through terracing, contour plowing, and other methods, and the preservation of soil moisture by leaving lands fallow and retaining trash on the ground. A related conservation initiative was the Shelterbelt Program, undertaken by the Forest Service, in which 220 million trees were planted on the Plains to hold the soil, serve as windbreaks, and slow evaporation. Finally, Bennett and his colleagues favored the creation of local, farmer-run soil conservation districts, reasoning that farmers would be more likely to adopt conservation techniques advocated by their neighbors than those passed down by the government.

People in the Dust Bowl region figured that their only real problem was a lack of rain that they hoped would be temporary. But of the New Deal's two programmatic thrusts, they found that of the SCS more attractive. The region was filled with boosters who saw a bright future for the Plains and who had invested their lives and fortunes in that vision. The plan proposed by Gray and the Great Plains Committee implicitly blamed the people on the Plains for the problems of the region and proposed what amounted to an agricultural retreat. Plains people could live with an end to the opening of new lands, largely accomplished by the Taylor Grazing Act of 1934, which removed remaining federal lands from entry and put them under the Bureau of Land Management, but they bristled at the suggestion that existing farms should be returned to grass. People who foresaw a region of prosperous farms and bustling towns and cities could hardly welcome such a program. Even partial land retirement worried those who feared that a shrinking tax base would increase their own burdens. Opposition from the region combined with budgetary constraints to dramatically limit land retirement. In the end only 11.3 million submarginal acres were removed from crop production and put into national grasslands.

The SCS implicitly blamed the people of the Plains for being poor farmers, but at least it saw a future for the area compatible with that envisioned by boosters. For a time, the SCS seemed to make progress in helping farmers live with the realities of their region, but changes proved to be more temporary than permanent. In the 1940s the rains came back, and after World War II farmers in the Dust Bowl began irrigating with water pulled up from the Ogallala aquifer, a water-saturated gravel bed that underlies much of the region. Abundant water, from whatever source, reduced or eliminated the necessity of practices predicated on the scarcity of moisture.

Today we can see how little progress has been made in conservation. Farmers on the Plains oppose the swampbuster and sodbuster provisions of farm legislation, designed to keep highly erodable lands in grass and conserve moisture, and they rip out shelterbelts to facilitate the use of larger farm machinery. Wind erosion continues to be a problem, as anyone who has seen a spring dust storm on the Plains can readily confirm, and it has been estimated that the United States loses nine tons of topsoil *per acre a year* to the erosive action of wind and water. It is a sign of the times that budget cutters periodically suggest the abolition of the SCS, which seems to many to have become irrelevant. Clearly, we are well positioned to learn whether the Dust Bowl was a unique phenomenon or a preview of things to come.

WORLD WAR II

New Deal farm programs were so contradictory and multifaceted that it was difficult for contemporaries to judge what their effects would be. On the one hand, Roosevelt and his agricultural advisors expressed a genuine commitment to the family farm and a sympathy for agriculture's underdogs, and the people on the bottom half of rural society reciprocated with their affection and their votes. On the other hand, the economic benefits of the programs had flowed disproportionately to large-scale commodity producers, even though the relatively privileged frequently complained bitterly about government activism in agriculture in general and such agencies as the FSA in particular. World War II made it clear that the New Deal had done nothing to overturn established power relationships in agriculture and had, indeed, reinforced them.

The response of government and agriculture to World War II was shaped by the World War I experience. The previous conflict had taken place less than a quarter century earlier; most policy makers and agricultural leaders had experienced it as adults, and many had held responsible positions during the first war. Consequently, most significant farm-policy actors went into the war with firm ideas of what they wanted out of agriculture and for agriculture and a clear sense of how they might best get it.

Nobody wanted a repetition of the heavy-handed social control that had so divided rural America in 1917–18. Nor did this seem necessary in light of the

230 remarkable level of national unity after Pearl Harbor. Many rural Americans had been isolationists up until the Japanese attack and subsequent German entry plunged the country into a two-front war, but even the ethnic Germans among them did not feel the ambivalence toward Hitler they had felt toward Kaiser Wilhelm. The remarkable unanimity of rural opinion meant that no Committee on Public Information propagandized rural Americans, county agents did not try to mobilize them against their neighbors, and home guards and other vigilante units were not formed.

The government also avoided exercising tight control over food and agricultural production goods. During the First World War, the USDA received sweeping powers over seed, fertilizer, and other productive resources, which it seldom used, and the Food Administration got controls over food that it exercised vigorously. This time, the government sought to leave as much authority as possible with rural people themselves.

It was impossible to fight a modern war without some economic controls, but those usually benefited agriculture instead of handicapping it. The threat of inflation led in 1942 to the imposition of price controls on most raw materials and manufactured items purchased by farmers, but controls were not placed on food prices until the following year. Petroleum and tires were rationed, but farmers received special allocations of these crucial items. Machinery and labor were in short supply, but the government did what it could to provide farmers with a sufficiency of both. Further lightening the hand of government for some was the fact that most controls were administered locally by County War Boards run through the Extension Service. In practice, this meant that in most localities the Farm Bureau carried out policies.

The Farm Bureau was as powerful in setting national agricultural policy as it was in administering it locally. One area in which that organization exercised its clout with considerable effect was farm labor. In 1942, Farm Bureau lobbying succeeded in getting Congress to grant draft deferments to all laborers producing so-called essential crops, including tobacco. The next year, the Farm Bureau got control over farm labor moved from the War Manpower Commission to the USDA, which was prohibited at bureau insistence from using federal funds to establish housing standards, set wages and hours, or promote collective bargaining among farmworkers. It was allowed to hold unwilling workers on the land by threatening them with the draft, however, a power it used effectively in the cotton South.

The importance of agriculture for the war effort combined with the political power of organized farmers to create a highly favorable government pricing policy. Production controls were suspended, but income supports were kept in place, despite the fact that the economic conditions that had originally justified them no longer operated. In 1941, Congress set commodity loan levels at 85 percent of parity, then raised them the next year to 90 percent. Nineteen forty-three loan rates were set at 110 percent of parity, despite President Roosevelt's angry complaint that greedy farmers wanted "a pound of flesh."[4] Government income and price supports had clearly made the transition from bad times to good. They were no longer economically necessary, but they had become politically invulnerable. Some critics wondered, though, whether programs could be restructured in such a way as to limit aid to the most comfortable farmers and wean producers away from basic commodities that were normally produced in surplus.

After the war, Charles Brannan, President Harry Truman's secretary of agriculture, suggested a basic restructuring of the farm program. Brannan favored high income supports for producers of basic commodities but only on the first $25,700 worth of the commodity a farmer marketed. The second major part of the Brannan plan involved encouraging production of perishable crops by the provision of deficiency payments to farmers to make up the difference between market prices and target prices set as a percentage of parity. Brannan hoped to discourage commodity surpluses, increase the production of fruits, vegetables, dairy products, and other items that would enrich the American diet, and limit the degree to which the largest farmers could be rewarded.

Whatever the strengths of the Brannan plan, it aroused intense opposition from the Farm Bureau. The Bureau opposed the plan because it aimed to change a system under which the organization's largest members had thrived and, perhaps more important, because it was backed by the Farmers Union, the bureau's weaker rival for dominance in organized agriculture. Congress's defeat of the Brannan plan was yet another sign of the political dominance of the Farm Bureau, as well as of the endurance of the farm program that had been outlined in the dark days of 1933.

During the war, high price support for commodities and the end of acreage restrictions combined to push production ahead. For example, wheat and rice production both rose by about 50 percent between 1939 and 1945. High production together with high prices inflated agricultural incomes dramatically, albeit unevenly. Net farm income rose by a staggering 156 percent

232 between 1939 and 1944 alone. Similar prosperity during World War I had intoxicated farmers, removing their inhibitions against purchasing expensive land. Those farming in the early 1940s remembered their earlier experience, as well as the two decades of hard times since. Consequently, farmers paid off mortgages and replenished bank accounts, expanding only carefully and prudently. One result of farmer conservatism was that land prices advanced only about 50 percent during the war. In a sense, farmers drew lessons from history that had become less valid. New Deal price-support programs had substantially reduced the risks of commercial agriculture while rewarding expansion, but most producers had yet to realize it.

Throughout the war conservatives and liberals argued over the effects of government programs on agricultural production. Conservatives contended that the war showed what farmers could do with the government off their backs, while liberals countered that price supports had induced the surge in production. What both missed was that much of the increase in production was due to a technical and scientific revolution that was in its early stages, a revolution that would transform agriculture and rural life after the war.

ELEVEN

The Production Revolution
and Its Consequences

In the USDA's *Yearbook of Agriculture* for 1940, historian Paul Johnstone contrasted the "old ideals" of agriculture with its "new ideas."[1] While the public continued to perceive farming in a traditional and often romantic way, Johnstone emphasized "profound differences between rural life today and a century ago," particularly in such areas as "increased commercialization, more advanced technology . . . [and] wider adoption of material things from the city." Even more significant, to Johnstone's mind, was the change in rural culture and in the ways rural people thought, "the gradual alteration of habits, customs, institutions, and ideas that has constituted the social or cultural adaptation to material change."

Johnstone was a perceptive observer who was able to cut through myth and rhetoric, some of it from farmers themselves, to the reality of the agricultural enterprise. Over the previous century, farming had become a more sophisticated endeavor, the material standards of rural people had come to approximate those of urbanites, and habits of mind and ways of looking at things had changed along the way.

What Johnstone could see in 1940 virtually everyone who observed agriculture could see in 1970 or 1980. During the generation after the appearance of his classic article, agriculture underwent a revolution in productivity

234 spurred by machines, chemicals, and improved plant and animal breeds. One of his contemporaries on a farm produced enough to feed about ten people. By the late eighties, the average farmer fed ninety other people.

As farmers became more productive their businesses changed. Farmers had to be more sophisticated, better educated, more technologically literate, more willing to use complex business strategies, and more highly capitalized. As farming became more demanding, fewer people were able to succeed at it, and as farmers became more productive, fewer of them were needed. The result was an exodus from the countryside beside which earlier rural-to-urban migrations paled into insignificance.

Those who stayed lived richer material lives than any of their predecessors on the land had ever enjoyed. There were fewer of them, but they were less isolated. Their horizons could be—and were—as broad as those of many urbanites. And they enjoyed all the comforts and conveniences of urban middle-class people, without the physical insecurity that often accompanied city life.

Johnstone could see the direction of things, but even one as prescient as he would have been stunned by the pace of change in the fifty years after his article appeared in the *Yearbook of Agriculture*.

THE PRODUCTIVITY REVOLUTION

The revolution in productivity that shaped so much of the agriculture we know today began in earnest during World War II, spurred by the combination of high prices and the labor shortage confronting farmers. The Civil War and World War I had presented farmers with similar challenges and had similar effects, but the innovations emerging during World War II reinforced and built on one another in a particularly dynamic way.

The first of the three major contributors to the rise in agricultural productivity during and after World War II was the introduction of improved varieties of crops and animals. Plant and animal improvement was due mainly, but by no means exclusively, to the work of publicly supported agricultural scientists in the USDA and in state land-grant colleges and experiment stations. Their work was rooted in the early years of the twentieth century, when Gregor Mendel's insights into the process of genetic inheritance were discovered and applied, and it began to pay dividends on the public's investment in the 1930s and 1940s.

The most spectacular success of early crop breeders was hybrid corn.

Corn was an attractive experimental subject for plant scientists because it is a genetically simple plant and its fertilization is relatively easy to control. In the early years of the century, geneticists discovered that by crossing two, and then four, inbred lines they could produce corn plants with more desirable characteristics than those demonstrated by parents or grandparents. Seed companies saw the opportunity for profit in the work of basic scientists. Seed houses were especially interested in hybrid corn because the seed produced vigorous plants for one year only. Because farmers could not produce their own seed, they had to return to the vendor every year. Henry A. Wallace, then an agricultural scientist and entrepreneur, sold the first hybrid corn seed in 1926, but hybrids did not really become popular in the corn belt until the 1930s, when farmers operating under AAA acreage reductions became obsessed with increasing yields. By the end of World War II, most corn grown in the country was hybrid corn.

Results in other areas of plant and animal improvement were less dramatic, and true hybrids were difficult to develop in most cultivars, but selective breeding changed virtually every crop and animal produced commercially. Selective breeding of dairy cattle, as well as the increasing use of green silage for winter feeding, doubled the milk production of the average cow between 1940 and 1980. Today good dairy cows produce more than 20 thousand pounds of milk in a year.

Much plant improvement has addressed particular farmers' problems. On the northern Plains, for example, agronomists at the North Dakota Agricultural Experiment Station developed area-specific spring wheats that matured rapidly, tolerated drought, resisted rust, and were high in protein. In California, experiment station scientists bred a tomato that ripened uniformly and had a tough skin, two prerequisites for effective mechanical harvesting.

Other breeding programs aimed at making products more attractive to consumers. For example, through selective breeding of chickens, researchers were able to develop a bird that matured quickly, converted feed into weight efficiently, and had only white feathers (the noticeability of holes on the flesh from dark feathers repelled some consumers).

Since 1980, conventional plant and animal breeding have been increasingly supplemented—and sometimes supplanted—by biotechnology, a broad term encompassing a number of specific technologies within the life sciences. Gene-splicing, a fairly rudimentary biotechnology, offers a quick

236

way to do what conventional breeders have always done, but other biotechnologies offer the possibility of creating new life-forms, such as bacteria to kill insects, introducing new characteristics into cultivars from dissimilar plants, or synthesizing natural substances. Bovine somatatrophin, a synthetic hormone that promises to raise milk production by 15 percent, is an example of the successful application of this biotechnology. While much biotechnology lies more in the realm of potential than performance, it will probably be the source of most of the major breakthroughs in agricultural science in the foreseeable future.

The second major source of increases in productivity was mechanization. The tractor remained the single most important machine on the farm, and continual improvements and adaptations made it ever-more convenient and flexible. In 1939 there were 1.445 million tractors on American farms, or about two for every nine farms. By 1945, there were 2.354 million tractors in use, or two for every five farms. The adoption of tractors accelerated over the next quarter century, so that by 1970 there were 1.6 tractors *per farm* in the United States. In 1987 the number of tractors per farm stood at 2.2. In the swish of a tail the horse and mule became obsolete.

Tractors facilitated the use of some machinery, and a number of other implements were converted from tractor drawn to self-propelled. In 1940 there were 190 thousand combine harvester-threshers on American grain farms, almost all of them tractor drawn, and by 1945 their numbers had doubled. In 1970 American farmers were using 850 thousand combines, virtually all of them self-propelled. The mechanization of some labor-intensive crops proceeded when self-propelled cotton pickers appeared in the 1940s, with self-propelled tobacco harvesters introduced in the 1960s.

Electrical power on the farm was another factor that encouraged mechanization, especially in some enterprises. Between 1940 and 1945 the number of milking machines on American farms more than doubled, to 365 thousand. Electricity also allowed dairy farmers to store large quantities of fluid milk in refrigerated facilities for relatively long periods of time. On the Great Plains, farmers used powerful gas- or electric-powered pumps to pull underground water to the surface, where, beginning in 1952, they irrigated with center-pivot sprinkler systems.

A range of mostly petroleum-based chemicals provided the third ingredient that fueled the productivity revolution. In 1939 Ciba-Geigy, a Swiss chemical company, introduced DDT (dichlorodiphenyltrichloroethane), the first in what proved to be a series of hydrocarbon-based insecticides. During the war it was used by the military to fumigate barracks and delouse troops, but afterward it became available to farmers. DDT was by no means the first chemical insecticide—arsenates had been particularly popular—but it was so effective against such a broad range of insects that it appeared to be the panacea for which entomologists had been searching for a century. Ironically, though, the very effectiveness of DDT proved to be a curse. For one thing, it led to a deemphasis of research on biological pest control, a more environmentally benign method. Second, it was indiscriminate, eliminating desirable insects along with undesirable ones. Third, its tendency to build up in living tissue and attack the nervous system threatened human and animal health. And finally, while it was remarkably effective for a time, insects did develop a resistance to it. These problems did not appear immediately, however, and for twenty years DDT was a powerful tool for farmers.

Another important chemical released to farmers in 1945 was 2,4-dichlorophenoxyacetic acid, a broad-leaf-weed herbicide popularly known as 2,4-D. This herbicide is actually a growth hormone, which scientists discovered caused some weeds and cultivars to grow themselves to death. Farmers using 2,4-D minimized cultivation and hoeing, saving labor and fuel and limiting erosion. Soon more herbicides appeared to deal with grasses and other weeds on which 2,4-D was ineffective. Because weeds, like insects, cut yields, herbicides helped farmers become more productive.

Shortly after the end of the war an important new nitrogen fertilizer was also introduced to farmers. Anhydrous ammonia, a gas that liquifies when it comes in contact with air, could be applied conveniently by injection of the pressurized gas into the soil through prongs. It was a boon to producers of corn and other nitrogen-hungry crops. Farmers using anhydrous ammonia no longer needed to follow such practices as rotating between nitrogen-fixing and nitrogen-depleting crops or spreading animal manure on their fields. Some critics have argued that anhydrous ammonia thereby encouraged poor farming practices, and its overuse also led to nitrogen contamination of water supplies in many areas. However, it was even more significant than herbicides and insecticides in raising yields.

In addition to these and other chemicals, such as fungicides, scientists developed a range of antibiotics and growth hormones for animals, the best known of which is DES, a growth accelerator for cattle. In combination, the cascade of chemicals provided farmers with deceptively simple answers to

238 problems that had plagued them and their predecessors since the dawn of time.

New varieties, machines, and chemicals were significant enough alone, but when combined they produced sweeping changes. Nowhere was this combination more revolutionary than in the cotton South. The New Deal inadvertently began the transformation of southern agriculture by encouraging the adoption of tractors, but farmers who bought the "steel mules" still needed substantial labor for weeding and picking. As long as workers lived close by, supported in part by federal furnish, sufficient labor could be had. But World War II saw a labor shortage in the cotton belt, despite the heroic efforts of the USDA, leading farmers to search for ways to do without workers entirely.

Mechanical cotton pickers had been used as early as World War I, especially in California, but these early stripper types took all bolls, whether ripe or not, and so much trash that quality suffered and cleaning and ginning were major problems. During World War II, International Harvester introduced a spindle harvester that took cotton from opened bolls only. Government scientists pitched in, especially at the Mississippi Agricultural Experiment Station, developing varieties of cotton in which the bolls grew to a relatively uniform height and ripened at about the same time. Chemicals also played an important role. DDT killed pests, 2,4-D eliminated chopping—and thus the need for choppers—and defoliants eased the way for mechanical pickers by killing foliage on cotton plants prior to harvest.

By 1950 a southern enclosure movement was well under way. As late as 1940 there were still over 783 thousand croppers in the South. By 1959, when the USDA stopped counting them, there were only 194 thousand. Where cotton was grown, it was produced mainly by substantial farmers dependent on machinery and chemicals. Increasingly, it was not produced at all, as farmers tired of competing with large-scale growers in California, Arizona, and west Texas put in soybeans or alfalfa and ran cattle on their lands. In many parts of the South today the land betrays no hint of the cotton agriculture nor of the slave labor and sharecropping systems that were such an important part of its history. Even the black farmer has become an endangered species. In 1987 there were fewer than 23 thousand left in the country, of whom a mere two thousand sold products worth at least $25,000 per year.

The effect of the southern enclosure on sharecroppers was mixed. Sharecropping was an enterprise with no future, even when no one could foresee that it would end. For most sharecroppers—70 percent of whom were blacks in 1940—it was a life of privation, which helped keep them a degraded caste in America. There was little potential for improvement in the material or physical realities of their lives until they left sharecropping, nor were they likely to enjoy the rights other Americans enjoyed. It is difficult to imagine a successful Civil Rights movement in the rural South had blacks remained economically and socially subordinate to white landlords.

On the other hand, relatively few opportunities were available to most former sharecroppers. The persistence of racism and their lack of education and skills appropriate for a sophisticated modern economy doomed many to continuing marginality. The demise of sharecropping also meant the deterioration of strong communities with durable churches, schools, and voluntary organizations that underpinned and bolstered the family. Sustaining institutions and strong families proved easier to maintain in the rural South than outside of it.

Outside of the cotton South, the changes that came with the production revolution were somewhat less sweeping, in part because most of the country had a foretaste of them earlier in the century. But change was the rule everywhere, and everywhere its results were mixed. The clearest beneficiaries of the surge in agricultural productivity have been consumers. In 1945 the average American spent 36.4 percent of his or her income on food, beverages, and tobacco. By 1970 that figure had fallen to 23.2 and stands at barely 16 percent today. Science, machinery, and chemicals assure that crops will be more dependable, quality less variable, farm operations more timely, yields higher, and losses to pests minimal. Government commodity programs help assure that supplies will be abundant. As a group, Americans are the most lavishly fed people in the world. Indeed, we have so much that we devote substantial resources to storage and disposal of surplus food. We suffer from obesity and spend billions every year to lose weight. These are problems, but they are problems that most of the peoples in the world would like to have.

Substantial commercial farmers have derived some benefits as well. The tools at their disposal give them greater control over their production, diminishing some of the anxieties and stresses of farming. They are highly sophisticated people, manipulating machinery, chemicals, and capital beyond the dreams of their parents and grandparents. With growing sophistication has come a degree of self-confidence and self-respect that is positive. Today's farming is characterized by less drudgery. Machines and chemicals have replaced muscle that farmers and their families historically supplied. The farmer is no longer the stooped and weathered fellow wearing dirty overalls but a respected businessperson.

Modern farming is a highly capitalized enterprise. In 1945 the average farm was worth $11,800, or $60.51 an acre. Twenty-five years later, the average farm was worth about $90,000, or about $241 per acre, and by 1990 the average farm was worth $390,000, or nearly $850 per acre. Farming has clearly become big business.

The problem farmers confronted through most of the postwar period was that their returns did not keep pace with the value of their investment. The domestic market was a mature one that grew at a slower rate than agricultural production. As in the twenties, consumers preferred foods that were highly processed and tended to substitute fresh fruits and vegetables for starches and carbohydrates. Synthetic materials boomed, diminishing the share of the textile market held by cotton and wool. Farmers were also hurt by consumers' greater sophistication. People ate greater varieties of foods and were quick to switch from one meat or fruit to another when prices were temporarily high. There were still hungry people in America, and such federal programs as food stamps and the school lunch program helped farmers feed them, but as a general rule there was no domestic growth market for agriculture.

Foreign markets were also unpromising, especially prior to 1970. The United States restricted trade with the Soviet Union, China, and their allies as a Cold War measure. As a creditor nation with a strong currency, we were frequently viewed as the vendor-of-last-resort by potential buyers. Our quality standards for such products as wheat and butter were lower than those of some of our competitors, further diminishing our customer base. And European nations that had been customers subsidized their farmers lavishly, diminishing our market and even creating export competition for us.

There were a lot of hungry people in the developing world, but one of the reasons they were hungry was that they could not afford to purchase food. Congress addressed this problem in 1954 with Public Law 480. This legislation allowed food sales to developing countries in local currency, which was then spent by the United States on infrastructure development in the recipient country. The law also provided for simply giving surpluses away for famine or disaster relief. Congress hoped Public Law 480 would help poor countries develop into paying customers, and it did help farmers by diminishing surpluses, but it was not the most desirable way of developing markets.

People in poor countries also lacked the resources to feed themselves. The United States Agency for International Development, other federal agencies, and American philanthropic organizations attacked this problem by sponsoring the green revolution. The green revolution involved enhancing food self-sufficiency in developing countries through irrigation, chemical fertilization, and the introduction of area-specific crop varieties, such as the high-yielding semidwarf wheats developed by Norman Borlaug and his associates in Mexico. In some cases, relatively simple solutions worked wonders. In India, for example, the replacement of wicker with corrugated metal storage facilities allowed as much as half of the grain harvest to be saved from moisture and vermin. The green revolution was so successful that a number of countries became self-sufficient and even became exporters competing with American farmers. To make developing countries self-sufficient in food was one of the most selflessly humane actions of the modern age, but it did little to enhance market possibilities for American farmers.

Weak demand restrained agricultural prices, but farmers' costs for seed, machinery, chemicals, and land advanced smartly. The result was a cost-price squeeze that constricted agricultural incomes. In the quarter century after 1945 the price of farm products rose by only 41 percent, while the consumer-price index soared by 116 percent.

One answer to relatively low incomes had always been to diversify and "live at home." Diversification of the traditional sort was difficult for postwar farmers, however. Federal agricultural programs actually discouraged diversification, both because they placed price floors under a few commodities and because they required that farmers grow set minimums of the crops in question over a period of years to qualify for loans. Then there was the expense of diversification. A wheat grower might also grow barley but was less likely to make the necessary capital investment to raise potatoes as well. There was also the problem of markets. Local markets for specialty products shrank as the country was increasingly bound together into a national marketing and transportation system. Moreover, dairies no longer wanted milk from small producers who could not afford refrigerated tanks or large herds. And poultry producers discovered they could not compete with the large-

Two combines harvesting wheat on the Great Plains during the 1960s.
Courtesy of the North Dakota Institute for Regional Studies and North Dakota University Libraries, Fargo.

scale, low-cost broiler and egg factories sprinkled across the nation by agribusiness firms. On the other hand, farmers could and did diversify by bringing more nonfarm income into the family. In 1945, 26 percent of farm income came from off the farm; twenty-five years later, 47 percent came from nonfarm sources.

Shrinking unit margins also led farmers to consider ways of producing more units, which frequently meant expansion. Modern machinery made expansion easier and, to a large degree, necessary. A $5,000 tractor is less expensive in real terms if it can be used on two hundred rather than one hundred acres. Between 1945 and 1970 the average farm nearly doubled in size, from 195 to 373 acres. As had been the case during the twenties, the middle-sized farmer—large enough not to have time to hold a second job but too small to achieve economies of scale—was most likely to be squeezed out. In the quarter century after the end of the war the number of farms larger than five hundred acres increased by twenty-eight percent to 367 thousand, while the number of farms between 100 and 500 acres declined by over 40 percent.

Expansion seemed unavoidable to many who wanted to survive in postwar agriculture, but it was a risky proposition. In 1945 the average farm returned an annual income to its owner equal to 17.5 percent of its value. But the value of land, machinery, and buildings rose so much faster than prices that in 1970 the average farmer's yearly income was only 6.4 percent of the value of the farm. With such minimal returns in prospect, expanding farmers were gambling, and many found it difficult to break even, let alone earn a profit. Small wonder that so many farmers were willing to sell out or that young people lacking capital concluded they had little chance of getting started in farming.

All of these rather dry economic realities affected real human beings. The cost of money, or machinery, or insecticide, and the price of soybeans, or rice, or cattle, kept people awake at night and determined how well their families would live—or even if they would continue to live—on the land. If farming had ever been a carefree enterprise, it was not any longer. During and after World War II, many decided that farming was not for them, and the revolution in productivity made their decision easier. In macroeconomic terms of factor allocation, the revolution in productivity mainly involved the substitution of capital for labor. Machines and chemicals created surplus people just as surely as they created surplus commodities. When those people left, their leaving affected rural society and institutions, and when they came to urban places, their coming affected urban society and institutions.

THE GREAT RURAL-TO-URBAN MIGRATION

In 1940, 30.547 million people, or 23 percent of the nation, lived on farms. In 1970, the farm population stood at 9.712 million people, or less than 5 percent of all Americans. In one generation, farmers went from being a major demographic group to being a marginal one. A small part of the reason for this decline was a falling rural birthrate. In modern agriculture, children were no longer needed for family labor, and the economics of farm inheritance and farm building made it difficult for families to assure futures for very many. Moreover, rural women increasingly anticipated lives that were not dominated by bearing and raising children. In 1940 the rural birthrate still exceeded the urban rate by 77 percent, but by 1970 it was only 16 percent higher. By 1990 there were only 1.95 children in the average farm family, compared to 1.83 in the average nonfarm family.

The main reason for the dramatic decline in farm population was unprecedented migration. The rural exodus began as the economy of the country picked up in response to the beginning of World War II in Europe, then accelerated when the United States entered the conflict. During the Great Depression, population had built up in most rural areas because young men and women who might have moved to cities in prosperous economic times remained on farms. These were the people who were most likely to leave for military service or defense jobs. Between 1939 and 1944, 8.711 million people moved off farms, 3.145 million in 1942 alone. In 1945 there was a temporary reversal of this trend as some young people came home, but the migration resumed in 1946. Between that year and 1970, another 21.454 million people left farms. So many left that farm life became an anomaly, even in rural America. In 1940, 53 percent of rural people still lived on farms; by 1970, only 18 percent did so.

Structural economic factors were primarily responsible for spurring this massive migration. As farmers became more productive, they required less labor. The average farmer in 1970 could feed about three times as many people as he or she could twenty-five years before; in other words, one-third as many workers could feed the same number of consumers. For those who desired to remain in farming, the cost of entry, narrowing margins, and the greater business and technical sophistication required all served as deterrents.

The United States was fortunate that the revolution in productivity occurred in conjunction with the longest sustained period of urban economic growth and prosperity in the history of the country. The strength of the urban commercial and industrial economy in the quarter century after World War II meant that most of the rural migrants were absorbed with relatively little pain—indeed, they helped spur growth in the urban economy. The strong national economy made the experience of postwar migrants much different from that of their Dust Bowl predecessors a few years before and prevented them from becoming subjects of national concern or even, really, any part of the national consciousness.

Rural-to-urban migration was not attributable solely to economics, however significant that factor was. Young people, especially, continued to be drawn to cities by the supposed excitement and stimulation of life there. The battle over which style of living was superior had been won long before, as far as most Americans were concerned, but the victorious cities continued to take prisoners. It also became increasingly common for elderly farm people to retire in towns. The decreasing likelihood that their children would take over the farm, and thus be there to look after them, and the relative convenience of town living made it seem a good idea. Government programs also played a role. For example, the Soil Bank program during the Eisenhower administration allowed farmers to remove their entire farms from production and induced tens of thousands to move away. Finally, the dynamic of the process of migration fed on itself. With everyone seeming to leave, those who had never thought about it began to, and those who had thought about it were moved to action. The fact that one was likely to have friends or relatives in this or that town made one's migration all the more feasible and comfortable.

Migrants from the farm were not an undifferentiated mass. The main characteristic that distinguished them involved the degree of choice they were able to exercise. Those most likely to choose migration from the farm tended to be young people, not yet encumbered with property or dependent family members, or older farmers retiring to town. They were often people with some financial resources on which to draw, at least until they established themselves in new locations. Young migrants-by-choice often had some off-farm experiences, frequently in the military service or in college.

246

Such experiences broadened their horizons, gave them some familiarity with nonrural customs and lifestyles, and often provided them with skills that were marketable in a modern urban economy. They were also usually able to exercise a good deal of choice regarding when they migrated and to what specific place they went.

Other migrants, such as many of the displaced croppers from the cotton belt, enjoyed less choice. They were likely to be people who had intended to spend a life in agriculture but had been unable to do so. They were more likely to be married people with dependent children. They were less likely to have much foreknowledge of urban life, work, and customs and were less likely to have much beyond muscle to offer urban employers. Finally, the circumstances of their leaving and their relative poverty meant that they were less able to time their migration to their advantage or to enjoy as much choice of destination. Their need for support and their unfamiliarity with urban life inclined them to go where friends and kin were already established.

At first glance, it is hard to see that much about this population hemorrhage was positive for rural America. At the local level, migration made it difficult and often impossible to maintain institutions and communities. Churches and local lodges and clubs died for lack of membership, and even consolidated schools became too small to be sustained as independent entities. Depopulation meant that fewer taxpayers had to shoulder the burden for essential public services. Small towns that were dependent on the business of farmers from the local area declined when increasing numbers of merchants and professionals found that demand for the goods and services they offered was insufficient to sustain them. All of these results can be charted or quantified. Less easy to measure was the effect of migration on rural morale, the degree to which it heightened rural people's sense of isolation, and the impact it had on neighborhood and kinship groups that had been so important in sustaining farm people, especially women.

The effects of migration seemed negative in other ways as well. Depopulation appeared to be paralleled by the polarization of the rural social structure between the rich and the poor. It was the middle class that seemed to be leaving, and that had serious implications for the rural community. In 1947, rural sociologist Walter Goldschmidt published a study of two California farm communities, one with numerous small farmers and the other with a handful of large growers.[2] The former enjoyed a vital and sustaining community life, while the latter was a sterile place socially divided between rich and poor.

Goldschmidt's suggestion that social polarization and spreading impoverishment were in rural America's future received confirmation in the 1960s, when stunned researchers discovered that poverty was a more prominent feature of rural than of urban life. Indeed, as late as 1990 the rural poverty rate stood at 16.3 percent, while the national poverty rate was only 13.5 percent. This high level of poverty was at once a sobering reminder of the price paid for agricultural restructuring and an indication that rural-to-urban migration was far from over.

Rural depopulation also had implications for agriculture's political power. If farmers became a marginalized and trivial portion of the population, would their interests be sacrificed to those of urban groups? The increasing interest of nonfarm groups in agricultural policy seemed to suggest as much. Supreme Court decisions in the sixties mandating congressional and legislative redistricting on a one-person, one-vote basis further heightened fears of rural insignificance.

While it is not difficult to conceive how migration has been negative for the rural community, it might be worthwhile to speculate about what rural America would be like had this movement not taken place. What would all these people have done had they stayed? Would they have been able to find occupations that satisfied them and contributed to society, or would they have become part of an underutilized, underemployed, and largely wasted labor pool? And what sorts of lives would such people live? The examples of an overpopulated countryside we have had in the United States—the postbellum cotton South, for instance—and those, like Bangladesh or El Salvador, that exist in the contemporary world do not suggest that it is a circumstance in which an acceptable modern material standard of living can be achieved. Indeed, the continuing differential between urban and rural incomes and the persistence of rural poverty suggest that, from a purely economic standpoint of factor distribution, not enough migration has yet taken place, despite the stunning population hemorrhage from the countryside since World War II.

While those who left may have weakened the rural community in some ways by their leaving, then, it is probably generally true that they benefited themselves and society by migrating. They composed a source of labor that helped fuel the commercial and industrial boom of the postwar years, and they provided social enrichment to the urban places to which they went. Moreover, their leaving enhanced economic opportunities for those who remained in the countryside, where fewer people remained to share the shrinking pie.

Migration was not positive for all rural migrants, however. Many blacks displaced from southern agriculture had little but muscle to offer urban employers at a time when machines were replacing muscle in urban as well as rural work. The forklift truck was the urban equivalent of the mechanical cotton picker, displacing hundreds of thousands who had earned their daily bread by the sweat of their brows. Black migrants were further handicapped in coming to cities where racism was more subtle than in the rural South but no less effective in limiting their prospects. And they came to places where the conditions of work and life made it harder to maintain families and where sustaining institutions were weaker, less intimate, and less empowering. In contrast to the Okies, the travails of these migrants received little attention. Because they were black they were expected to suffer, they lived in inner cities away from the public eye, and a rich nation could easily afford the conscience money it took to meet their most elemental needs. But the existence and the suffering of the urban underclass today is eloquent testimony to the reality that the great exodus from rural America was not always positive and did not necessarily result in greater opportunities for migrants.

MODERN RURAL LIFE

One result of the production revolution was that successful farmers became what the USDA and others had long hoped they would become. What agricultural reformers had desired for nearly a century—that farming would become an enterprise requiring specialized technical knowledge and that farmers would be accomplished, self-confident, and respected professionals—increasingly became reality after World War II. Another traditional hope of reformers—that rural life would approximate urban life in grace, convenience, and material comfort—was also largely realized during these years.

Rural life in America had historically involved a good deal of isolation, but that was largely eliminated in the decades following World War II. Rural people participated more fully than ever before in the larger American culture. They had the same appliances and conveniences in their homes urban people had, they dressed as urban people dressed, they consumed the same national products urban people consumed, and they read the same magazines and watched the same television programs at the same time urban people watched them. To live in the countryside no longer meant that one inevitably accepted a degree of material deprivation.

Isolation was diminished in other ways as well. Rural people had a broader range of experiences—and often broader horizons—than their parents or grandparents had enjoyed. They were more likely to have been in the service or attended college, and often they brought back spouses from outside the community who had their own unique perspectives. They were more likely to travel and to have a circle of friends that extended beyond the locality.

The dramatic increase in physical mobility has further diminished isolation. More dependable automobiles and dramatically improved road systems after World War II gave farmers greater potential mobility, and the reality that they were less often tied to farmsteads by young children or livestock allowed them to take advantage of it. Modernity has shattered the tyranny that distance traditionally exercised over rural lives.

A farmer living in Bartholomew County, Indiana, ten miles from Columbus, at the turn of the century might get to town a couple of times a month. A twenty-mile round-trip would take a team all day, so one would not embark on it on a whim. To go fifty miles farther, to Indianapolis, would have been a major undertaking. The farmer would have to take the team into Columbus, put it up in a livery stable, and then take the train. A family probably only went to Indianapolis once a year, usually a couple of weeks before Christmas. It was simply too far away, and it would have been too much trouble to have neighbors look after livestock.

By 1930 the Bartholomew County farmer probably would have had a Model T. He or she could get into Columbus in half an hour, if the roads were dry and clear, as they sometimes were, and might be able to get to Indianapolis and back in a day, if everything worked out all right, as it sometimes did. The farmer would have had to get back in a day, though, because there were animals to care for, and the family would probably have been too large for everyone to go along.

Forty years later, the Bartholomew County farm family could have run in to Columbus and returned in half an hour when convenience goods—a loaf of bread, some cotter pins, or a pair of jeans, for example—were needed, or to attend a high school basketball game or buy an ice cream sundae. Indianapolis was now only an hour away. The family might go there once a week, or more often, with little inconvenience. More of their discretionary spending on big-ticket items like furniture, appliances, or fancy clothing would be done in the metropolis, and it would not be rare for them to go to Indianapolis for a nice dinner or a movie. Now the family would probably go to Chicago a couple of times a year, and when the kids had left home the parents might have started wintering in Florida.

As rural people have become more like urban people and as their experiences have become less unique, their family roles have changed as well. While every member of the family has been mightily affected by the changes that have transpired over the past half century, the alterations in the lives of women and children have been most pronounced.

At the end of World War II the lives of farm women still revolved mainly around the farm. They were mainly responsible for maintaining farm homes, which might have been somewhat more convenient if they had electricity and modern water systems but which remained demanding in families that were still relatively large and with which hired men frequently lived. They continued to play a vital role in the farm economy as well. Women tended vegetables and fruit, raised chickens, milked cattle, butchered and canned, baked bread, made soap, and carried out many of the other tasks that had burdened their foremothers.

Most of those traditional tasks had either changed dramatically or passed from the scene entirely well before 1970. Women remain primary homemakers, but with fewer children and hired men and more modern conveniences the demands of that enterprise can be less onerous. State health regulations and the rise of massive, vertically integrated agribusiness firms doomed most female economic enterprises. Virtually nobody butchers or makes soap anymore, and canning and baking are more often hobbies than necessary activities.

Rural reformers, from Grange leaders to home extension agents, hoped that heightened domesticity would replace economic activities as the latter withered away, but it has not worked out that way. Some farm women substituted traditional male tasks for those they no longer performed. In Wisconsin, for example, surveys showed that women devoted more time to commercial farm work in 1975 than they had in 1950. There are two main reasons for this development. First, as more men took off-farm jobs and as hired men were eliminated, a greater burden fell on women. And second, modern machinery was easier for women to handle than traditional tools had been.

Farm work allowed women to continue to supplement the family income, albeit in a manner slightly different from the traditional ways. Farm women also help provide family subsistence by working off the farm, as nearly 45 percent under the age of sixty-five did in 1988. At one time women supplemented the farm income with egg money or a cream check. Today they more commonly deliver a paycheck from the school district or the Wal-Mart store. As women have left the home to support the family, they have become separated, to some degree, from the farm and the rural neighborhood. Some feminist scholars argue that women who were removed from farmwork were trivialized, disempowered, and diminished in status. Such a view reflects a romanticization of the traditional work of farm women and an overly harsh judgment of what they do now. Some women were empowered by farmwork; but for others, scouring milk cans and slaughtering chickens was drudgery, and many farm women today find that their off-farm work adds a new dimension to their lives. Most urban women who work outside the home find satisfaction and even fulfillment in their jobs; is there any reason to think that rural women are different?

The lives of rural children have also changed dramatically. The traditional American farm was an educational institution in which boys and girls learned their future occupations by working with their parents. The apprenticeship was a long one. It began when a child was old enough to concentrate on doing simple tasks like gathering eggs and hoeing gardens, intensified when the child achieved the physical maturity to do the same tasks as an adult, and concluded when the child moved away, usually to establish her or his own family.

Child labor is a much less prominent feature on modern farms. Rural children are still expected to help out—you see them at calving time, driving grain trucks at harvest, doing the wash, and preparing supper—but it is now universally accepted that they will spend most of their childhood and adolescent years going to school, that they will enjoy such extracurricular activities as band or basketball, and that they probably will go to college. This last point highlights the parallel between the decline of child labor and the diminished importance of the farm as an educational institution. The farm today is mainly a place where people grow up. When they have reached adulthood, they are more likely to leave and become accountants or computer programmers or retail clerks than they are to follow in their parents' footsteps.

Socially, culturally, materially, and in terms of life experiences, rural life was converging with urban life in the decades following World War II. It could never become exactly the same, not least because the farm was both a home and a business in a way most urban establishments could never be. But there was no question that rural life was closer to urban life than ever before. It all made Paul Johnstone's observations of 1940 all the more prescient.

TWELVE

Agriculture and Rural Life
at the End of the Twentieth Century

The 1970s and 1980s were a crucial period in the history of rural America. The 1970s saw a rise in demand for American agricultural products that triggered a boom in farming of the sort not seen since the World War I period. Farmers expanded their operations, bidding the price of land up dramatically in the expectation that the future would be bright, and young people entered what suddenly appeared to be a promising endeavor in impressive numbers. Temporarily rich, at least on paper, farmers began acting and thinking rich, building expensive houses, buying pleasure boats, joining country clubs, and wintering in warm climates.

During the golden age of agriculture, prospering farmers had been criticized by urbanites who complained that they had not kept pace with the modern world. Prospering farmers in the seventies were beset by a new set of critics who complained that they were all too much part of the modern world. These observers argued that farmers had become indistinguishable from other profit-maximizing businesspeople in their obsession with the bottom line and their lack of concern for the community and the environment.

The seventies boom deflated at the end of the decade, with disastrous consequences for many overextended farmers. Rural hardship spurred the de-

254 velopment of new farm organizations, some of which included sympathetic urbanites, and a general national outpouring of concern for downtrodden farmers that was reflected both in the popular culture and in tangible government aid. The agricultural depression did not alter the structure of the farm sector or the conditions under which modern farmers operated. Nor did it reverse the physical and material standards of rural life. One thing it did do, however, was to spur a reexamination of farming and rural life by those who continued to be involved in it, an endeavor that involved significant degrees of redirection and recommitment.

THE BOOM OF THE SEVENTIES

In the quarter century following World War II, demand for American agricultural products was anemic. The domestic population grew at a slower rate than agricultural production, and foreign demand lacked vitality due to a number of political and economic factors. The result was a cost-price squeeze on farmers and low returns on the farm investment. That situation changed rather quickly and dramatically in the early seventies due to a number of unrelated developments extrinsic to agriculture.

Beginning in the late 1950s the United States experienced a deteriorating trade balance. While Americans purchased more cheap foreign nondurable goods such as clothes, durable goods such as automobiles and consumer electronics, and raw materials such as petroleum, foreign purchases of American products failed to keep pace. American trade woes had no single cause, but one problem was that the government supported the value of the dollar at an artificially high level. In 1971, President Richard Nixon decided that the United States should allow the dollar to float, meaning that the United States would no longer support the dollar's value relative to that of other currencies. The immediate effect of this action was to devalue the dollar and thus make American products—including agricultural products—cheaper for foreign customers.

Other factors further improved the outlook for American agricultural exports. In 1972, as part of his policy of achieving détente—or understanding—with the Communist powers, President Nixon concluded an agreement with the Soviet Union under which that country committed itself to purchase substantial quantities of wheat and feed grains over the next several years. Simultaneously, dramatic rates of economic growth in developing countries, especially those producing oil and other strategic commodities, put them in the position to purchase American food. Adverse climatic developments cut crop yields in many parts of the world, including Western Europe, enhancing demand for American products and diminishing competition confronting American farmers. In combination with a surging inflation that pushed all prices up, these developments led to a rise in farm prices unparalleled since World War II. Indeed, between 1972 and 1974 wheat prices doubled and corn prices tripled.

Policy makers and farmers alike responded to this unanticipated reversal of fortune promptly, energetically, and ultimately inappropriately. The Nixon administration, seeing agricultural exports as the magic bullet that would kill the nation's balance of payments deficit, lifted acreage controls and urged farmers to plant fencerow to fencerow. As a result, more than 40 million acres were brought into production, some for the first time. To individual farmers, Secretary of Agriculture Earl Butz provided the advice, "get bigger, get better, or get out," and many did. Butz and most other observers believed that agricultural consolidation was the wave of the future as it had been of the recent past, and they thought rising farm prices removed the risk inherent in expansion.

Butz was popular with commercial agriculturalists—during Nixon's 1972 reelection campaign midwesterners held up placards reading Vote for Nixon, Farmers. Don't Lose your Butz—and his words were music to their ears. Many farmers had waited for years for their enhanced productivity to pay off, and they didn't hesitate to strike when the iron was hot. They were joined in the land market by beginning farmers, usually young and well educated, who concluded that agriculture finally offered rewards commensurate with the labor and the risk, and by older farmers concerned about providing enterprises of adequate scale for the agricultural world in which their children would apparently live. The result was a dizzying spiral in land prices, as values rose by over 220 percent between 1971 and 1980.

In retrospect, it was a situation fraught with risk. Interest rates were high, though they frequently lagged behind double-digit inflation, and farmers sometimes paid rates of 15 percent or more per year to buy land so expensive that crop production was insufficient to cover the cost of interest. This was considered to be a temporary situation. With crop prices advancing steadily and land values leaping ahead by one-fifth every year, what was expensive land today would look like a bargain tomorrow. Agricultural lenders, who could normally be counted on to be sober, added to the mania. Rural banks and the Farmers Home Administration encouraged borrowers to think big and refused to lend to farmers they considered to be too small or whose expansion plans they judged to be insufficiently ambitious. Lenders also encouraged borrowers to engage in risky leveraging strategies, in which paper equities served as collateral for further loans. For example, a farmer who purchased land for $500 an acre one year and who found it was worth $600 the next year could use the $100 equity as collateral to buy more $600-an-acre land. It was a good strategy for expansion as long as prices were rising, which most observers believed they would continue to do, but it compounded debtors' problems when the price trend reversed.

Expansion was not the only risky farmer behavior in the frothy days of the seventies. Many farmers on wheat-and-cattle and corn-and-hog operations got rid of their livestock, preferring to concentrate on the production of bread and feed grains. Not only were grains more lucrative, but producing them was a lot less work than caring for animals. The problem was that meat and grain prices historically move in opposite directions, cushioning diversified farmers to some degree against risk. During the seventies some farmers convinced themselves that risk was a thing of the past, but they learned to their distress that it is always present.

For a while, though, farmers had a wonderful time. With more leisure time and more paper wealth they started acting rich. They joined country clubs, took up golf, enjoyed cruises, bought summer cabins, and wintered in warm places. In the Midwest, a growing number of farmers were referred to as "CBF" farmers, for corn, beans, and Florida. Some even refused to be called farmer anymore, preferring "grower" or "agribusinessman" as more appropriate to their station.

The evolution of farmers and farming would have gratified many of the traditional critics and reformers of rural life. One can easily imagine how pleased such people as Justin Morrill or the members of the Country Life Commission would have been with the sophisticated, professional, and businesslike agriculture that had emerged by the seventies. For others, though, the development of business behaviors and standards by farmers represented a threat to all that was good about rural life. Wendell Berry, Kentucky essayist and poet, was a particularly articulate critic of modern agriculture.[1] To him, farming was valuable mainly as a way of life that allowed people to relate to one another and to the land in a caring, sharing, and loving manner. Berry argued that when farming became a business, land was no more than another factor of production, and neighbors were no more than other businesspeople whose land one coveted.

Berry and other critics of modern agriculture, such as Kansas agricultural scientist Wes Jackson, drew on a tradition of "romantic agrarianism" that stretched back to the early twentieth century and was articulately represented by such figures as Ralph Borsodi and the Nashville Agrarians.[2] While romantic agrarians criticized developments in agriculture, their main dispute had always been with the larger American society and its values. Romantic agrarians believed rural life offered a desirable alternative in an overly industrialized capitalist society. As rural life and values more closely approximated those of the larger society, romantic agrarians were understandably distressed.

Their deep cultural alienation led Berry and others of similar mind to overly romanticize the rural past and to articulate unfair expectations for the behavior of farm people, but romantic agrarians did highlight the downside of changes in farming and rural life. In 1993 I met a corn and soybean farmer at a branch agricultural experiment station field day. Soybean prices had dropped a few days before, and this farmer complained that "I should have been at my computer, locking in the price, but I was on the tractor that day." When farmers consider farming a diversion from their main enterprise, it is clear that Wendell Berry has something significant to tell us.

Other critics of the new agriculture focused on rural poverty and relationships in farming between the rich and the poor. Far from being the middle-class utopia of popular imagination, rural America is a class society in which gaps between classes are deep and are widening. The nation had focused on the problem of rural poverty during the 1930s in reference especially to the Dust Bowl migrants, but that concern proved to be ephemeral (see chapter 10). In 1960 respected broadcast journalist Edward R. Murrow made the television documentary "Harvest of Shame," which exposed the lives of poverty and hopelessness lived by migrant agricultural laborers on the Atlantic coast. The effectiveness of "Harvest of Shame" was enhanced by CBS's decision to air it on Thanksgiving evening. Murrow's documentary enraged farm groups, which succeeded in getting him called before a hostile congressional committee to defend himself against charges that he had besmirched the American way of life, but social concern for the rural poor never went away. Indeed, Lyndon Johnson's War on Poverty, César Chávez's efforts to organize farmworkers, and Jim Hightower's *Hard Tomatoes, Hard Times* kept the problem of rural poverty in the public consciousness, as did scathing investigations of the adverse effects of federal crop subsidy and reclamation programs on the rural underclass.[3]

Important though they were, concerns about rural people, classes, and communities paled into insignificance next to concerns about the relationship between agriculture, the environment, and human and animal health. Initial concerns about the environmental costs of the new agriculture focused on chemicals. In 1962, biologist Rachel Carson published *Silent Spring*, an exposé of the harmful effects of DDT on wildlife.[4] Birds, animals, and fish ingested DDT by drinking water or eating plants, animals, and insects that contained the pesticide. Instead of being flushed through the system, as other toxic substances often were, DDT built up in tissues, eventually disrupting reproduction and fatally attacking the nervous system. The Agricultural Research Service of the USDA denied Carson's allegations and aided those chemical interests that attacked her, despite the fact that it knew that most of what she charged was correct. Most state experiment stations and agricultural groups refused to consider the points Carson made, establishing themselves in an unfortunate adversarial position in relation to what became a growing environmental movement.

DDT was banned for domestic use after the truth of Carson's charges was proved, but this was only the beginning of a long series of challenges, usually successful, to agricultural chemicals shown to be harmful to animal or human life. Removal of dangerous substances could prevent further harm, but the consequences of the chemical revolution in agriculture continued. In 1986, one-third of Iowa's wells contained pesticides, and half of Nebraska's municipal water systems were similarly contaminated. Because many of these compounds do not break down naturally, they are likely to be with us for a long time. Even relatively benign agricultural chemicals can become harmful in large concentrations. In many parts of the corn belt, water supplies carry such high concentrations of nitrogen—which has been linked to birth defects and some cancers—that people are advised to drink bottled water.

In recent years some farmers have become concerned about the health risks of chemical use. They wonder whether this neighbor's liver cancer or that neighbor's miscarriage might somehow be connected to agricultural chemicals. But the most common reaction of farmers to the environmental movement has been anger and hostility. Farmers consider themselves to be good people who feed and clothe others, and until relatively recently they were unused to being questioned regarding how they went about it. They also operate in a business in which narrow margins dictate that they use all the tools at their disposal to produce to the maximum. Farmers argue that environmentalists are excessive and hysterical, pointing out that people have overreacted to chemicals that have no proven ill effects on humans or that are found in plant and animal matter in such minuscule concentrations as to be harmless.

Moreover, while even the most trivial risks involved in the use of a chemical seem to receive extravagant attention, the rewards it delivers tend to be ignored. Living in a society in which people seem unwilling to take even the most remote health risk and in which science now has the ability to measure the presence of contaminants even at the parts-per-trillion level, some farmers wonder whether they will long be able to use any chemicals at all. However valid their points might be, however, in their response to environmentalists farmers have too often appeared to demonstrate the worst aspects of being businesspeople without reflecting the best. Instead of being nature's partners, as Jefferson saw them, they have come off as nature's enemies, recklessly endangering the environment in their single-minded concentration on the bottom line. At the same time, they have ignored the first rule of a successful business—the customer is always right.

Closely related to the issue of the new agriculture and the environment is that of the sustainability of the present agricultural system. When people talk about agricultural sustainability, they are raising the question of whether our resource-intensive agriculture can continue indefinitely. Specifically, they wonder whether the quantities and integrity of soil, water, petroleum, and other resources currently devoted to agriculture can be maintained. If the resource base of our agriculture is depleted and not replaced, then the level of agricultural production will eventually decline to the point where the population dependent on it cannot be sustained.

Some of the threats to sustainability that critics of the new agriculture highlight arise from our dependence on finite resources. Within the space of a couple of generations our agriculture has become heavily petroleum-based. Not only are most of our machines powered by gasoline or diesel fuel, but most of our agricultural chemicals are petroleum-based as well. Even a temporary interruption of the supply of petroleum, half of which we import, would potentially threaten our agricultural system. Another threat to the sustainability of the new agriculture lies in the declining genetic diversity of our food crops. Where we once grew hundreds of varieties of wheat or corn, we now concentrate on a relative handful of high yielders with other desirable characteristics. As a practical matter, we have only one breed of chicken. This lack of genetic diversity puts us at risk that some insect or disease could devastate an entire crop lacking natural resistance. Genetics threaten sustainability in other ways as well. Some insects and weeds have developed resistance to chemicals that once killed them, raising the prospect of a superbug or superweed in our future with the potential to wipe out a crop.

Those concerned about the sustainability of our system also worry about the integrity of our soil and water resources. Soil erosion remains a problem, and some argue it is even more serious now than it was during the 1930s. Soil erosion is one problem to which some farmers have responded promptly. Sobering discoveries, such as that half of Iowa topsoil was lost in the century and a quarter after settlement, increased the popularity of no-till or minimum tillage systems in which soil preparation and cultivation were limited. Unfortunately, limited tillage systems involve greater use of insecticides and herbicides that present their own threats to the soil. While we do not commonly think of soil as a living thing, it is teeming with microorganisms that break down organic matter into nitrogen. Excessive use of chemicals kills these beneficial microorganisms, turning the soil into little more than an anchor for chemically produced crops.

The degradation of water resources further imperils agricultural sustainability. Irrigation mobilizes salts held in the soil or added to it by agricultural chemicals. When the land is not or cannot be well drained or when the water table rises, salinization threatens productivity. Irrigation return-flows and runoff from agricultural land increase the salts in water courses and sometimes contaminate them with such deadly minerals as selenium. Exhaustion of water supplies is another problem. For those who indict the new agriculture for its destruction of irreplaceable resources in the interests of short-term economic gain, there is no better example than the depletion of the Ogallala aquifer. The Ogallala underlies the central and southern Plains, including much of the old Dust Bowl region (see chapter 10). In 1945 it contained as much as three billion acre-feet of water (an acre-foot is the amount of water needed to cover an acre of land to a depth of one foot), an amount equal to what the Mississippi River has carried over the last two hundred

Modern chicken facility in New Mexico.
Copyright by the Progressive Farmer *(1970). Reprinted with permission.*

years. After World War II farmers began tapping the Ogallala and bringing
its waters to the surface with powerful pumps. They used flow techniques or
center-pivot sprinklers to grow such thirsty crops as alfalfa, corn, and cotton. They took the water from the ground so rapidly and spread it so lavishly
that by 1990 it was half gone, and observers estimated that the water level
would be depleted by the first years of the twenty-first century to the point
where pumping costs would be prohibitive. If this timetable holds, a natural
resource millions of years in the making will have been destroyed in less than
two generations.

The complaints of the critics of the new agriculture generally irritated
farmers, even those who could see some validity to them. For generations
farmers had been criticized for not being enough like urban people; now
they were lambasted for demonstrating too many of the traits associated with
industrial capitalism. The insult was bad enough, but the prospect of injury
also appeared when critics interested themselves in the making of agricultural policy. Between the 1930s and the 1960s farm policy was made by one
of those collegial, back-scratching iron triangles for which Washington is so
famous, or infamous. Friendly congressional committees, supportive bu-

reaucrats from the USDA, and lobbyists from established farm organizations and commodity groups made farm policy. They did not always agree on the answers, but they always asked the same questions. By the early 1970s these policy makers were joined by an earnest and insistent array of public-interest groups. The new participants in farm policy debates were not much interested in peanut subsidies or marketing agreements for wheat. But they were interested in justice for farm workers, nutrition and food safety, the environment, world hunger, consumers' rights, water quality, agricultural sustainability, and numerous other issues besides.

The new groups could not be excluded from the policy-making process, however much the agricultural establishment would have liked to ignore them. In the first place, farmers ask for resources from all taxpayers, and all interested citizens have the right to suggest how the money should be spent. In the second place, by 1990 only 46 of the country's 435 congressional districts could still be classified as farm oriented. There were not enough farmers and representatives serving them in Congress to make farm policy any more, so coalition building became necessary. Declining farm political power began to be reflected in legislation, such as the 1985 farm bill that included swampbuster, sodbuster, and other environmental protections, as well as funding for research in low-input, sustainable agriculture, provisions enjoying little support from old-line farm groups. In about a century, farmers had gone from majority, to minority, to subminority within the minority interested in agricultural policy. It is a trend unlikely to be reversed.

THE AGRICULTURAL DEPRESSION

Beginning in 1977 the agricultural economy's buoyancy faded. The initial problem for American producers was twofold. First, the market worked. High prices for agricultural commodities called forth greater supplies, as farmers all over the world intensified production and farmed more marginal acres. The second problem for American producers was that the climatic difficulties that had beset much of the world proved to be temporary, with the result that our competitors' production returned to normal.

Then, between 1979 and 1981 a series of events sent agriculture spiraling into its most serious crisis in half a century. Beginning in October of 1979, the Federal Reserve Board under the leadership of Chairman Paul Volcker raised interest rates as a means of curbing inflation. Volcker's action created difficulties for farmers in three ways. First, it raised the cost of borrowing for farm debtors and dissuaded purchasers from bidding up land prices. Second, it cooled inflation, the debtor's friend. And finally, high interest rates raised the value of the dollar, making American farm products more expensive on international markets. American exports were further imperiled early in 1980, when President Jimmy Carter responded to the Soviet invasion of Afghanistan by declaring an embargo on wheat and feed-grain sales to the Russians. Not only did this action close off an important new market for American farmers, it also raised questions in the minds of many of our customers about the United States' reliability as a supplier. Finally, the centerpiece of President Ronald Reagan's domestic program, as revealed shortly after his inauguration in 1981, was a massive tax cut. This tax reduction assured that budget deficits would be high and guaranteed that inflation would be fought by the high interest rates that were deviling farmers.

The result of all this was a decline in farm prices that affected most commodities but was especially pronounced in food grains and feed grains. In 1979 farm prices stood at 71 percent of parity, but they declined steadily, bottoming out at 51 percent of parity in 1986. At that point farm prices were at a lower level relative to the prices farmers paid than they had been at the depth of the Great Depression.

While all commercial farmers felt the effects of this downturn, the ones most seriously hurt were those who had participated most enthusiastically in the boom. Farmers who specialized in wheat, corn, or soybeans were reminded painfully that livestock buffer incomes against shocks. Those who embraced lavish lifestyles were reminded that, while farmers might look rich on paper, they act rich at their peril. The situation faced by borrowers was both ironic and pitiful. Many were young, well-educated farmers who were now imperiled through no fault of their own. Others had followed the advice of the agricultural establishment by expanding during the boom and had been praised thereby for being good managers, in contrast to their more conservative neighbors who were often stigmatized as poor managers. Many had been trying to provide for their children's future in agriculture, but now they faced the loss not only of what they had purchased but also of what they already owned. It is unfortunate when anyone loses a job or a business. But the farm is also a home, often put together painstakingly over several generations. Thus losing one's farm is losing one's home, and its loss frequently represents a betrayal not only of one's children but of one's parents and grandparents as well. Small wonder that this tragic situation produced so much alcoholism, so many nervous breakdowns, and so many violent deaths.

Agriculture was not well prepared politically to address its disappointing reversal of fortunes. Farmers had become such a tiny portion of the electorate that their clout was limited at best. A further difficulty was that such old-line organizations as the Farm Bureau and the Farmers Union had lost much of their fire and had become more interested in such member services as insurance sales than in the making of farm policy. The traditional organizations were also harmed by the rise of commodity groups, especially after World War II. Commodity groups organized the producers of single commodities, such as hogs or cotton. Organization on a commodity basis was indirectly encouraged by federal programs, which were commodity based, and it magnified the effectiveness of farmers with a narrow range of concerns and problems and a few limited goals. Commodity groups were not effective in dealing with problems that had an impact on agriculture as a whole.

The times seemed to call for a new grassroots movement, and it appeared in the American Agriculture Movement (AAM), founded by farmers living in the Campo, Colorado, area in 1977. The AAM was based on the proposition that traditional farm organizations had become overly bureaucratized and detached from their members and that commodity groups were too narrow. Only a new mass organization that developed from the bottom up, the AAM reasoned, could truly solve farmers' increasing difficulties. The AAM was commonly portrayed by the press as a latter-day manifestation of Populism, but it was quite a modern group in many ways. It skillfully used advanced communications technology to create and then mobilize an organization, and it was shrewd in exploiting the electronic media, taking a page from the Civil Rights and other contemporary protest movements. The AAM garnered maximum favorable publicity by staging tractorcades and other protests at locations accessible to metropolitan media representatives and at times convenient for television stations with dinner-hour deadlines to meet.

The AAM initially sponsored a farm strike, but that was doomed to failure because few commercial farmers—and none with mortgages—could afford not to plant. It quickly became obvious that government aid was a more feasible answer, and in the spring of 1978 several hundred AAM members took a tractorcade to Washington, D.C., to demand relief. Impressed by the farmers' resolve and by the favorable media attention they received, Congress increased price supports by 11 percent. Unfortunately, the AAM was less sophisticated in political matters than it was in media manipulation, and many members took their victory as a defeat because it failed to give them all that they wanted. Frustrated, bitter, and sometimes violent people assumed a more prominent role in the organization, leading moderates to withdraw. A January 1979 tractorcade to Washington was dominated by extremists who snarled traffic, drove tractors into the reflecting pool between the Capitol and the Washington Monument, and scuffled with police. The 1979 demonstration was a public-relations disaster, and an organization that had lived by the media now died by the media. Part of the AAM moved toward becoming a more conventional lobbying group, while its fringes proved to be fertile recruiting grounds for right-wing hate groups and other extremists who blamed the Tri-Lateral Commission, the Federal Reserve Board, Jews, and others for farmers' problems.

Groups outside of agriculture also provided support for farmers during the eighties. Remarkably, farmers drew sympathy from some of the same sorts of people who had been most critical of them in the seventies. In North Dakota, for example, the American Civil Liberties Union went to court to force the Farmers Home Administration to follow its own rules in farm foreclosure proceedings. In Iowa, a disparate liberal aggregation of churches, community activists, unions, academics, and others came together to form the Iowa Farm Unity Coalition, which lobbied for agricultural relief, mediated between lenders and farm borrowers, and provided counseling services for farm families under stress.

Show business discovered the farm crisis as well. The 1984 film *Country* concerned the efforts of a couple, portrayed by Sam Shepard and Jessica Lange, to save their Iowa farm from foreclosure. In that same year, Mel Gibson and Sissy Spacek struggled to save their farm from floodwaters and grasping bankers in *The River*. The eighties also saw Willie Nelson launch a series of Farm Aid concerts to help agencies trying to protect farmers from foreclosure. It was obvious that there was a residual belief outside of rural America that farming was special and that the family farm deserved preservation. Certainly, no one considered holding "druggist aid" or "gas-station-operator aid" concerts in behalf of other small businesspeople.

Urban sympathy and rural political action helped farmers achieve substantial aid during the eighties. Debtors received some relief when Farmers Home Administration procedures were liberalized and when the debts of farmers whose situations were not considered hopeless were restructured. Its conservative tone did not prevent the Reagan administration from creating programs that lavished money on commercial producers. In 1981, the Payment-In-Kind program gave farmers government-held surplus crops in return for their removing land from production, and the 1985 farm bill created the Conservation Reserve Program, under which 40 million acres of highly erodible land was removed from production. By 1986 nearly 3 percent of the federal budget was going into agricultural subsidies, which averaged about $13,000 per farm. Such subsidization was justified as a means of saving the family farm, and the fact that the vast majority of even very large farms were family owned lent credence to that justification. In 1986, however, as in 1936, all family farmers were not treated equally. Federal largesse was received in equal measure by large farmers, who composed only 15 percent of all recipients, and small farmers, who composed 80 percent; and the 2 percent of farmers grossing over $500,000 per year received 15 percent of all the benefits.

BEYOND THE DEPRESSION

As the distribution of benefits from federal agricultural programs shows, the farm crisis of the 1980s failed to reverse most of the long-term trends in agriculture. Many of the farmers who had expanded during the seventies went under during the eighties, but their lands were acquired by others whose operations were at least as large and sometimes larger. In 1981 the average farm in the United States had 424 acres. Ten years later the average farm had 467 acres. Bigger farms continued to mean fewer farms. There were about 2.44 million farms in 1981 and fewer than 2.105 million a decade later. Of these, only a relative handful were economically significant. Nearly half of the farms in the country in 1991 were weekend or hobby farms with less than $10,000 in annual gross sales. Only a little more than 15 percent had gross sales in excess of $100,000 per year, and a mere 40 thousand had gross sales worth over $500,000.

As the number of farms dwindled the farm population declined as well. In 1981 the farm population stood at 5.82 million, or 2.5 percent of the nation's total. By 1990 only 4.591 million people, or 1.8 percent of Americans, still lived on farms. Farm people had gone from majority, to minority, to curiosity. Even in the countryside farmers were becoming anomalous. At the end of World War II over half of rural people still lived on farms, but in 1990 only about 10 percent did.

The downturn of the eighties did not reverse any trends, but it did stimulate some rethinking about the future of agriculture and of rural America. Many farmers looked to make their farms more sustainable as economic units. During the Great Depression fifty years before, this had meant living-at-home and doing without, but these were no longer viable options for most farm families. Farmers' capital needs and living standards committed them to commercial production. They could not get through these hard times by buying a flock of chickens, making their own soap, and burning corn for coal. It was possible, however, to enhance sustainability by diversifying within a commercial context. One means of diversifying was to continue the trend of depending less on farm income by getting an off-farm job, or a second off-farm job. Another means of diversifying was to bring animals back into grain operations. Hogs and cattle demand attention that small grains or corn and soybeans do not, but they also provide steady cash flow and reduce income volatility. Other farmers tried new commercial crops, such as crambe (an oil seed) or amaranth (a high-protein small grain with cosmetic and pharmaceutical applications), grew Christmas trees, or raised exotic animals such as buffalo or ostriches. Some farmers, responding to the growing market provided by affluent health-conscious Americans, produced natural foods through organic methods in which chemical pesticides and fertilizers were not used. In 1980, most farmers viewed organic producers, or alternative agriculturalists, with bemused contempt, as latter-day hippies with harebrained notions of how farming should be done. But their successes in the market have quieted the skeptical, and today alternative agriculturalists are an increasingly respected and numerous component of the farming community.

Alternative agriculturalists showed how economic and environmental sustainability could be compatible. Unfortunately, the struggle of farmers to survive economically sometimes had dire environmental implications. Some pushed their farms hard, putting on more chemicals, draining wetlands, breaking unbroken acres, and taking shortcuts that imperiled long-term sustainability. But others took a fresh look at the new agriculture and wondered whether the increased yields were worth the cost. There was a new receptivity to those suggesting ways to get along with fewer off-farm inputs, less anhydrous ammonia, insecticide, or herbicide. And farmers no longer automatically regarded yield as the main index of their success. A few more bugs and weeds lowered yield, but was eradicating them economically wise when crops often sold below the cost of production anyway? It was the kind of question farmers began seriously to consider, and sometimes the answer was no.

Farmers were also increasingly inclined to "just say no" to science. A generation of farmers who had grown up believing that science had the solution to their problems has become skeptical of the changes coming out of laboratories in land-grant schools and agribusiness. Wisconsin farmers protested bitterly when their agricultural experiment station researched bovine somatatrophin, which will increase milk production in a country that already produces more than can be sold profitably. And other farmers are dubious about biotechnological advances, which they suspect will mainly increase the profits of agribusiness firms at the expense of producers.

Cutting upstream expenses is one way of enhancing economic sustainability in agriculture. Capturing downstream profits is another. As producers of commodities to which others add substantial value, farmers find themselves enjoying a shrinking share of every dollar spent on food. In 1988, only 12 percent of what the consumer spent on potatoes went to the farmer, and only 7 percent of the cost of a loaf of bread went to the producer of the wheat. Everywhere farmers are looking to increase their participation in agricultural processing and food production. In North Dakota durum wheat farmers have built a factory to turn their product into pasta. Other farmers are processing potatoes, slaughtering buffalo, and turning corn into sweeteners. These are risky enterprises, because they compete with billion-dollar multinational firms, but many farmers believe they are necessary if agriculture is to be economically viable.

Farmers were concerned about enhancing their abilities to survive economically in part because they remained strongly committed to rural life. Physically and materially, rural living was less distinct from urban living than ever before, and rural people had no desire to go back to outhouses and kerosene lamps or to surrender their microwave ovens and VCRs. But rural people did see differences between rural and urban life that made the former desirable. An extensive survey of rural attitudes conducted for the National Rural Electric Cooperative Association by the Roper Organization in 1992 showed that a large majority of respondents scored their communities high in terms of personal values, community spirit, quality of life, and friendliness. More remarkable, in light of chronic economic difficulties and out-migration, was the surveyors' finding that two-thirds of rural people were optimistic about the future of their communities.

My own more anecdotal evidence lends support to the findings of the Roper Organization. For years I have taught a class called History of Rural America. Sometimes, on exams, I offer students the option of writing essays on the differences between rural and urban life. The results are provocative. A woman from western Minnesota tells how a farmer's neighbors brought in his crop when he became ill. A man from a town of two hundred in central North Dakota writes of the "kindness and closeness" of people in his area and notes that "everyone watches out for everyone else." A young woman from a western North Dakota cattle ranch points out that everyone in her town goes to high school basketball games, not because there is nothing else to do but because they all know the players and care about them. The daughter of a wheat farmer writes of "a shared joy in a small community when an accomplishment is attained," and a young man notes that one never locks a house or car in his area. An older student who spent six years erecting communications towers in the Great Plains and Midwest remembers how farmers were always glad to lend a tractor to pull a truck from the mud or move equipment around a site. He mentions that all the people in rural cafes would talk to him and that motorists on rural roads invariably waved to oncoming drivers.

Instead of leading farmers to wash their hands of their life or turn their backs on rural America in disgust, the hard times of the 1980s seemed to lead to a recommitment to rural life and a determination to nurture whatever is unique in it. The revival of quilting and other rural crafts is indicative of this attitude. And the popularity of rural fairs and celebrations recreating past modes of living and working, such as the Western Minnesota Steam Threshers' Reunion, reflects nostalgia but also a determination to keep cherished traditions alive.

A few years ago I interviewed a farmer in central North Dakota. While we sat at a formica kitchen table strewn with business papers, he spoke of how he and his wife had raised ten children on the farm and of their concern about providing for all of their kids. During the seventies they had expanded dramatically, more than doubling their two-section farm by purchasing land from neighbors. He had been a wheat-and-cattle raiser, but now he had gone into small grains exclusively in response to the surging market. When the depression hit he lost most of what he had bought and would have lost his original farm had not relatives helped him with loans. He had survived, and now he was doing what the times demanded. He was feeding cattle again, to minimize his risks. He was thinking seriously about costs. He made his machinery go longer, and he doctored his cattle himself. He had cut back on his chemical use, in part because of the cost and in part because he worried about his health. Several neighbors had died of cancer, and he figured the chemicals had something to do with it.

He drove me around his farm, as proud farmers like to do, telling me about a son who had a spread across the county line and gossiping a bit about neighbors I did not know. Here he stopped to point out his father's original farmstead, there to show me the dairy operation of one son whose wife taught school in town, and over here to shout at another son to put on a mask while he applied herbicide to a field. This man was a survivor. The countryside is full of them, and we are all the richer for it.

Notes

PREFACE AND ACKNOWLEDGMENTS

1. Richard Hofstadter, *The Age of Reform* (New York: Vintage, 1955), 23.

2. Frederick Jackson Turner's great seminal work is "The Significance of the Frontier in American History," American Historical Association, *Annual Report for the Year 1893* (Washington, D.C.: American Historical Association, 1894), 199–227. John D. Hicks's most important historical contribution is *The Populist Revolt: A History of the Farmers' Alliance and the People's Party* (Minneapolis: University of Minnesota Press, 1931).

3. Paul Gates reviewed his own early work and that of his students in "Research in the History of American Land Tenure: A Review Article," *Agricultural History* 28 (July 1954): 121–26.

4. Joseph Schafer, *The Social History of American Agriculture* (New York: Macmillan, 1936).

5. Robert Swierenga, "The New Rural History: Defining the Parameters," *Great Plains Quarterly* 1 (fall 1981): 211–23.

CHAPTER 2. THE RURAL DEVELOPMENT
OF ENGLISH NORTH AMERICA

1. The Tuggle family is followed in Darrett Rutman and Anita Rutman, *A Place in Time: Middlesex County, Virginia, 1650–1750* (New York: Norton, 1984).

2. The creation of Sudbury is detailed in Sumner Chilton Powell, *Puritan Village: The Formation of a New England Town* (Middletown, Conn.: Wesleyan University Press, 1963).

3. The Andover experience is recounted by Philip A. Greven Jr., *Four Generations: Population, Land, and Family in Colonial Andover, Massachusetts* (Ithaca: Cornell University Press, 1970).

CHAPTER 3. MATURITY AND ITS DISCONTENTS

1. Rutman and Rutman, *A Place in Time.*

2. The movements of John Pulliam and his descendants are followed in John Mack Faragher, *Sugar Creek: Life on the Illinois Prairie* (New Haven: Yale University Press, 1986).

3. Greven, *Four Generations.*

4. These later Ballards are examined in Laurel Thatcher Ulrich, *A Midwife's Tale: The Life of Martha Ballard, Based on Her Diary, 1785–1812* (New York: Knopf, 1990).

5. James T. Lemon, *"The Best Poor Man's Country": A Geographical Study of Early Southeastern Pennsylvania* (New York: W. W. Norton, 1976).

CHAPTER 4. AGRICULTURE AND ECONOMIC GROWTH IN THE NEW REPUBLIC

1. Thomas Jefferson, *Notes on the State of Virginia* (Chapel Hill: University of North Carolina Press, 1955), 164–65.

2. David F. Allmendinger Jr., *Ruffin: Family and Reform in the Old South* (New York: Oxford University Press, 1990).

3. Jeremy Atack and Fred Bateman, "Was There Ever an 'Agrarian Democracy' in America? The American Middle West in 1860," in Frederick V. Carstensen, Morton Rothstein, and Joseph A. Swanson, eds., *Outstanding in His Field: Perspectives on American Agriculture in Honor of Wayne D. Rasmussen* (Ames: Iowa State University Press, 1993), 69–89.

4. Quoted in Joan E. Cashin, *A Family Venture: Men and Women on the Southern Frontier* (New York: Oxford University Press, 1991), 66.

5. Faragher, *Sugar Creek.*

6. Jane Marie Pederson, *Between Memory and Reality: Family and Community in Rural Wisconsin, 1870–1970* (Madison: University of Wisconsin Press, 1992).

7. Elizabeth A. Perkins, "The Consumption Frontier: Household Consumption in Early Kentucky," *Journal of American History* 78 (Sept. 1991): 486–510.

8. Quoted in Fredric Trautman, ed. and trans., "Eight Weeks on a St. Clair

County Farm in 1851: Letters by a Young German," *Journal of the Illinois State Historical Society* 75 (autumn 1982): 176–77.

9. Quoted in R. Douglas Hurt, "Pork and Porkopolis," *Cincinnati Historical Society Bulletin* 40 (fall 1992): 198.

10. Jeremy Atack and Fred Bateman, *To Their Own Soil: Agriculture in the Antebellum North* (Ames: Iowa State University Press, 1987), 224.

11. Fred Bateman and Jeremy Atack, "The Profitability of Northern Agriculture in 1860," *Research in Economic History* 4 (1979): 119.

CHAPTER 5. RURAL LIFE IN THE YOUNG NATION

1. Kathryn Kish Sklar, *Catharine Beecher: A Study in American Domesticity* (New York: Norton, 1973).

2. John Muir, *The Story of My Boyhood and Youth* (Boston: Houghton Mifflin, 1913), 203.

3. Pederson, *Between Memory and Reality.*

4. Quoted in Walter D. Kamphoefner, Wolfgang Helbich, and Ulrike Sommer, eds., *News From the Land of Freedom: German Immigrants Write Home*, trans. Susan Carter Vogel (Ithaca: Cornell University Press, 1991), 70.

5. Frederick Law Olmsted, *The Papers of Frederick Law Olmsted*, vol. 2, *Slavery and the South, 1852–1857*, ed. Charles E. Beveridge and Charles Capen McLaughlin (Baltimore: Johns Hopkins University Press, 1981), 206. Emphasis in original.

6. James C. Curtis. *Andrew Jackson and the Search for Vindication* (Boston: Little, Brown, 1976), 8.

7. Harvey A. Levenstein, *Revolution at the Table: The Transformation of the American Diet* (Oxford: Oxford University Press, 1988), 5.

8. Cashin, *A Family Venture*, 114–15.

9. Jackson's deathbed scene is recounted in Arthur M. Schlesinger Jr., *The Age of Jackson* (Boston: Little, Brown, 1945), 447.

CHAPTER 6. THE UNMAKING AND REMAKING OF THE RURAL SOUTH

1. Quoted in David B. Danbom, " 'Dear Companion': Civil War Letters of a Story County Farmer," *Annals of Iowa* 47 (fall 1984): 538–39.

2. Quoted in Edward D. Eddy Jr., "The Land-Grant Movement," in *Land-Grant Centennial Fact Book* (Washington, D.C.: American Association of Land-Grant Colleges and State Universities, 1962), 2.

3. Ted Ownby, "The Defeated Generation at Work: White Farmers in the Deep South, 1865–1890," *Southern Studies* 23 (winter 1984): 325–47.

4. Gilbert C. Fite, "The Agricultural Trap in the South," *Agricultural History* 60 (fall 1986): 38–50.

5. Roger L. Ransom and Richard Sutch, *One Kind of Freedom: The Economic Consequences of Emancipation* (Cambridge: Cambridge University Press, 1977), 28.

6. Margaret Jones Bolsterli, ed., *Vinegar Pie and Chicken Bread: A Woman's Diary of Life in the Rural South* (Fayetteville: University of Arkansas Press, 1965), 99.

7. Quoted in Frank Freidel, *F. D. R. and the South* (Baton Rouge: Louisiana State University Press, 1965), 99.

CHAPTER 7. RURAL AMERICA
IN THE AGE OF INDUSTRIALIZATION

1. Fred A. Shannon, *The Farmer's Last Frontier: Agriculture, 1860–1897* (New York: Holt, Rinehart and Winston, 1961), 152.

2. Robert P. Wilkins and Wynona H. Wilkins, *North Dakota: A Bicentennial History* (New York: Norton, 1977), 76.

3. John Opie, *Ogallala; Water for a Dry Land* (Lincoln: University of Nebraska Press, 1993), 65.

4. Timothy J. Kloberdanz, "Volksdeutsche: The Eastern European Germans," in William C. Sherman and Playford V. Thorson, eds., *Plains Folk: North Dakota's Ethnic Heritage* (Fargo: North Dakota Institute for Regional Studies, 1988): 157.

5. E. V. Smalley, "The Isolation of Life on Prairie Farms," *Atlantic Monthly* 72 (Sept. 1893): 379.

6. Quoted in Walker D. Wyman, ed., *Frontier Woman: The Life of a Woman Homesteader on the Dakota Frontier* (River Falls: University of Wisconsin–River Falls Press, 1972), 13.

7. Edgar W. Howe, *The Story of a Country Town* (Atchison, Kans.: Howe and Company, 1883).

8. Richard Dugdale, *"The Jukes": A Study in Crime, Pauperism, Disease and Heredity* (New York: G. P. Putnam's Sons, 1877).

9. Pederson, *Between Memory and Reality.*

10. Virginia E. McCormick, ed., *Farm Wife: A Self-Portrait* (Ames: Iowa State University Press, 1990).

CHAPTER 8. PROSPERITY AND ITS DISCONTENTS

1. Bolton Hall, *Three Acres and Liberty* (New York: Macmillan, 1907).

2. *Report of the United States Country Life Commission* (Washington, D.C.: Government Printing Office, 1909), 3.

3. Quoted in David B. Danbom, *The Resisted Revolution: Urban America and the Industrialization of Agriculture, 1900–1930* (Ames: Iowa State University Press, 1979), 88.

4. Ibid., 102.

5. Dan Lewis, Joe Young, and Walter Donaldson, "How Ya Gonna Keep 'Em Down on the Farm (After They've Seen Paree)," 1919.

CHAPTER 9. FROM THE BEST OF TIMES TO THE WORST

1. H. Thomas Johnson, *Agricultural Depression in the 1920's: Economic Fact or Statistical Artifact* (New York: Garland, 1985).

2. Pederson, *Between Memory and Reality.*

3. Kenneth Hassebrock, *Rural Reminiscences: The Agony of Survival* (Ames: Iowa State University Press, 1990), 122.

4. Wheeler McMillan, *Too Many Farmers* (New York: Morrow, 1929).

5. E. R. McIntyre, "Hic Jacet—the Hick," *Independent* 116 (Apr. 10, 1926): 421–22.

6. Quoted in Beulah Meier Pelton, *We Belong to the Land: Memories of a Midwesterner* (Ames: Iowa State University Press, 1984), 144.

7. For depression era back-to-the landism, see David B. Danbom, "Romantic Agrarianism in Twentieth-Century America," *Agricultural History* 65 (fall 1991): 1–12.

8. Hassebrock, *Rural Reminiscences*, 177.

CHAPTER 10. THE NEW DEAL AND RURAL AMERICA

1. Rexford G. Tugwell, "The Resettlement Idea," *Agricultural History* 33 (Oct. 1959): 161.

2. Pamela Riney-Kehrberg, "Separation and Sorrow: A Farm Woman's Life, 1935–1941," *Agricultural History* 67 (spring 1993): 189.

3. This report is explored in Donald Worster, *Dust Bowl: The Southern Plains in the 1930s* (Oxford: Oxford University Press, 1979).

4. Quoted in Richard Polenberg, *War and Society: The United States, 1941–1945* (Philadelphia: Lippincott, 1972): 31.

CHAPTER 11. THE PRODUCTION REVOLUTION AND ITS CONSEQUENCES

1. Paul H. Johnstone, "Old Ideals versus New Ideas in Farm Life," *Farmers in a Changing World: The Yearbook of Agriculture 1940* (Washington, D.C.: Government Printing Office, 1940), 140.

2. Walter Goldschmidt, *As You Sow* (New York: Harcourt Brace, 1947).

276   CHAPTER 12. AGRICULTURE AND RURAL LIFE
                       AT THE END OF THE TWENTIETH CENTURY

1. See, especially, Wendell Berry, *The Unsettling of America: Culture and Agriculture* (San Francisco: Sierra Club Books, 1977).

2. Danbom, "Romantic Agrarianism."

3. Jim Hightower, *Hard Tomatoes, Hard Times: A Report of the Agribusiness Accountability Project on the Failure of America's Land Grant College Complex* (Cambridge: Schenkman, 1973).

4. Rachel Carson, *Silent Spring* (Boston: Houghton Mifflin, 1962).

Suggestions

for Further Reading

CHAPTER I. RURAL EUROPE AND PRE-COLUMBIAN AMERICA
Life and labor in European villages have drawn a good deal of attention in recent years. Some important contributions include Peter Laslett, *The World We Have Lost* (New York: Charles Scribner's Sons, 1965); Carlo M. Cipolla, *Before the Industrial Revolution: European Society and Economy, 1000–1700* (New York: Norton, 1976); Fernand Braudel, *The Structures of Everyday Life* (New York: Harper and Row, 1981); Jerome Blum, ed., *Our Forgotten Past: Seven Centuries of Life on the Land* (London: Thames and Hudson, 1982); Emmanuel LeRoy Ladurie, *The French Peasantry 1450–1660* (Berkeley: University of California Press, 1987); and G. E. Mingay, *A Social History of the English Countryside* (London: Routledge, 1990). For European agriculture specifically, see B. H. Slicher Van Bath, *The Agrarian History of Western Europe: A.D. 500–1800* (New York: St. Martin's, 1963); and Joan Thirsk, ed., *The Agrarian History of England and Wales, vol. 4, 1500–1640* (Cambridge: Cambridge University Press, 1967).

For the impact of economic and political changes on European villages, see Joan Thirsk, *English Peasant Farming: The Agrarian History of Lincolnshire from Tudor to Recent Times* (London: Mathuen, 1957); W. G. Hoskins, *The Midland Peasant: The Economic and Social History of a Leicestershire Village* (London: Macmillan, 1957), and *Provincial England: Essays in Social and Economic History* (London: Macmillan, 1965); Eric Kerridge, *The Agricultural Revolution* (New

York: Augustus M. Kelley, 1968); William N. Parker and Eric L. Jones, eds., *European Peasants and Their Markets: Essays in Agrarian Economic History* (Princeton: Princeton University Press, 1975); and Robert C. Allen, *Enclosure and the Yeoman* (Oxford: Clarendon, 1992).

For aspects of Indian agriculture and society, especially in the Woodland Culture, see Howard S. Russell, *Indian New England Before the Mayflower* (Hanover, N.H.: University Press of New England, 1980); Neal Salisbury, *Manitou and Providence: Indians, Europeans, and the Making of New England, 1500–1643* (New York: Oxford University Press, 1982); William Cronon, *Changes in the Land: Indians, Colonists, and the Ecology of New England* (New York: Hill and Wang, 1983); and R. Douglas Hurt, *Indian Agriculture in America: Prehistory to the Present* (Lawrence: University Press of Kansas, 1987).

For the Columbian Exchange, see Alfred W. Crosby, *The Columbian Exchange: Biological and Cultural Consequences of 1492* (Westport, Conn.: Greenwood, 1972), and *Ecological Imperialism: The Biological Expansion of Europe, 900–1900* (Cambridge: Cambridge University Press, 1986); Richard White, *Land Use, Environment, and Social Change: The Shaping of Island County, Washington* (Seattle: University of Washington Press, 1980); and Timothy Silver, *A New Face on the Countryside: Indians, Colonists, and Slaves in South Atlantic Forests, 1500–1800* (Cambridge: Cambridge University Press, 1990).

CHAPTER 2. THE RURAL DEVELOPMENT OF ENGLISH NORTH AMERICA

A good deal of excellent work has been done on the colonial Chesapeake in recent years. Among the volumes the reader might wish to consult are Edmund S. Morgan, *American Slavery—American Freedom: The Ordeal of Colonial Virginia* (New York: W. W. Norton, 1975); Carville V. Earle, *The Evolution of a Tidewater Settlement System: All Hallow's Parish, Maryland, 1650–1783* (Chicago: University of Chicago Geography Department, 1975); Gloria Main, *Tobacco Colony: Life in Early Maryland, 1650–1720* (Princeton: Princeton University Press, 1982); Darrett B. Rutman and Anita H. Rutman, *A Place in Time: Middlesex County, Virginia, 1650–1750* (New York: W. W. Norton, 1984); Allan Kulikoff, *Tobacco and Slaves: The Development of Southern Cultures in the Chesapeake, 1680–1800* (Chapel Hill: University of North Carolina Press, 1986); James R. Perry, *The Formation of a Society on Virginia's Eastern Shore, 1615–1655* (Chapel Hill: University of North Carolina Press, 1990); and Lois Green Carr, Russell R. Menard, and Lorena S. Walsh, *Robert Cole's World: Agriculture and Society in Early Maryland* (Chapel Hill: University of North Carolina Press, 1991).

The early history of New England in general, and Massachusetts Bay in particular, is among the most intensively studied topics in American history. Included among the many significant works on this subject are William Haller Jr., *The Puritan Frontier: Town-Planting in New England Colonial Development* (New York: Columbia University Press, 1951); Sumner Chilton Powell, *Puritan Village: The Formation of a New England Town* (Middletown, Conn.: Wesleyan University Press, 1963); Darrett B. Rutman, *Husbandmen of Plymouth: Farms and Villages in the Old Colony, 1620–1692* (Boston: Beacon, 1967); Philip A. Greven Jr., *Four Generations: Population, Land, and Family in Colonial Andover, Massachusetts* (Ithaca: Cornell University Press, 1970); Kenneth A. Lockridge, *A New England Town: The First Hundred Years: Dedham, Massachusetts, 1636–1736* (New York: W. W. Norton, 1970); Howard S. Russell, *A Long, Deep Furrow: Three Centuries of Farming in New England* (Hanover, N.H.: University Press of New England, 1976); and David Grayson Allen, *In English Ways: The Movement of Societies and the Transferal of English Local Law and Custom to Massachusetts Bay in the Seventeenth Century* (Chapel Hill: University of North Carolina Press, 1981).

For early South Carolina agriculture, see Peter A. Coclanis, *The Shadow of a Dream: Economic Life and Death in the South Carolina Low Country, 1670–1920* (New York: Oxford University Press, 1989). For Dutch rural life in New Netherland, see David Steven Cohen, *The Dutch-American Farm* (New York: New York University Press, 1992). James T. Lemon's *"The Best Poor Man's County": A Geographical Study of Early Southeastern Pennsylvania* (New York: W. W. Norton, 1976) is the best introduction to the course of development in colonial Pennsylvania. The importance of British origins to the nature of development in colonial America, including Pennsylvania, is vigorously upheld by David Hackett Fischer, *Albion's Seed: Four British Folkways in America* (New York: Oxford University Press, 1989). The significance of the Finns in introducing techniques of frontier settlement is provocatively advanced in Terry S. Jordan and Matti Kaups, *Backwoods Frontier: An Ethnic and Ecological Interpretation* (Baltimore: Johns Hopkins University Press, 1989).

CHAPTER 3. MATURITY AND ITS DISCONTENTS

For general economic developments in colonial America, see Alice Hanson Jones, *Wealth of a Nation to Be: The American Colonies on the Eve of the Revolution* (New York: Columbia University Press, 1980); Edwin J. Perkins, *The Economy of Colonial America* (New York: Columbia University Press, 1980); and John J. McCusker and Russell R. Menard, *The Economy of British America, 1607–1789* (Chapel Hill: University of North Carolina Press, 1985). Colonial labor systems are profitably explored by several contributors to Stephen Innes, ed., *Work and Labor in Early America* (Williamsburg, Va.: Institute of Early American History and Culture, 1988). For consumption patterns among colonists, see Carole

Shammas, *The Pre-Industrial Consumer in England and America* (Oxford: Clarendon, 1990).

The issue of the level of market participation by colonial farmers and their consciousness of market—as opposed to communal—motivations has become a major one among historians in recent years. For an introduction to the points at issue, see James A. Henretta, "Families and Farms: *Mentalité* in Pre-Industrial America," *William and Mary Quarterly* 35 (Jan. 1978): 3–32; Darrett B. Rutman, "Assessing the Little Communities of Early America," *William and Mary Quarterly* 43 (Apr. 1986): 163–78; and Allan Kulikoff, "The Transition to Capitalism in Rural America," *William and Mary Quarterly* 46 (Jan. 1989): 120–44.

For agriculture and society in Maryland and Virginia, see, in addition to previously mentioned works, Lewis Cecil Gray, *History of Agriculture in the Southern United States to 1860* (Washington, D.C.: Carnegie Institution, 1933); Robert D. Mitchell, *Commercialism and Frontier: Perspectives on the Early Shenandoah Valley* (Charlottesville: University Press of Virginia, 1977); Richard R. Beeman, *The Evolution of the Southern Backcountry: A Case Study of Lunenburg County, Virginia 1746–1832* (Philadelphia: University of Pennsylvania Press, 1984); T. H. Breen, *Tobacco Culture: The Mentality of the Great Tidewater Planters on the Eve of Revolution* (Princeton: Princeton University Press, 1985); Lois Green Carr, Philip D. Morgan, and Jean B. Russo, eds., *Colonial Chesapeake Society* (Williamsburg, Va.: Institute of Early American History and Culture, 1988); John Solomon Otto, *The Southern Frontiers, 1607–1860: The Agricultural Evolution of the Colonial and Antebellum South* (Westport, Conn.: Greenwood, 1989), and Lois Green Carr and Russell R. Menard, "Land, Labor, and Economies of Scale in Early Maryland: Some Limits to Growth in the Chesapeake System of Husbandry," *Journal of Economic History* 49 (June 1989): 407–18.

For South Carolina, see Peter H. Wood, *Black Majority: Negroes in Colonial South Carolina from 1670 Through the Stono Rebellion* (New York: W. W. Norton, 1974); Daniel C. Littlefield, *Rice and Slaves: Ethnicity and Slave Trade in Colonial South Carolina* (Baton Rouge: Louisiana State University Press, 1981); Albert E. Cowdrey, *This Land, This South: An Environmental History* (Lexington: University Press of Kentucky, 1983); Henry C. Dethloff, *A History of the American Rice Industry, 1685–1985* (College Station: Texas A&M University Press, 1988); Joyce E. Chaplin, "Tidal Rice Cultivation and the Problem of Slavery in South Carolina and Georgia, 1760–1815," *William and Mary Quarterly* 49 (Jan. 1992): 29 61; and Judith A. Carney, "From Hands to Tutors: African Expertise in the South Carolina Rice Economy," *Agricultural History* 67 (summer 1993): 1–30.

For New England, see the community studies cited previously, as well as Charles S. Grant, *Democracy in the Connecticut Frontier Town of Kent* (New York:

Columbia University Press, 1961); Robert Gross, *The Minutemen and Their World* (New York: Hill and Wang, 1976); Christopher M. Jedrey, *The World of John Cleaveland: Family and Community in Eighteenth-Century New England* (New York: W. W. Norton, 1979); Douglas Lamar Jones, *Village and Seaport: Migration and Society in Eighteenth-Century Massachusetts* (Hanover, N.H.: University Press of New England, 1981); Stephen Innes, *Labor in a New Land: Economy and Society in Seventeenth-Century Springfield* (Princeton: Princeton University Press, 1983); John Frederick Martin, *Profits in the Wilderness: Entrepreneurship and the Founding of New England Towns in the Seventeenth Century* (Chapel Hill: University of North Carolina Press, 1991); Kenneth Lockridge, "Land, Population and the Evolution of New England Society, 1630–1790," *Past and Present* 39 (1968): 62–80; and Bettye Hobbs Pruitt, "Self-Sufficiency and the Agricultural Economy of Eighteenth-Century Massachusetts," *William and Mary Quarterly* 41 (July 1984): 333–64.

For Pennsylvania, see Peter C. Mancall, *Valley of Opportunity: Economic Culture Along the Upper Susquehanna, 1700–1800* (Ithaca: Cornell University Press, 1991); James T. Lemon, "Household Consumption in Eighteenth-Century America and Its Relationship to Production and Trade: The Situation Among Farmers in Southeastern Pennsylvania," *Agricultural History* 41 (Jan. 1967): 59–70; D. E. Ball and G. M. Walton, "Agricultural Productivity Change in Eighteenth-Century Pennsylvania," *Journal of Economic History* 36 (March 1976): 102–17; and Joan M. Jensen, "Butter Making and Economic Development in Mid-Atlantic America from 1750 to 1850," *Signs* 13 (summer 1988): 813–29, as well as previously cited works.

CHAPTER 4. AGRICULTURE AND ECONOMIC GROWTH IN THE NEW REPUBLIC

For Jeffersonian agrarianism, see Thomas Jefferson, *Notes on the State of Virginia* (Chapel Hill: University of North Carolina Press, 1955); Daniel J. Boorstin, *The Lost World of Thomas Jefferson* (Boston: Beacon, 1948); and Merrill D. Peterson, *The Jefferson Image in the American Mind* (New York: Oxford University Press, 1960). For popular agrarianism and agrarian reform, see Clarence H. Danhof, *Change in Agriculture: The Northern United States, 1820–1870* (Cambridge: Harvard University Press, 1969); Tamara Plakins Thornton, *Cultivating Gentlemen: The Meaning of Country Life among the Boston Elite, 1785–1860* (New Haven: Yale University Press, 1989); and David F. Allmendinger Jr., *Ruffin: Family and Reform in the Old South* (New York: Oxford University Press, 1990).

For the agricultural economy and the expansion of agriculture, see R. Carlyle Buley, *The Old Northwest: Pioneer Period, 1815–1840* (Bloomington: Indiana University Press, 1950); Paul W. Gates, *The Farmer's Age: Agriculture, 1815–*

282   *1860* (New York: Holt, Rinehart and Winston, 1960); James E. Davis, *Frontier America, 1800–1840: A Comparative Demographic Analysis of the Frontier Process* (Glendale, Calif.: Arthur H. Clark Company, 1977); Jeremy Atack and Fred Bateman, *To Till Their Own Soil: Agriculture in the Antebellum North* (Ames: Iowa State University Press, 1987); Ronald Hoffman, John J. McCusker, Russell R. Menard, and Peter J. Albert, eds., *The Economy of Early America: The Revolutionary Period, 1763–1790* (Charlottesville: University Press of Virginia, 1988); Thomas D. Clark and John D. W. Guice, *Frontiers in Conflict: The Old Southwest, 1795–1830* (Albuquerque: University of New Mexico Press, 1989); Sue Headlee, *The Political Economy of the Family Farm: The Agrarian Roots of American Capitalism* (New York: Praeger, 1991); and John Solomon Otto, "Southern 'Plain Folk' Agriculture: A Reconsideration," *Plantation Society in the Americas* 2 (Apr. 1983): 29–36.

Other important works on life in the West include Richard A. Bartlett, *The New Country: A Social History of the American Frontier, 1776–1890* (New York: Oxford University Press, 1974); Robert V. Hine, *Community on the American Frontier: Separate But Not Alone* (Norman: University of Oklahoma Press, 1981); and *The American West: An Interpretive History* (Boston: Little, Brown, 1984); John Mack Faragher, *Sugar Creek: Life on the Illinois Prairie* (New Haven: Yale University Press, 1986); Joan E. Cashin, *A Family Venture: Men and Women on the Southern Frontier* (New York: Oxford University Press, 1991); Jane Marie Pederson, *Between Memory and Reality: Family and Community in Rural Wisconsin, 1870–1970* (Madison: University of Wisconsin Press, 1992); Allan Bogue, "Land Credit for Northern Farmers, 1789–1940," *Agricultural History* 50 (Jan. 1976): 68–100; Jeremy Atack and Fred Bateman, "Self-Sufficiency and the Marketable Surplus in the Rural North, 1860," *Agricultural History* 58 (July 1984): 296–315; Daniel Dupre, "Ambivalent Capitalists on the Cotton Frontier: Settlement and Development in the Tennessee Valley of Alabama," *Journal of Southern History* 56 (May 1990): 215–40; and Elizabeth A. Perkins, "The Consumption Frontier: Household Consumption in Early Kentucky," *Journal of American History* 78 (Sept. 1991): 486–510.

For urbanization, industrialization, and their implications for rural life, see, especially, Michael P. Conzen, *Frontier Farming in An Urban Shadow: The Influence of Madison's Proximity on the Agricultural Development of Blooming Grove, Wisconsin* (Madison: State Historical Society of Wisconsin, 1971); Margaret Walsh, *The Manufacturing Frontier: Pioneer Industry in Antebellum Wisconsin, 1830–1860* (Madison: State Historical Society of Wisconsin, 1972), and *The Rise of the Midwestern Meat Packing Industry* (Lexington: University Press of Kentucky, 1982); Roberta Balstad Miller, *City and Hinterland: A Case Study of Urban*

Growth and Regional Development (Westport, Conn.: Greenwood, 1979); Jonathan Prude, *The Coming of Industrial Order: Town and Factory Life in Rural Massachusetts, 1810–1860* (Cambridge: Cambridge University Press, 1983); Morton Owen Shapiro, *Filling Up America: An Economic-Demographic Model of Population Growth and Distribution in the Nineteenth-Century United States* (Greenwich, Conn.: JAI Press, 1986); Christopher Clark, *The Roots of Rural Capitalism: Western Massachusetts, 1780–1860* (Ithaca: Cornell University Press, 1990); William Cronon, *Nature's Metropolis: Chicago and the Great West* (New York: W. W. Norton, 1991); Charles Sellers, *The Market Revolution: Jacksonian America, 1815–1846* (New York: Oxford University Press, 1991); and Richard L. Bushman, "Family Security in the Transition from Farm to City, 1750–1850," *Journal of Family History* 6 (fall 1981): 238–56.

For farmers' adjustments to and attitudes toward change, see David C. Klingaman and Richard K. Vedder, eds., *Essays in Nineteenth Century Economic History: The Old Northwest* (Athens: Ohio University Press, 1975); Hal S. Barron, *Those Who Stayed Behind: Rural Society in Nineteenth-Century New England* (Cambridge: Cambridge University Press, 1984); Lou Ferleger, ed., *Agriculture and National Development: Views on the Nineteenth Century* (Ames: Iowa State University Press, 1990); J. Ritchie Garrison, *Landscape and Material Life in Franklin County, Massachusetts, 1770–1860* (Knoxville: University of Tennessee Press, 1991); Winifred Barr Rothenberg, *From Market-Places to a Market Economy: The Transformation of Rural Massachusetts, 1750–1850* (Chicago: University of Chicago Press, 1992); Fred Bateman and Jeremy Atack, "The Profitability of Northern Agriculture in 1860," *Research in Economic History* 4 (1979): 87–125; Paul D. Escott, "Yeoman Independence and the Market: Social Status and Economic Development in Antebellum North Carolina," *North Carolina Historical Review* 66 (July 1989): 275–300; Richard L. Bushman, "Opening the American Countryside," in James A. Henretta, Michael Kammen, and Stanley N. Katz, eds., *The Transformation of Early American History: Society, Authority, and Ideology* (New York: Alfred A. Knopf, 1991): 239–56; and Thomas Dublin, "Rural Putting-Out Work in Early Nineteenth-Century New England: Women and the Transition to Capitalism in the Countryside," *New England Quarterly* 64 (Dec. 1991): 531–73.

CHAPTER 5. RURAL LIFE IN THE YOUNG NATION

For the rural family and especially the role of women therein, readers should refer to Nancy F. Cott, *The Bonds of Womanhood: Woman's Sphere in New England, 1780–1835* (New Haven: Yale University Press, 1977); Mary Beth Norton, *Liberty's Daughters: The Revolutionary Experience of American Women, 1750–1800*

284 (Boston: Little, Brown, 1980); Carolyn E. Sachs, *The Invisible Farmers: Women in Agricultural Production* (Totowa, N.J.: Rowman and Allenheld, 1983); Jane Turner Censer, *North Carolina Planters and Their Children, 1800–1860* (Baton Rouge: Louisiana State University Press, 1984); Joan M. Jensen, *Loosening the Bonds: Mid-Atlantic Farm Women, 1750–1850* (New Haven: Yale University Press, 1986); Sally McMurry, *Families and Farmhouses in Nineteenth-Century America: Vernacular Design and Social Change* (New York: Oxford University Press, 1988); Laurel Thatcher Ulrich, *A Midwife's Tale: The Life of Martha Ballard, Based on Her Diary, 1785–1812* (New York: Alfred A. Knopf, 1990); Nancy Grey Osterud, *Bonds of Community: The Lives of Farm Women in Nineteenth-Century New York* (Ithaca: Cornell University Press, 1991); John Mack Faragher, "History from the Inside-Out: Writing the History of Women in Rural America," *American Quarterly* 33 (winter 1981): 537–57; and Nancy Grey Osterud, "Gender and the Transition to Capitalism in Rural America," *Agricultural History* 67 (spring 1993): 14–29.

Those interested in the rural neighborhood and its institutions should look at Malcolm J. Rohrbough, *The Trans-Appalachian Frontier: People, Societies, and Institutions, 1775–1850* (New York: Oxford University Press, 1978); Wayne E. Fuller, *The Old Country School: The Story of Rural Education in the Middle West* (Chicago: University of Chicago Press, 1982); Carl F. Kaestle, *Pillars of the Republic: Common Schools and American Society, 1780–1860* (New York: Hill and Wang, 1983), Orville Vernon Burton, *In My Father's House Are Many Mansions: Family and Community in Edgefield, South Carolina* (Chapel Hill: University of North Carolina Press, 1985); Robert C. Kenzer, *Kinship and Neighborhood in a Southern Community: Orange County, North Carolina, 1849–1881* (Knoxville: University of Tennessee Press, 1987); Curtis D. Johnson, *Islands of Holiness: Rural Religion in Upstate New York, 1790–1860* (Ithaca: Cornell University Press, 1989); and Thomas C. Hubka, "Farm Family Mutuality: The Mid-Nineteenth-Century Maine Farm Neighborhood," *Annual Proceedings of the Dublin Seminar for New England Folklife* (1986): 13–23.

Some of the more stimulating volumes on immigrants in rural America include Jon Gjerde, *From Peasants to Farmers: The Migration from Balestrand, Norway, to the Upper Middle West* (Cambridge: Cambridge University Press, 1985); Walter D. Kamphoefner, *The Westfalians: From Germany to Missouri* (Princeton: Princeton University Press, 1987); and Robert C. Ostergren, *A Community Transplanted: The Trans-Atlantic Experience of a Swedish Immigrant Settlement in the Upper Middle West, 1835–1915* (Madison: University of Wisconsin Press, 1988). For some insights into daily life, see Jack Larkin, *The Reshaping of Everyday Life, 1790–1840* (New York: Harper and Row, 1988); Harvey A. Levenstein, *Revolution At the Table: The Transformation of the American Diet* (Oxford: Oxford

University Press, 1988); and James H. Cassedy, *Medicine in America: A Short History* (Baltimore: Johns Hopkins University Press, 1991).

The historical literature on slavery is so impressive and so monumental that one hesitates to mention any works for fear of slighting some. My view of the slave and southern communities draws heavily on John W. Blassingame, *The Slave Community: Plantation Life in the Antebellum South* (New York: Oxford University Press, 1972); Eugene D. Genovese, *Roll, Jordan, Roll: The World the Slaves Made* (New York: Random House, 1974), and *The Black Family in Slavery and Freedom, 1750–1925* (New York: Vintage, 1977); Lawrence W. Levine, *Black Culture and Black Consciousness: Afro-American Folk Thought from Slavery to Freedom* (New York: Oxford University Press, 1977); George W. McDaniel, *Hearth and Home: Preserving a People's Culture* (Philadelphia: Temple University Press, 1982); Bertram Wyatt-Brown, *Southern Honor: Ethics and Behavior in the Old South* (Oxford: Oxford University Press, 1982); Jacqueline Jones, *Labor of Love, Labor of Sorrow: Black Women, Work, and the Family from Slavery to the Present* (New York: Vintage, 1985); Deborah Gray White, *Ar'n't I a Woman? Female Slaves in the Plantation South* (New York: W. W. Norton, 1985); James Oakes, *Slavery and Freedom: An Interpretation of the Old South* (New York: Alfred A. Knopf, 1990); Drew Gilpin Faust, "Culture, Conflict, and Community: The Meaning of Power on an Ante-Bellum Plantation," *Journal of Social History* 14 (fall 1980): 83–97; Peter Kolchin, "Reevaluating the Antebellum Slave Community: A Comparative Perspective," *Journal of American History* 70 (Dec. 1983): 579–601; and Richard H. Steckel, "A Dreadful Childhood: The Excess Mortality of American Slaves," *Social Science History* 10 (winter 1986): 427–65.

For slavery and the Southern economy, see, especially, Gavin Wright, *The Political Economy of the Cotton South: Households, Markets, and Wealth in the Nineteenth Century* (New York: W. W. Norton, 1978); Fred Bateman and Thomas Weiss, *A Deplorable Scarcity: The Failure of Industrialization in the Slave Economy* (Chapel Hill: University of North Carolina Press, 1981); Frederick F. Siegel, *The Roots of Southern Distinctiveness: Tobacco and Society in Danville, Virginia, 1780–1865* (Chapel Hill: University of North Carolina Press, 1987); Robert William Fogel, *Without Consent or Contract: The Rise and Fall of American Slavery* (New York: W. W. Norton, 1989); Roger L. Ransom, *Conflict and Compromise: The Political Economy of Slavery, Emancipation, and the American Civil War* (Cambridge: Cambridge University Press, 1989); Heywood Fleisig, "Slavery, the Supply of Agricultural Labor, and the Industrialization of the South," *Journal of Economic History* 36 (Sept. 1976): 572–97; and Ralph V. Anderson and Robert E. Gallman, "Slaves as Fixed Capital: Slave Labor and Southern Economic Development," *Journal of American History* 64 (June 1977): 24–46.

286   CHAPTER 6. THE UNMAKING AND REMAKING
OF THE RURAL SOUTH

For the rural North during the Civil War and especially the technological revolution therein, see Allan G. Bogue, *From Prairie to Corn Belt: Farming on the Illinois and Iowa Prairies in the Nineteenth Century* (Chicago: University of Chicago, 1963); John T. Schlebecker, *Whereby We Thrive: A History of American Farming, 1607–1972* (Ames: Iowa State University Press, 1975); R. Douglas Hurt, *American Farm Tools from Hand Power to Steam Power* (Manhattan, Kansas: Sunflower University Press, 1982); Wayne D. Rasmussen, "The Impact of Technological Change on American Agriculture, 1862–1962," *Journal of Economic History* 22 (Dec. 1962): 578–91; R. Douglas Hurt, "Out of the Cradle: The Reaper Revolution," *Timeline* 3 (Oct./Nov. 1986): 38–51; and Nancy Grey Osterud, "Rural Women During the Civil War: New York's Nanticoke Valley, 1861–1865," *New York History* 62 (Oct. 1990); 357–385. Many of the sources I drew on for the rural South during the Civil War were mentioned previously, but readers might also want to look at Clarence L. Mohr, *On the Threshold of Freedom: Masters and Slaves in Civil War Georgia* (Athens: University of Georgia Press, 1986).

For the hopes of the freedpeople after the war, see Leon F. Litwack, *Been in the Storm So Long: The Aftermath of Slavery* (New York: Vintage, 1980); Elizabeth Rauh Bethel, *Promiseland: A Century of Life in a Negro Community* (Philadelphia: Temple University Press, 1981); Charles L. Flynn Jr., *White Land, Black Labor: Caste and Class in Late Nineteenth-Century Georgia* (Baton Rouge: Louisiana State University Press, 1983); Michael W. Fitzgerald, *The Union League Movement in the Deep South: Politics and Agricultural Change During Reconstruction* (Baton Rouge: Louisiana State University Press, 1989); Eric Foner, *A Short History of Reconstruction, 1863–1877* (New York: Harper and Row, 1990); Michael L. Lanza, *Agrarianism and Reconstruction Politics: The Southern Homestead Act* (Baton Rouge: Louisiana State University Press, 1990); Ira Berlin, Steven F. Miller, and Leslie S. Rowland, "Afro-American Families in the Transition from Slavery to Freedom," *Radical History Review* 42 (fall 1988): 89–121; and Edna Greene Medford, "Land and Labor: The Quest for Black Economic Independence on Virginia's Lower Peninsula, 1865–1880," *Virginia Magazine of History and Biography* 100 (Oct. 1991): 567–82.

Sharecropping and the crop-lien system have been fruitfully explored by many scholars. Among the works on which I have leaned most heavily are Eric Foner, *Nothing But Freedom: Emancipation and Its Legacy* (Baton Rouge: Louisiana State University Press, 1983); Michael Wayne, *The Reshaping of Plantation*

Society: The Natchez District, 1860–1880 (Baton Rouge: Louisiana State University Press, 1983); Thavolia Glymph and John J. Kushma, eds., *Essays on the Post-bellum Southern Economy* (Arlington: University of Texas at Arlington, 1985); William Cohn, *At Freedom's Edge: Black Mobility and the Southern White Quest for Racial Control 1861–1915* (Baton Rouge: Louisiana State University Press, 1991); Jay R. Mandle, *Not Slave, Not Free: The African American Economic Experience Since the Civil War* (Durham, N.C.: Duke University Press, 1992); Stewart E. Tolnay, "Black Family Formation and Tenancy in the Farm South, 1900," *American Journal of Sociology* 90 (Sept. 1984): 305–25; Lee J. Alston, "Race Etiquette in the South: The Role of Tenancy," *Research in Economic History* 10 (1986): 199–211; Donald L. Winters, "Postbellum Reorganization of Southern Agriculture: The Economics of Sharecropping in Tennessee," *Agricultural History* 62 (fall 1988): 1–19; and Robert Tracy McKenzie, "Freedmen and the Soil in the Upper South: The Reorganization of Tennessee Agriculture, 1865–1880," *Journal of Southern History* 59 (Feb. 1993): 63–84.

For white small farmers after the Civil War, see Steven Hahn, *The Roots of Southern Populism: Yeoman Farmers and the Transformation of the Georgia Upcountry, 1850–1890* (New York: Oxford University Press, 1983); William F. Holmes, "Whitecapping: Agrarian Violence in Mississippi, 1902–1906," *Journal of Southern History* 35 (May 1969): 165–85; Ted Ownby, "The Defeated Generation at Work: White Farmers in the Deep South, 1865–1890," *Southern Studies* 23 (winter 1984): 325–47; and David F. Weiman, "The Economic Emancipation of the Non-Slaveholding Class: Upcountry Farmers in the Georgia Cotton Economy," *Journal of Economic History* 45 (Mar. 1985): 71–93.

Some other valuable works on the economy and society in the rural South after the Civil War include Nell Irvin Painter, *Exodusters: Black Migration to Kansas After Reconstruction* (New York: Knopf, 1977); Roger L. Ransom and Richard Sutch, *One Kind of Freedom: The Economic Consequences of Emancipation* (Cambridge: Cambridge University Press, 1977); Gilbert C. Fite, *Cotton Fields No More: Southern Agriculture, 1865–1980* (Lexington: University Press of Kentucky, 1984); Gavin Wright, *Old South, New South: Revolutions in the Southern Economy Since the Civil War* (New York: Basic, 1986); Peter A. Coclanis, "The Rise and Fall of the South Carolina Low Country: An Essay in Economic Interpretation," *Southern Studies* 24 (summer 1985): 143–66, Gilbert C. Fite, "The Agricultural Trap in the South," *Agricultural History* 60 (fall 1986): 38–50; Tamara Miner Haygood, "Cows, Ticks, and Disease: A Medical Interpretation of the Southern Cattle Industry," *Journal of Southern History* 52 (Nov. 1986): 551–64; Ronald L. Lewis, "From Peasant to Proletarian: The Migration of Southern Blacks to the Central Appalachian Coal Fields," *Journal of Southern History* 55

287

(Feb. 1989): 77–102; and Carville Earle, "The Price of Precocity: Technical Choice and Ecological Constraint in the Cotton South, 1840–1890," *Agricultural History* 66 (summer 1992): 25–60.

CHAPTER 7. RURAL AMERICA
IN THE AGE OF INDUSTRIALIZATION

For the Great Plains, see Walter Prescott Webb, *The Great Plains* (Boston: Ginn and Company, 1931); James C. Malin, *The Grasslands of North America: Prolegomena to Its History* (Lawrence, Kansas: James C. Malin, 1956); Ian Frazier, *Great Plains* (New York: Penguin, 1989); and Norman J. Rosenberg, "Climate of the Great Plains Region of the United States," *Great Plains Quarterly* 7 (winter 1987): 22–32.

For ranching, see Robert R. Dykstra, *The Cattle Towns* (Lincoln: University of Nebraska Press, 1968); Charles L. Wood, *The Kansas Beef Industry* (Lawrence: Regents Press of Kansas, 1980); Terry G. Jordan, *Trails to Texas: Southern Roots of Western Cattle Ranching* (Lincoln: University of Nebraska Press, 1981); Jack Jackson, *Los Mestiños: Spanish Ranching in Texas, 1721–1821* (College Station: Texas A&M University Press, 1986); and Jimmy M. Skaggs, *Prime Cut: Livestock Raising and Meatpacking in the United States, 1607–1983* (College Station: Texas A&M University Press, 1986).

For farming on the Plains, see Everett Dick, *The Sod-House Frontier, 1854–1890* (Lincoln: University of Nebraska Press, 1937); Fred A. Shannon, *The Farmer's Last Frontier: Agriculture, 1860–1897* (New York: Holt, Rinehart and Winston, 1961); Gilbert C. Fite, *The Farmer's Frontier, 1865–1900* (New York: Holt, Rinehart and Winston, 1966); and Hiram M. Drache, *The Challenge of the Prairies: Life and Times of Red River Pioneers* (Fargo: North Dakota Institute for Regional Studies, 1970). For other aspects of life on the Plains, see Craig Miner, *West of Wichita: Settling the High Plains of Kansas, 1865–1890* (Lawrence: University Press of Kansas, 1986); Paula M. Nelson, *After the West Was Won: Homesteaders and Town-Builders in Western South Dakota, 1900–1917* (Iowa City: University of Iowa Press, 1986); and Glenda Riley, *The Female Frontier: A Comparative View of Women on the Prairie and the Plains* (Lawrence: University Press of Kansas, 1988).

For some of the impacts of industrialization on rural people, see Lewis Atherton, *Main Street on the Middle Border* (Bloomington: Indiana University Press, 1954); Earl W. Hayter, *The Troubled Farmer, 1850–1900: Rural Adjustment to Industrialism* (DeKalb: Northern Illinois University Press, 1968); Richard Lingeman, *Small Town America: A Narrative History, 1620–the Present* (Boston: Houghton Mifflin, 1980); Fred W. Peterson, *Homes in the Heartland: Balloon Frame Farmhouses in the Upper Midwest, 1850–1920* (Lawrence: University Press of Kansas, 1992); and Nancy Grey Osterud, "The Valuation of Women's Work: Gender and the Market in a Dairy Farming Community During the Late Nineteenth Century," *Frontiers* 10 (1988): 18–24. For the Grange, see D. Sven Nordin, *Rich Harvest: A History of the Grange, 1867–1900* (Jackson: University Press of Mississippi, 1974); Donald B. Marti, *Women of the Grange: Mutuality and Sisterhood in Rural America, 1866–1920* (Westport, Conn.: Greenwood, 1991); and Thomas A. Woods, *Knights of the Plow: Oliver H. Kelley and the Origins of the Grange in Republican Ideology* (Ames: Iowa State University Press, 1991).

The Alliance movement and Populism are among the most intensely studied phenomena in American political history. A few of the significant works include John D. Hicks, *The Populist Revolt: A History of the Farmers' Alliance and the People's Party* (Minneapolis: University of Minnesota Press, 1931); Theodore Saloutos, *Farmer Movements in the South, 1865–1933* (Lincoln: University of Nebraska Press, 1960); Peter Argersinger, *Populism and Politics: William Alfred Peffer and the People's Party* (Lexington: University Press of Kentucky, 1974); Robert C. McMath Jr., *Populist Vanguard: A History of the Southern Farmers' Alliance* (Chapel Hill: University of North Carolina Press, 1975); Lawrence Goodwyn, *The Populist Moment: A Short History of the Agrarian Revolt in America* (Oxford: Oxford University Press, 1978); Donna A. Barnes, *Farmers in Rebellion: The Rise and Fall of the Southern Farmers Alliance and People's Party in Texas* (Austin: University of Texas Press, 1984); Theodore R. Mitchell, *Political Education in the Southern Farmers' Alliance, 1887–1900* (Madison: University of Wisconsin Press, 1987); Scott G. McNall, *The Road to Rebellion: Class Formation and Kansas Populism, 1865–1900* (Chicago: University of Chicago Press, 1988); Norman Pollack, *The Humane Economy: Populism, Capitalism, and Democracy* (New Brunswick: Rutgers University Press, 1990); Julie Roy Jeffrey, "Women in the Southern Farmers' Alliance: A Reconsideration of the Role and Status of Women in the Late-Nineteenth Century South," *Feminist Studies* 3 (fall 1975): 72–91; and William F. Holmes, "Populism: In Search of Context," *Agricultural History* 64 (fall 1990): 26–58.

CHAPTER 8. PROSPERITY AND ITS DISCONTENTS

This chapter draws heavily on my own work, especially *The Resisted Revolution: Urban America and the Industrialization of Agriculture, 1900–1930* (Ames: Iowa State University Press, 1979), "The Agricultural Extension System and the First World War," *Historian* 41 (Feb. 1979): 315–31, and "Rural Education Reform and the Country Life Movement, 1900–1920," *Agricultural History* 53 (Apr. 1979): 462–74.

More recent works on agricultural expansion and economic development in this period include Barbara Allen, *Homesteading in the High Desert* (Salt Lake

City: University of Utah Press, 1987); William M. Parker and Stephen J. De-Canio, "Two Hidden Sources of Productivity Growth in American Agriculture, 1860–1930," *Agricultural History* 56 (Oct. 1982): 648–62; and Theodore R. Mitchell and Robert Lowe, "To Sow Contentment: Philanthropy, Scientific Agriculture, and the Making of the New South: 1906–1920," *Journal of Social History* 24 (winter 1990): 317–40. For the impact of the automobile, see Reynold M. Wik, *Henry Ford and Grass-roots America* (Ann Arbor: University of Michigan Press, 1972); Michael L. Berger, *The Devil Wagon in God's Country: The Automobile and Social Change in Rural America, 1893–1929* (Hamden, Conn.: Archon, 1979); Hal S. Barron, "And the Crooked Shall Be Made Straight: Public Road Administration and the Decline of Localism in the Rural North, 1870–1930," *Journal of Social History* 26 (fall 1992): 81–103; and Mary Neth, "Leisure and Generational Change: Farm Youths in the Midwest, 1910–1940," *Agricultural History* 67 (spring 1993): 163–84.

For the Country Life Movement and some of its facets, see William L. Bowers, *The Country Life Movement in America, 1900–1920* (Port Washington, N.Y.: Kennikat, 1974); Thomas and Marilyn Wessel, *4-H: An American Idea, 1900–1986: A History of 4-H* (Chevy Chase, Md.: National 4-H Council, 1982); William A. Link, *A Hard Country and a Lonely Place: Schooling, Society, and Reform in Rural Virginia, 1870–1920* (Chapel Hill: University of North Carolina Press, 1986); Thomas J. Morain, *Prairie Grass Roots: An Iowa Small Town in the Early Twentieth Century* (Ames: Iowa State University Press, 1988); Wayne D. Rasmussen, *Taking the University to the People: Seventy-Five Years of Cooperative Extension* (Ames: Iowa State University Press, 1989); Paula Baker, *The Moral Frameworks of Public Life: Gender, Politics, and the State in Rural New York, 1870–1930* (Oxford: Oxford University Press, 1991); Katherine Jellison, *Entitled to Power: Farm Women and Technology, 1913–1963* (Chapel Hill: University of North Carolina Press, 1993); and Roy Alden Atwood, "Routes of Rural Discontent: Cultural Contradictions of Rural Free Delivery in Southeastern Iowa, 1898–1917," *Annals of Iowa* 48 (summer–fall 1987): 264–73.

For the rural-to-urban migration of blacks in this period, see Peter Gottlieb, *Making Their Own Way: Southern Blacks' Migration to Pittsburgh, 1916–30* (Urbana: University of Illinois Press, 1987); and Jack Temple Kirby, "The Southern Exodus, 1910–1960: A Primer for Historians," *Journal of Southern History* 69 (Nov. 1983): 585–600. The best work on land settlement is Paul K. Conkin's *Tomorrow a New World: The New Deal Community Program* (Binghamton, N.Y.: American Historical Association, 1959). Some important works touching on irrigation in this period include Michael C. Robinson, *Water for the West: The Bureau of Reclamation, 1902–1977* (Chicago: Public Works Historical Society, 1979); Donald Worster, *Rivers of Empire: Water, Aridity, and the Growth of the*

American West (New York: Oxford University Press, 1992); and Donald J. Pisani, "Reclamation and Social Engineering in the Progressive Era," *Agricultural History* 57 (Jan. 1983): 46–63. For the Nonpartisan League, see Robert L. Morlan, *Political Prairie Fire* (Minneapolis: University of Minnesota Press, 1959); and for the American Farm Bureau Federation and its relationship to the Extension Service, see Grant McConnell, *The Decline of Agrarian Democracy* (Berkeley: University of California Press, 1953).

CHAPTER 9. FROM THE BEST OF TIMES TO THE WORST

The best treatment of the agricultural depression of the twenties is James H. Shideler, *Farm Crisis, 1919–1923* (Berkeley: University of California Press, 1957). H. Thomas Johnson, *Agricultural Depression in the 1920's: Economic Fact or Statistical Artifact* (New York: Garland, 1985), argues that no real depression occurred. For McNary-Haugenism, see Gilbert C. Fite, *George N. Peek and the Fight for Farm Parity* (Norman: University of Oklahoma Press, 1954). For cooperation, see Joseph G. Knapp, *The Rise of American Cooperative Enterprise, 1620–1920* (Danville, Ill.: Interstate Printers and Publishers, 1969), and *The Advance of American Cooperative Enterprise, 1920–1945* (Danville, Ill.: Interstate Printers and Publishers, 1973); David E. Hamilton, *From New Day to New Deal: American Farm Policy from Hoover to Roosevelt, 1928–1933* (Chapel Hill: University of North Carolina Press, 1991); and Elizabeth Hoffman and Gary D. Libecap, "Institutional Choice and the Development of U.S. Agricultural Policies in the 1920s," *Journal of Economic History* 51 (June 1991): 397–411. For the impact of the twenties on rural material life, see Claude S. Fischer, "Technology's Retreat: The Decline of Rural Telephony in the United States, 1920–1940," *Social Science History* 11 (fall 1987): 295–327; and Katherine Jellison, "Women and Technology on the Great Plains," *Great Plains Quarterly* 8 (summer 1988): 145–57.

For mechanization and its impact, see Reynold M. Wik, *Steam Power on the American Farm* (Philadelphia: University of Pennsylvania Press, 1953); Gilbert C. Fite, *American Farmers: The New Minority* (Bloomington: Indiana University Press, 1981); Robert C. Williams, *Fordson, Farmall, and Poppin' Johnny: A History of the Farm Tractor and Its Impact on America* (Urbana: University of Illinois Press, 1987); Robert E. Ankli and Alan L. Olmstead, "The Adoption of the Gasoline Tractor in California," *Agricultural History* 55 (July 1981): 213–30; and Peter Berck, "A Note on the Real Cost of Tractors in the 1920s and 1930s," *Agricultural History* 59 (Jan. 1985): 66–71.

Some valuable works on the Great Depression in rural America include Paul E. Mertz, *New Deal Policy and Southern Rural Poverty* (Baton Rouge: Louisiana State University Press, 1978); Andrew Gulliford, *America's Country Schools*

(Washington, D.C.: Preservation, 1984); Nan Elizabeth Woodruff, *As Rare as Rain: Federal Relief in the Great Southern Drought of 1930–1931* (Urbana: University of Illinois Press, 1985); Lawrence J. Nelson, "Welfare Capitalism on a Mississippi Plantation in the Great Depression," *Journal of Southern History* 50 (May 1984): 225–50; and Lee J. Alston and T. J. Hatton, "The Earnings Gap between Agricultural and Manufacturing Laborers, 1925–1941," *Journal of Economic History* 51 (Mar. 1991): 83–99.

For rural women in the Great Depression, see Deborah Fink, *Open Country, Iowa: Rural Women, Tradition, and Change* (Albany: State University of New York Press, 1986), and *Agrarian Women: Wives and Mothers in Rural Nebraska, 1880–1940* (Chapel Hill: University of North Carolina Press, 1992); Catherine McNicol Stock, *Main Street in Crisis: The Great Depression and the Old Middle Class on the Northern Plains* (Chapel Hill: University of North Carolina Press, 1992); Dorothy Schwieder and Deborah Fink, "Plains Women: Rural Life in the 1930s," *Great Plains Quarterly* 8 (spring 1988): 79–88; and Kathleen R. Babbitt, "The Productive Farm Woman and the Extension Home Economist in New York State, 1920–1940," *Agricultural History* 67 (spring 1993): 83–101.

Some works on agricultural unrest include John L. Shover, *Cornbelt Rebellion: The Farmers Holiday Association* (Urbana: University of Illinois Press, 1965); Lowell K. Dyson, *Red Harvest: The Communist Party and American Farmers* (Lincoln: University of Nebraska Press, 1982); Robert E. Snyder, *Cotton Crisis* (Chapel Hill: University of North Carolina Press, 1984); and Kim E. Nielsen, "Who Were These Farm Radicals? The Douglas County Farm Holiday Association," *Minnesota History* 51 (fall 1989): 270–80.

CHAPTER 10. THE NEW DEAL AND RURAL AMERICA

For New Deal agriculture programs, see Murray R. Benedict and Oscar C. Stine, *The Agricultural Commodity Programs: Two Decades of Experience* (New York: Twentieth Century Fund, 1956); Christiana McFadyen Campbell, *The Farm Bureau and the New Deal: A Study of National Farm Policy, 1933–1940* (Urbana: University of Illinois Press, 1962); Van L. Perkins, *Crisis in Agriculture: The Agricultural Adjustment Administration and the New Deal, 1933* (Berkeley: University of California Press, 1969); Theodore Saloutos, *The American Farmer and the New Deal* (Ames: Iowa State University Press, 1981); Michael W. Schuyler, *The Dread of Plenty: Agricultural Relief Activities of the Federal Government in the Middle West, 1933–1939* (Manhattan, Kans.: Sunflower University Press, 1989); and John Mack Hansen, *Gaining Access: Congress and the Farm Lobby, 1919–1981* (Chicago: University of Chicago Press, 1991).

A few of the many important works on the New Deal and Southern agriculture include David Eugene Conrad, *The Forgotten Farmers: The Story of Sharecroppers in the New Deal* (Urbana: University of Illinois Press, 1965); Donald H. Grubbs, *Cry from the Cotton: The Southern Tenant Farmers' Union and the New Deal* (Chapel Hill: University of North Carolina Press, 1971); Paul E. Mertz, *New Deal Policy and Southern Rural Poverty* (Baton Rouge: Louisiana State University Press, 1978); Anthony J. Badger, *Prosperity Road: New Deal, Tobacco, and North Carolina* (Chapel Hill: University of North Carolina Press, 1980); Pete Daniel, *Breaking the Land: The Transformation of Cotton, Tobacco, and Rice Cultures Since 1880* (Urbana: University of Illinois Press, 1985); Jack Temple Kirby, *Rural Worlds Lost: The American South, 1920–1960* (Baton Rouge: Louisiana State University Press, 1987); Bruce J. Schulman, *From Cotton Belt to Sunbelt: Federal Policy, Economic Development, and the Transformation of the South, 1938–1980* (New York: Oxford University Press, 1991); Pete Daniel, "The Transformation of the Rural South, 1930 to the Present," *Agricultural History* 55 (July 1981): 231–48; Jack Temple Kirby, "The Transformation of Southern Plantations, c. 1920–1960," *Agricultural History* 57 (July 1983): 257–76; Lawrence J. Nelson, "The Art of the Possible: Another Look at the 'Purge' of the AAA Liberals in 1935," *Agricultural History* 57 (Oct. 1983): 416–35; and Alexander Yard, "'They Dont Regard My Rights At All': Arkansas Farmworkers, Economic Modernization, and the Southern Tenant Farmers Union," *Arkansas Historical Quarterly* 47 (autumn 1988): 201–28.

For New Deal activities on behalf of the rural poor, see Sidney Baldwin, *Poverty and Politics: The Rise and Decline of the Farm Security Administration* (Chapel Hill: University of North Carolina Press, 1968); and Donald Holley, *Uncle Sam's Farmers: The New Deal Communities in the Lower Mississippi Valley* (Urbana: University of Illinois Press, 1975). An interesting piece on conservative opposition is James C. Carey, "The Farmers' Independence Council of America, 1935–1938," *Agricultural History* (Apr. 1961): 70–77. For rural electrification and its implications, see Michael J. McDonald and John Muldowny, *TVA and the Dispossessed: The Resettlement of Population in the Norris Dam Area* (Knoxville: University of Tennessee Press, 1982); David E. Nye, *Electrifying America: Social Meanings of a New Technology, 1880–1940* (Cambridge: MIT Press, 1990); Don F. Hadwiger and Clay Cochran, "Rural Telephones in the United States," *Agricultural History* 58 (July 1984): 221–38; and Katherine Jellison, "'Let Your Cornstalks Buy a Maytag': Prescriptive Literature and Domestic Consumerism in Rural Iowa, 1927–1939," *The Palimpsest* 69 (fall 1988): 132–39.

For the Dust Bowl, see Brian W. Blouet and Frederick C. Luebke, eds., *The Great Plains: Environment and Culture* (Lincoln: University of Nebraska Press, 1979); Paul Bonnifield, *The Dust Bowl: Men, Dirt, and Depression* (Albuquerque:

294 University of New Mexico Press, 1979); Donald Worster, *Dust Bowl: The Southern Plains in the 1930s* (Oxford: Oxford University Press, 1979); R. Douglas Hurt, *The Dust Bowl: An Agricultural and Social History* (Chicago: Nelson-Hall, 1981); Donald Worster, "The Dirty Thirties: A Study in Agricultural Capitalism," *Great Plains Quarterly* 6 (spring 1986): 107–16.

For Dust Bowl migrants, see Walter Stein, *California and the Dust Bowl Migration* (Westport, Conn.: Greenwood, 1973); James N. Gregory, *American Exodus: The Dust Bowl Migration and Okie Culture in California* (New York: Oxford University Press, 1989); and James C. Malin, "The Turnover of Farm Population in Kansas," *Kansas Historical Quarterly* 4 (Nov. 1935): 339–72. For specific government programs, see R. Douglas Hurt, "The National Grasslands: Origin and Development in the Dust Bowl," *Agricultural History* 59 (Apr. 1985): 246–59, and "Federal Land Reclamation in the Dustbowl," *Great Plains Quarterly* 6 (spring 1986): 94–106; and Douglas Helms, "Conserving the Plains: The Soil Conservation Service in the Great Plains," *Agricultural History* 64 (spring 1990): 58–73. For the Ogallala aquifer, see John Opie, *Ogallala: Water for a Dry Land* (Lincoln: University of Nebraska Press, 1993). For agriculture during World War II, see Walter W. Wilcox, *The Farmer in the Second World War* (Ames: Iowa State College, 1947); and Nan Elizabeth Woodruff, "Pick or Fight: The Emerging Farm Labor Program in the Arkansas and Mississippi Deltas During World War II," *Agricultural History* 64 (spring 1990): 74–85.

CHAPTER II. THE PRODUCTION REVOLUTION
AND ITS CONSEQUENCES

For the productivity revolution, see John T. Shover, *First Majority—Last Minority: The Transforming of Rural Life in America* (De Kalb: Northern Illinois University Press, 1976); Jim Hightower, *Hard Tomatoes, Hard Times: A Report of the Agribusiness Accountability Project on the Failure of America's Land Grant College Complex* (Cambridge, Massachusetts: Schenkman Publishing, 1973); Thomas D. Isern, *Custom Combining on the Great Plains: A History* (Norman: University of Oklahoma Press, 1981); Deborah Fitzgerald, *The Business of Breeding: Hybrid Corn in Illinois, 1890–1940* (Ithaca: Cornell University Press, 1990); John Fraser Hart, *The Land That Feeds Us* (New York: W. W. Norton, 1991); Richard H. Day, "The Economics of Technological Change and the Demise of the Sharecropper," *American Economic Review* 57 (June 1967): 427–49; Willis Peterson and Yoav Kislev, "The Cotton Harvester in Retrospect: Labor Displacement or Replacement?" *Journal of Economic History* 46 (Mar. 1986): 199–216; and Dana D. Dalrymple, "Changes in Wheat Varieties and Yields in the United States, 1919–1984," *Agricultural History* 62 (fall 1988): 20–36. For DDT, see Thomas Dunlap, *DDT: Scientists, Citizens, and Public Policy* (Princeton: Princeton University

Press, 1981); and John H. Perkins, *Insects, Experts, and the Insecticide Crisis* (New York: Plenum, 1982).

See Walter Goldschmidt, *As You Sow* (New York: Harcourt, Brace, 1947), for a famous study of the social ramifications of big agriculture, and Harold T. Pinkett, "Government Research Concerning Problems of American Rural Society," *Agricultural History* 58 (July 1984): 365–72, for the reluctance of the research establishment to study them. Some interesting pieces on the rural exodus include Deborah Fink, "Rural Women and Family in Iowa," *International Journal of Women's Studies* 7 (Jan.-Feb. 1984): 57–69, and "'Mom, It's a Losing Proposition': The Decline of Women's Subsistence Production on Iowa Farms," *North Dakota Quarterly* 52 (winter 1984): 26–33; Pete Daniel, "Going Among Strangers: Southern Reactions to World War II," *Journal of American History* 77 (Dec. 1990): 886–911; Peter Gottlieb, "Rethinking the Great Migration: A Perspective from Pittsburgh," in Joe William Trotter Jr., ed., *The Great Migration in Historical Perspective: New Dimensions of Race, Class, and Gender* (Bloomington: Indiana University Press, 1991): 68–82; and Gavin Wright, "Economic Consequences of the Southern Protest Movement," in Armstead L. Robinson and Patricia Sullivan, eds., *New Directions in Civil Rights Studies* (Charlottesville: University Press of Virginia, 1991): 175–83.

For changes in rural life, see Lowry Nelson, *American Farm Life* (Cambridge: Harvard University Press, 1954); Thomas E. Williams, "Rural America in an Urban Age, 1945–1960," in Robert H. Bremner and Gary W. Reinhard, eds., *Reshaping America: Society and Institutions, 1945–1960* (Columbus: Ohio State University Press, 1982): 147–61; and Cornelia Butler Flora and Jan L. Flora, "Structure of Agriculture and Women's Culture in the Great Plains," *Great Plains Quarterly* 8 (fall 1988): 195–205.

CHAPTER 12. AGRICULTURE AND RURAL LIFE
AT THE END OF THE TWENTIETH CENTURY

Some interesting works on the new agriculture include Wes Jackson, *New Roots for Agriculture* (San Francisco: Friends of the Earth, 1980); David E. Brewster, Wayne D. Rasmussen, and Garth Youngberg, *Farms in Transition: Interdisciplinary Perspectives on Farm Structure* (Ames: Iowa State University Press, 1983); Pierre Crosson, "Agricultural Land: A Question of Values," *Agriculture and Human Values* 2 (fall 1985): 6–13; and Thomas L. Daniels, "A Rationale for the Support of the Medium-Sized Family Farm," *Agriculture and Human Values* 6 (fall 1989): 47–53. For some works on the environment, see J. G. Hawkes, *The Diversity of Crop Plants* (Cambridge: Harvard University Press, 1983); Pete Daniel, "A Rogue Bureaucracy: The USDA Fire Ant Campaign of the 1950s," *Agricultural History* 64 (spring 1989): 99–114; and Linda J. Lear, "Bombshell in Beltsville: The USDA and the Challenge of Silent Spring," *Agricultural History* 66 (spring 1992): 151–70.

For the downturn of the late seventies and eighties, see William P. Browne, *Private Interests, Public Policy, and American Agriculture* (Lawrence: University Press of Kansas, 1988); Mark Friedberger, *Shake-Out: Iowa Farm Families in the 1980s* (Lexington: University Press of Kentucky, 1989), Osha Gray Davidson, *Broken Heartland: The Rise of America's Rural Ghetto* (New York: Free Press, 1990); Neil E. Harl, *The Farm Debt Crisis of the 1980s* (Ames: Iowa State University Press, 1990); Sonja Salamon, *Prairie Patrimony: Family, Farming, and Community in the Midwest* (Chapel Hill: University of North Carolina Press, 1992); William P. Browne and John Dinse, "The Emergence of the American Agricultural Movement, 1977–1979," *Great Plains Quarterly* 5 (fall 1985): 221–35; William Mueller, "How We're Gonna Keep 'Em Off of the Farm," *American Scholar* 56 (winter 1987): 57–67; and Mark Friedberger, "Women Advocates in the Farm Crisis of the 1980s," *Agricultural History* 67 (spring 1993): 224–34. For biotechnology and some of its implications, see Jack Ralph Kloppenburg Jr., *First the Seed: The Political Economy of Plant Biotechnology, 1492–2000* (Cambridge: Cambridge University Press, 1988); Lawrence Busch, William B. Lacy, Jeffrey Burkhardt, and Laura R. Lacy, *Plants, Power, and Profit: Social, Economic, and Ethical Consequences of the New Biotechnologies* (Cambridge, Massachusetts: Basil Blackwell, 1991); Frederick H. Buttel, "Agricultural Research and Farm Structural Change: Bovine Growth Hormone and Beyond," *Agriculture and Human Values* 3 (fall 1986): 88–98; Mark Sagoff, "Biotechnology and the Environment: What is at Risk," *Agriculture and Human Values* 5 (summer 1988): 26–35. The study of rural attitudes I mention is *Public Attitudes Toward Rural America and Rural Electric Cooperatives* (Roper Organization, June 1992).

Index

Index

Index

Index